MAN IS
THE MEASURE

MAN IS
THE MEASURE

*A Cordial Invitation to the Central
Problems of Philosophy*

REUBEN ABEL

Fp

THE FREE PRESS
A Division of Macmillan Publishing Co., Inc.
NEW YORK

Collier Macmillan Publishers
LONDON

The Free Press
A Division of Macmillan Publishing Co., Inc.
866 Third Avenue, New York, N.Y. 10022

Collier Macmillan Canada, Ltd.

Library of Congress Catalog Card Number: 75–16646

Printed in the United States of America

Paperback printing number

9   10

Hardbound printing number

1   2   3   4   5   6   7

Library of Congress Cataloging in Publication Data

Abel, Reuben
    Man is the measure.

    Bibliography: p.
    Includes index.
    1. Philosophy. 2. Man. 3. Cosmology.
I. Title.
B53.A23   128   75-16646
ISBN 0-02-900140-4
ISBN 0-02-900110-2 pbk.

COPYRIGHT ACKNOWLEDGMENTS

To
Marion
and
to
Ernest

sine quibus non

Contents

interaction of the social scientist with his subjects;
values; holism and contextuality of social facts;
"ideal types" . . . but differences in subject matter,
technique, and degree do not exempt areas of science from the common logic of justification . . .
Sociology of knowledge: social and historical coefficients in science; value judgments taken as facts;
ideology . . . but this is empirical and remediable,
not logical . . . Cultural relativity of conceptual
framework: we are imprisoned in implicit basic
presuppositions which we are not aware of . . .
but this too is empirical only, and surmountable
by continued growth.

. . . vagueness . . . ambiguity . . . context . . . can language be made perfect? . . . how language can mislead us . . . no meanings apart from words, although meanings are not identical with words . . . the functions of language: cognitive; expressive; performatory; others . . . ostension . . . "mental acts" can not alter established meanings . . . animal communication vs. human language . . . Chomsky vs. Skinner on how to explain this . . . no specific linguistic capacity need be postulated . . . language is continuous with other human activities.

20. Intention, Action, and Free Will   235

Intention as explanation for human actions . . . but difficult to clarify or pin-point . . . twenty-five questions . . . reasons for actions are not causes . . . human actions as logically primitive . . . but difficulties . . . freedom; determinism; fatalism . . . freedom from external compulsion: what is? . . . choice by dominant motive . . . responsibility . . . freedom does not prevent science of human behavior . . . self-determination by the growing person . . . every man is a self-made man.

21. Form in Art   249

Various senses of "art" . . . difficulties of classification . . . functions of art . . . the "imitation of nature" . . . art as a language . . . does not require unambiguous meanings . . . the artist's intention . . . "intentional fallacy" . . . variety of "true" interpretations . . . what is a "work of art"? . . . form . . . five quandaries . . . a status imputed to sensuous materials intentionally formed into a unity by a person, for the sake of doing so, and to evoke a response . . . some problems thus resolved . . . contemporary weakening of formal requirements . . . art as a criterion of the human?

Preface

I TRY in this book to bridge three different gulfs: first, the abyss that scares the layman away from professional philosophy; second, the no-man's land between philosophy and other sorts of intellectual inquiry; and third, the chasm that unhappily exists between the two disparate aims of philosophy, namely, critical analysis and speculative insight.

The first bridge has fallen into disrepair in our times, but was regularly traversed by many great philosophers in the Anglo-American tradition. I have in mind such notable figures as Bacon, Locke, Berkeley, Hume, Mill, Russell, James, Schiller, and Dewey. They all succeeded in imparting pleasure and profit to their professional colleagues, as well as to the reader who has no familiarity with technical philosophy; yet they did so without distorting or minimizing the problems, and without patronizing the novice.

The second gap I attempt to close is the one that segregates philosophy (narrowly defined) from other significant cognitive enterprises. Thus I comment upon or try to analyze philosophical problems in such diverse fields as psychology, anthropology, linguistics, psychoanalysis, physics, biological evolution, mathematics, historiography, poetry, and art.

The third gulf is a transatlantic one, both literally (that is, between the English-speaking nations and continental Europe) and figuratively. It firmly separates the analytic philosophers, who insist on logic, precision, and clarity, from the imaginative metaphysicians, who claim that their vision resists the rigor of those requirements.

I have also tried, on many of the issues in philosophy, to present a variety of points of view with which I do *not* agree, so that the reader will have some notion of why I argue as vehemently as I sometimes do. My own position will (I imagine) be variously referred to as pragmatist, or humanist, or naturalist, or empiricist, or instrumentalist, or positivist, or analytical, or neo-Kantian, or even existentialist. Dear reader, be chary! In order to be coherent, it is not necessary to carry a banner.

I owe a particular debt of gratitude to Ernest Nagel, who has lighted the way for a generation of American philosophers; to Sidney Hook, Paul Edwards, and Donald Levy, who have also gone over the entire manuscript; to my late mentors Felix Kaufmann and Horace M. Kallen; and to the editorial talents of Robert Wallace and Margaret Miner. But my debts are much greater. I have been thinking about these problems, as well as teaching, studying, reading, and discussing them for so long, and with such concentration, that I no longer can identify how much of this book is my own and how much has been absorbed. I make little effort to document the attribution which scholarship requires. If I had his audacity, I would repeat Wittgenstein's remark, in the preface to his *Tractatus*: "It is a matter of indifference to me whether the thoughts that I have had have been anticipated by someone else." After all, no one ever said anything for the first time! I would rather claim no originality for whatever is valuable here, and gratefully acknowledge my indebtedness to the great community of Philosophy.

Introduction: The Philosophic Enterprise

Man is the measure of all things: of those that are, that they are; and of those that are not, that they are not. — Protagoras

THIS BOOK is not an introduction to philosophy, although it invites the layman to consider most of the problems dealt with by philosophers; it is not a survey of philosophy, although it scrutinizes much of the philosophical terrain; and it is not a history of philosophy, although it discusses many of the important philosophical traditions.

My intention, rather, is to put forth a philosophical point of view about man and the world—a point of view boldly stated a long time ago by Protagoras, but perhaps never fully grasped, nor properly applied. We can best make sense, I maintain, of the great human enterprise by taking into account the fact that it is, peculiarly and unavoidably, human. All our attempts to understand the world, to "grasp this Sorry Scheme of Things entire,"—all of science, metaphysics, poetry, history, art, and religion—depend upon certain distinctive characteristics of *Homo sapiens*. And, it would be misleading to speak as if man were a clearly fixed datum. What man is can best be understood in terms of how he came to be what he now is and what (as the geneticists make us so vividly aware) he can make of himself in time to come. The human endeavor to apprehend the world is an open-ended process. My aim is to exhibit the "loose fit" between mind and the world, by analysis of some of the aspects and limitations of knowledge. I hope to make manifest a radical and irreducible anthropocentrism.

(The universe—so far as we can tell!—was not made for man. But neither is man the casual by-blow of nature. Intelligence is part of the world, not alien to it; it is nature becoming aware of itself. It is quite certain that there was a time when intelligent life did not exist on this planet; and it is perhaps equally certain that at some future time such life will no longer exist. However, it is not at all clear—as we see in Chapter 13—whether or not, and in what sense, the existence of intelligence on this earth may be called an accident.)

Thus, in the following chapters I argue that there is no such thing as *the* structure of the world. Any attempt to say how things really are, or what objectively exists, requires a set of concepts (or terms, or symbols); and these concepts are not dictated unequivocally by "the facts." Indeed, to refer to "the facts" or to "the given" as if it were obvious just what *is* given to us as fact is to disregard how the idiosyncrasies of human sensation, perception, and cognition select and shape "the facts." Nor is there any clear and unambiguous single meaning to "the truth." Can we assert that logic and mathematics, at least, are independent of human conceptualization, eternally subsistent in their crystalline purity? Is there a basic ultimate structure of mind? or of language? Can we reach the bedrock of certainty in knowledge of one's own self? Or does even self-knowledge have built-in limitations? Is "the past" irrevocably fixed and unalterable? Or is the notion of an absolute past no clearer than that of the absolute given? Does art produce a kind of knowledge, and serve as a criterion of the human? These questions are examined and clarified.

But the inevitable anthropocentrism of knowledge does not imply that rational scientific inquiry is futile. There are philosophers who are scornful of science; I am not among them. I know of few things more misguided than the recent proof by an esteemed philosopher that, since man's essence is unique, evolution is impossible. If the claims of a philosopher contradict those of a scientist, one or the other is confused or mistaken; but only prejudice will decide in advance. It is presumptuous for the philosopher to disparage the procedures of the scientist, and it is stultifying for the scientist to ignore the logical analysis of his concepts and suppositions. Science and philosophy are different kinds of intelligent inquiry, yet both are concerned with explaining the world. If in the long run they do not complement each other, the human enterprise will suffer. The absorption in philosophy without science may be illustrated by St. Simeon Stylites, who lived on top of a pillar for thirty-seven years; or by Cratylus, who, it is said, found language so unsatisfactory that he gave up talking altogether. Any philosopher who fears to lose his soul because of science is a lost soul to begin with.

Indeed, there is a recurring intellectual aberration that may be barbarously christened *epistemophobia:* an irrational fear of knowledge. This fear may appear as Gray's "where ignorance is bliss, 'tis folly to be wise"; or as Keats' "Philosophy will clip an Angel's wings." Or it may emerge in the many currents of superstition, mythology, mysticism, dogmatic supernaturalism, and opposition to reason, which swirl through much of the twentieth century. Or it may be seen in the remark of former Premier George Papadopoulos of Greece that schooling that "only broadened the child's mind" without fitting him for useful social work was dangerous; he added that much of the unrest in the world was due to excess knowledge, and concluded by asking "whether it is really useful for everybody to know everything."

I consider it profoundly irrational, and ultimately delusive, to base any notion of human happiness, or utility, or dignity, upon the value of self-deception or ignorance.

Philosophy is, as its etymology reveals, the love of wisdom. Such love may issue in speculative synoptic vision, or it may issue in methodical critical analysis. In either event, however, philosophy is the kind of insight into fundamental questions that first requires that we make clear exactly what we are asking. In order to be profound, it is neither necessary to be obscure, nor sufficient to be vague! Thus, when we ask such questions as, is knowledge ever certain? or, is knowledge possible without language? or, are any statements necessarily true?

or, does a computer think? or, how can a man be held account-able for his actions if all events have causes? or, is there a purpose in nature? or, are space and time infinitely divisible? we must analyze all these terms in order to ascertain how to proceed. But these philosophical questions differ from equally puzzling questions in science (such as, how did life originate? or, how many different kinds of subatomic particles are there? or, what causes cancer?) in that, usually, it is not additional facts that are needed. It has therefore been remarked that phi-losophical problems are not so much to be solved as to be dis-solved. In any event, they seldom have simple solutions. Some-times they have no solutions at all, which is part of what I mean by the loose fit of mind to the world. However, to realize this constraint is to enlarge our understanding. Even if philosoph-ical analysis does not always produce new knowledge, or get us as far along the road to enlightenment as we would wish, it is nonetheless essential that we prefer articulate reasoned uncer-tainty over inarticulate or irrational dogma.

Let us begin our inquiry with the traditional core of philos-ophy, namely, metaphysics.

I

Metaphysics: What in the World Is There?

THE PHILOSOPHER, the scientist, and the artist are all trying to describe the same world; they all want to tell us what is "really there." But they do it in different ways. The artist endeavors to convey his insights by painting limp watches, red mountains, and three-eyed women. The scientist aims at factual accuracy, predictability, and control. The philosopher seeks conceptual clarity and precision. Thus, the scientist relies on what he can observe, whereas the philosopher asks what "observe" means. Do you "observe" what is "really there" when using a microscope? or a telescope? or X rays? or television? The scientist and the philosopher, unlike the artist, are expected to give reasons for what they say; but they give different kinds of reasons.

Varieties of Metaphysics

Metaphysics is that branch of philosophy which attempts to comprehend the universe as a whole—not so much by examin-

1

ing it in detail (which is the procedure of science) as by analyzing and organizing the ideas and concepts by means of which
we examine and think about the world. Metaphysical presuppositions often determine the way we approach other central
problems in philosophy. Thus *materialism*, for example, is the
metaphysical theory that the motion of matter (which is anything that occupies space) can in principle account for all that
there is in the world; whatever exists can be explained by physical conditions. The difficulty materialism encounters is how to
fit consciousness and purposiveness into that format. *Idealism*
takes as the fundamental and irreducible feature of the universe
the existence of mind or spirit (whether subjective or objective, theist or pantheist). The drawback of idealism is that, in
all its many versions, it depreciates the commonsense world
of material things. The idealist in metaphysics, as we see in
the next few chapters, is likely to be a rationalist rather than
an empiricist in epistemology. Materialism and idealism are
both monistic metaphysical theories; that is, each claims that
there is only one kind of thing in the world. The metaphysics of *dualism*, however, posits two ultimate categories,
mind and matter, neither of which can be reduced to the
other. The dualist's problem is to explain how mind and
matter, if they are radically different, can ever influence
or affect each other (as we examine in Chapter 18).

There are many other metaphysical positions. Aristotle called
for eight (or sometimes ten) categories, or kinds of properties,
to describe the ultimate substances that "underlie everything
else." These are the categories we cite in Chapter 7 as determining whether a proposition is meaningful or not. Kant was the
first to recognize that certain alleged facts about the world are
not really properties of things, but rather of the ways in which
we organize our knowledge. Causality, for example, is not an
inherent attribute of events, but rather provides the form for
our cognitive discourse about the world; it is one of the categories of our understanding. Things cannot ever come within
our experience or sensibility except insofar as they conform to
those categories. Hegel devised some eighty metaphysical categories (such as quality, quantity, and measure) that go through
the stages of thesis, antithesis, and synthesis in a dialectical pro-

cess. Peirce worked out an unusual schema involving three metaphysical levels which he designated, appropriately, as first-ness, secondness, and thirdness.

These and other metaphysical doctrines have been attacked and defended over the centuries. The attacks are often violent, but never fatal; old philosophies do not die, they merely fade away. A metaphysics is not the sort of thing that can be proved or disproved by anything that happens; it need not submit to any test, since it can specify what a test is. *Hylozoism* (the view that all matter is alive) still has its advocates. *Solipsism* (the theory that only I exist) is irrefutable—Schopenhauer said that it needed not a refutation but a cure.

The term *reality* often enters the discussion at this point, but it is not of much help. All metaphysicians claim to distinguish what is "real" from what is mere "appearance," but they can seldom agree on a criterion. Plato said that the bed you sleep on is less real than the "Form," or "Idea," of "The Bed." Your bed may have lumps, but The Bed is perfect; your bed did not exist at one time and, someday, will disappear, but The Bed is eternal. Particular things for Plato are what they are because they "imitate" or "partake of" or "participate in" the Forms or Ideas; it is only these Forms that are truly real. Kant said that reality is "that which is connected with perception according to laws." Hegel epitomized idealism when he declared that the essence of reality is consciousness. William James said, "any-thing is real of which we find ourselves obliged to take account in any way." For Croce, "physical facts have no reality, whereas art . . . is eminently real." Other philosophers, however, have insisted that "reality" is forever hidden from us by a "veil of illusion." Thus the word "reality" tends to become a term of praise rather than a useful descriptive concept; it "carries an agreeable afflatus without dependence on any definite meaning," says Morris Cohen.

The Aim of Metaphysics: What Is There?

The aim of metaphysics is to account for all that there is, and only for what there is, in as simple, complete, and compendious a scheme as possible. The metaphysician wants to sort into the fewest categories all that the world contains. He wants to accommodate, for example, the potential energy of the water above Niagara Falls (which may never become actual) and the capacity of this grain of salt in my hand to be dissolved (which may never come to pass); but he does not want to be "conned" or cozened into providing room in his scheme for nonexistent or merely putative entities, such as the present Queen of France, or an imaginary solid gold mountain a mile high, even if philosophers can talk about them (which is one of the problems of meaning discussed in Chapter 7). Nelson Goodman makes the point thus:

> Some of the things that seem to me inacceptable without explanation are powers or dispositions, counterfactual assertions, entities or experiences that are possible but not actual, electrons, angels, devils and classes. . . . My sample listing of suspect notions is of course far from complete. . . . You may decry some of these scruples and protest that there are more things in heaven and earth than are dreamt of in my philosophy. I am concerned, rather, that there should not be more things dreamt of in my philosophy than there are in heaven or earth.

What, indeed, is there? There is a pen in my hand; a star in the sky; a hole in the carpet; a pain in my tooth; a ringing in my ears; a song in my heart; a redness in the sunset; a discussion in Congress; unrest in Ireland; a need for action; a duty to try; a possibility of success; a difference in size. Which of these are not "parts of the world"? The irreducible variety and plurality of "what there is" seems incontrovertible.

Yet philosophers and scientists have always tried to reduce this disorderly multiplicity. Thales declared simply that all things are water. Other ancient Greek thinkers added the other "elements"—earth, air, and fire. The growth of knowledge has indeed permitted many simplifications or *reductions*. Thus "caloric," which was once supposed to be the independent essence or principle of heat, has been reduced to the motion of molecules; the gene as the unit of heredity has been reduced to the chemical DNA; what was once called "satanic possession," to glandular imbalance. Reduction plays an important role in scientific explanation, as we see in Chapter 10. Some philosophers try to reduce "thing" to a group of sense data or sensibilia (Chapter 3); "proposition" to "sentence" (Chapter 7); and "person" to "body" (Chapter 17). The great difficulty with reduction is to accomplish it without committing the *reductive fallacy*—that would be to say that one thing is "nothing but" some other thing (for example, to say that the music of the violin is "nothing but the friction of horse's hair drawn over cat's gut" is to commit the reductive fallacy). A proper explanatory reduction, as we see in the progress of science (Chapter 10), does not eliminate any entity from the world, but is a more economical way of describing phenomena. Caloric *is not* something other than the motion of molecules, whereas music *is* something other than the vibration of strings. An example of successful reduction is Russell's reduction of "number" to a class of classes. He proposes that philosophers adopt the maxim "always substitute logical constructions for inferred entities." Whitehead likewise reduces "point" to a class of convergent volumes (why ever should anyone have to cope with the concept of an unextended spatial entity?). In their different ways, philosophers as diverse as Socrates, Descartes, Leibniz, Locke, Hume, and Wittgenstein have also sought by analysis to arrive at metaphysical simplicity.

Things and Events

One traditional approach to sorting out what there is in the world is a division into things and events. My pen, for example, is a *thing*; it occupies space, or exists in space. A discussion, however, is an *event*; it runs through time, or happens in time. Things, it is claimed, are substances, characterized by continuity; events are processes, characterized by change. But is this distinction exclusive? or quite clear? Is a river a thing or an event? how about a rainbow? an electron? a sense datum? (Chapter 3). Events must involve things, and can occur only to things. A discussion cannot exist without people who discuss; the flight of an arrow cannot occur without the arrow. And every thing changes through time; my pen now is not absolutely identical with the pen it was yesterday. Thus, the distinction is of limited usefulness. Among the philosophers who argue for the metaphysical primacy of events are Schopenhauer, Bergson, Cassirer, and Whitehead; their "process" philosophy is supported by Relativity Theory. In Engels' words, "The great basic thought" which dialectical materialism inherited from Hegel was "that the world is not to be comprehended as a complex of ready-made things but as a complex of processes." Wittgenstein, however, begins his *Tractatus*, "The world is all that is the case" (that is, states of affairs, or configurations of objects).

There are, of course, other metaphysical schemata to classify what there is. In his "logical atomism" Russell declares the ultimate constituents of the world to be particular things, qualities or attributes, relations, and facts. Dewey considers that the universe consists of fields (of interconnected things, events, and individuals). Other philosophers demand metaphysical autonomy for persons; for meanings; for actions; for sense data; for works of art; and for God or gods.

Naturalism

Having run through (with shameless speed) some of the great efforts to sort out what there is in the world, we can look at three other varieties of metaphysics. Naturalism intends the single category of Nature to encompass all that exists in space and time—the totality of processes and things, organic and inorganic. It asserts that there is only one order of existence and denies that there is anything super-natural or sub-natural. "Nature has neither kernel nor shell," says Goethe. Naturalism avoids the exclusive monism of both materialism and idealism, and the conceptual difficulty of dualism, by declaring that although matter is the basis of whatever exists, it does not exhaust whatever exists. Thus, man's thoughts and values, his hopes and ideals, his failures and illusions are part of the material world which has become self-conscious. Mind is not a miraculous creation, nor an intrusion from outside of Nature. The naturalist accuses the materialist of committing the reductive fallacy when the materialist says that mental states are "nothing but" molecules of matter (Chapter 18). However, the naturalist agrees with the materialist that whatever exists or happens can be explained in principle by the methods of science.

Absolute Idealism

One version of idealist metaphysics that proved very attractive in the nineteenth century, and that exemplifies some of the aesthetic appeal of monism, is well expressed by Tennyson:

> Flower in the crannied wall,
> I pluck you out of the crannies,
> I hold you here, root and all, in my hand,
> Litttle flower—but *if* I could understand
> What you are, root and all, and all in all,
> I should know what God and man is.

The world, thus, is seen as an indivisible concatenated whole; each part is what it is because of its place in this ideal whole. It would be a distortion to separate out any single element or fact. But William James and F. C. S. Schiller condemned this view as a "block universe." Russell argued that the world was, rather, a series of isolated facts, with no necessary connections between them. In his autobiography, Russell stormed:

> Academic philosophers, ever since the time of Parmenides, have believed that the world is a unity. . . . The most fundamental of my intellectual beliefs is that this is rubbish. I think the universe is all spots and jumps, without unity, without continuity, without coherence or orderliness or any of the other properties that governesses love . . . it consists of events, short, small and haphazard. Order, unity, and continuity are human inventions, just as truly as are catalogues and encyclopedias.

Mechanism

A third important metaphysics, one that expresses the scientific outlook of the seventeenth century, is *mechanism*. It sees the world as a huge clockwork, a composite machine that is entirely and uniquely determined by its component parts. Mechanism adds to materialism the hypothesis of determinism: the universe is a closed and self-contained material system of causes and effects. Whenever anything changes in *quality* (e.g., becomes warmer or prettier) , this is a mere epiphenomenon, a passive shadow of the changes in *quantity* or motion of the basic material particles. Thus, mechanism is simultaneously opposed (a) to idealism, dualism, and vitalism (which all assert that life or mind cannot be reduced to matter); (b) to dialectical materialism (which says that a composite whole cannot grow unless it has "internal contradictions"); and (c) to teleology (which maintains that there are goals or ends or purposes in the world—what Aristotle calls "final causes"—and that therefore you cannot really understand an acorn, for example, unless you know its goal is to become an oak tree; or clay, unless you know it can be made into a pot; or grapes, unless you know they can "make glad the hearts of men." ("Final causes" were extruded from Nature by Darwin; see Chapter 13.) The impact of the mechanist world view is perfectly expressed in Matthew Arnold's "Dover Beach":

> Ah, love, let us be true
> To one another! for the world, which seems
> To lie before us like a land of dreams,
> So various, so beautiful, so new,
> Hath really neither joy, nor love, nor light,
> Nor certitude, nor peace, nor help for pain;
> And we are here as on a darkling plain
> Swept with confused alarms of struggle and flight,
> Where ignorant armies clash by night.

But mechanism, like absolute idealism, has been found wanting. To begin with, neither of these metaphysical theories can account for the appearance of anything *new* in the world. (How science explains the emergence of novelty is discussed in Chapter 10.) Second, the mechanist image of the world as a huge clockwork is inadequate. A clock works by storing energy (for example, in the tension of a steel spring) and then releasing it. But there are more complex kinds of machines, such as the heat engine, which works not by storing energy but by transforming it (you feed it coal and water, which it transforms into steam, which drives a piston), and the computer, which stores and transforms not only energy but also information. Third (and most significantly), there are natural phenomena such as electromagnetism that cannot be explained mechanically at all. Physics now treats certain events (such as the emission of a single alpha particle) as in principle unpredictable. Hence, the basic premise of the metaphysics of mechanism is now rather dubious.

The model of the world as a great machine is responsible for such curious doctrines as Nietzsche's "eternal return." He claimed that if anything *can* happen, then it must, in the infinite past, already *have* happened. If the world is a clockwork, then it winds and unwinds and winds again. Mechanical processes are repeatable. David Hume wrote, "This world . . . with all its events, even the most minute, has before been produced and destroyed, and will again be produced and destroyed, without any bounds and limitations." If the world consists of a finite number of particles, which can be combined in only a finite number of ways, then any particular combination is bound to recur in infinite time. Moreover, if any one state of the world were indeed to reappear exactly, then the whole subsequent history of the world would have to be repeated exactly. But none of these ingenious speculations applies to our world, which is just not that simple a machine.

Determinism and Chance

Note carefully, however, that it is mechanism, and not determinism, which has been abandoned. *Determinism* may be defined as the doctrine that all events have causes; that is, whatever event occurs may be connected by general laws to other events. A large part of science consists of sets of equations that connect states of matter at one time with states of matter at other times. In classical Newtonian mechanics, these states are the position and momentum of particles. In thermodynamics, the states are pressure, volume, temperature, entropy, and free energy. And in quantum mechanics, the state is the psi function, or

probability state. This probability state does not represent imperfect or incomplete knowledge, but is all that there is to be
known. Some philosophers (Democritus and Spinoza, for example) have held that the concepts of necessity and impossibility
are complementary: whatever does actually happen must happen, and whatever does not actually happen cannot happen;
there is no middle ground of possibility or contingency; if we
were to say that it might or might not rain tomorrow, or that the
South might have won the Civil War, we would be showing our
ignorance of that which determines weather and wars. In modern physics, however, as we see in Chapters 12 and 16, probability
is an objective and inherent aspect of the world.

Determinism is much too valuable a postulate to abandon.
Like such other postulates as induction and the uniformity of
nature, however, it is not so much metaphysical as methodological; that is, it describes a feature of human endeavor, rather
than of the world. Curious men will never abandon the attempt
to find out what makes things go. James calls this effort "an
altar to an unknown god." However, we must differentiate determinism today from the bold but simplistic way in which it
was proclaimed by Laplace almost two centuries ago:

> [If] an Intellect at any given instant knew all the forces that
> animate nature, and the mutual position of the beings that com-
> pose it . . . nothing would be uncertain, for the future, even as
> the past, would be ever present before his eyes.

Nowadays, physics shows that no meaning can be assigned to "all
the forces . . . at any given instant," and that the "beings that
compose" the world are not things but conceptual waves of probability. Moreover, many natural phenomena such as clouds or
hydrodynamic turbulence seem to be irreducibly "stochastic";
that is, the number of individual events taking place at any one
time is so enormous that it is physically impossible to observe or
to note them all before they have changed. There is an upper
limit to the amount of data that can be fed into a computer, just
as there is an upper limit to how fast a human being can run.
And there is an upper limit to the precision or mechanical reliability of any actual computer. It cannot even theoretically be
made completely resistant to heat, friction, air pressure, cosmic
rays, gravitation, and wearing out. Thus, determinism, like other

methodological postulates, must take human limitations into account.

Determinism denies that there is any such thing as objective *chance*; it explains what may be called a "chance event" in one of the following six ways (which to a certain extent overlap) :

1. As an unexpected or unintended or psychologically surprising event. "I met him by chance in Samarra."

2. As a "lucky" event, that is, one in which some arbitrary action is followed by a desirable result. "I hit on the answer by pure chance."

3. As a case of probability. "There is a fifty-fifty chance of rain."

4. As a slight or unobserved change in initial conditions that produces a significant result. A mouse steps on the junction points of a railroad switch and "by chance" derails a train. A roulette ball teeters until a tiny puff of air blows it "by chance" onto my number.

5. As the complex interrelation between a large number of combined causes. A "chance" concurrence of unusual winds and tides sinks a ship. A perfect bridge hand is dealt "by chance."

6. As the intersection of two separate and independent causal series. Since physical laws all have a given domain, an event outside that domain is often called "chance"—a comet entering our solar system, for example, or a brick falling from a roof onto a passerby on the street.

These "chance" events may in fact be associated by laws with previous other events; they are not infractions of determinism. (There are, however, philosophers who deny universal determinism. Peirce, for example, believes that there is an element of genuine chance or spontaneity in the world; he calls it "tychism.")

Causality

The concept of *cause*, which is basic to determinism, has gone through many stages. Aristotle speaks of the "four causes of being": formal, material, efficient, and final; but these may be more accurately described as *aspects* of being, since they do not all precede what they are causes of. Bacon interprets cause as means to an end, the end being the control or manipulation of nature; thus, knowledge of causes amounts to power. Leibniz regards cause as sufficient reason; Descartes as ground or necessity or implication. But it is Hume who has had the greatest impact. No one has been able to refute his fundamental critique of the concept of causation: we do not ever observe one external event *compelling* another event to happen by necessity. We never see any glue connecting events; we note that a "cause" (e.g., the impact of one billiard ball on another) is in fact always associated with, or conjoined to, a given "effect" (the movement of the second billiard ball). Modern extensional or truth-functional logic therefore deals with "material implication" rather than necessity (Chapter 6). It is only by experience and experiment that we find out what causes what. If our predictions about which events are constantly conjoined are borne out, then we have a pragmatic verification of causality.

In addition to the fundamental difficulty that we cannot see or specify any necessary connection between cause and effect, there are these five problematic aspects to the notion of causality:

1. It used to be supposed (and still is, popularly) that some physical contact of the cause with the effect is needed—yet the moon and the sun cause the tides to rise from a distance.

2. The cause must clearly occur before the effect, or, at any rate, not later than the effect; but Relativity Theory complicates this apparently simple criterion of earlier and later (Chapter 12).

3. When events are analyzed, they often turn out to be less discrete than we would wish, in deciding what causes what. Brand Blanshard cites this example: we say that malaria is caused by the bite of the anopheles mosquito. But the bite does not in fact always produce the disease, so the cause must be not the bite, but the actual release of plasmodia into the bloodstream. But, again, malaria does not invariably ensue, so the cause must be the attack by the plasmodia on the victim's red blood corpuscles. Malaria is still not inevitable, however,

so the cause must be the loss of hemoglobin. But even this does not always produce malaria, so the cause must be that the tissues are deprived of oxygen. But this last "cause" of malaria is just what malaria is! Thus, what we do in sorting out causes and effects is to impose an intelligible structure of discrete events upon the continuous stream of occurrence; we do it in the way that is most useful for our purposes.

4. The constant conjunction of two events is a *necessary* condition for one to be the cause of the other, but it is not *sufficient*. Red and green traffic lights constantly succeed each other, but they do not cause each other. Both are caused by something else. The terminology of causation may thus be usefully supplemented: rain causes the streets to be wet; that is, rain is a sufficient but not a necessary condition, since the streets might have gotten wet in other ways. You can put out a fire by pouring water on it or by covering it with a blanket: either way is sufficient; neither way is necessary. But these two ways of putting out a fire have something in common; namely, they both deprive the fire of oxygen, and oxygen is necessary. It is an open question whether or not two or more sufficient conditions for an event always in fact have a factor in common, which would then be necessary. Do the many different causes of death, for example, have something in common? Do all the sufficient conditions behind contemporary social unrest —war, race prejudice, drugs, inflation, poverty, the decline of religion, the weakening of family ties—have a common factor (perhaps "insecurity")? No one can say whether or not the plurality of sufficient conditions with no underlying necessary conditions is an ultimate aspect of our world.

5. The selection and imputation of a cause often depends on our purposes and interests. That bad automobile accident on the highway yesterday, for example: was it caused by the icy pavement? or by a poorly designed roadway? or by a hole in the road? or by faulty brakes on the car? or by the driver's incompetence? or by his second martini? or by his marital problems? Any of these conditions might have sufficed. That recent outbreak of the plague in Asia: was the cause a microbe? or the flea that carried it? or the rat that spread it? or inefficient drainage? or poverty? What we decide to call *the* cause is em-

bedded in a context. It is linked to how we wish to impute responsibility, or to what we can correct most expeditiously, or to what we can correlate most widely. How much do we augment our understanding if we say that the cause of the Protestant Reformation was Martin Luther's constipation? (These questions appear again in Chapter 10 and in the appraisal of philosophies of history in Chapter 15.)

Universals

Included in my list of "what there is" is the redness in the sunset. Redness (like Plato's The Bed) is a *universal*: that is, unlike particular red things, which come into being and pass away, and which are only more or less pure red, Redness or Red is timeless, precise, and perfect. Is the universal "Red," which is not a thing, exactly the same as the class of red things in the world? That class of things constantly changes, and may disappear entirely. Would Red then have disappeared? or would it have lost its meaning? Is Red something more than the red things in the world? If I say, "The lion is fierce," do I mean to describe every lion in the world, so that my statement is falsified by the Cowardly Lion of Oz? If I say, "Woman is fickle," do I intend to include my wife?

Plato attempted, in his doctrine of the Forms, to explain why things fall into kinds, that is, why they are *what* they are. The Forms are an answer to Heraclitus, who said, you cannot step twice into the same river, since both you and the river have changed; and changing things resist rational explanation. The experience of our senses is concrete, discrete, and specific; but knowledge is of the whatness, or type, or species, or Form. Antisthenes, an ancient heckler, disputed with Plato: I see my bed, he said, but not The Bed. To which Plato replied, that is because you have eyes but no mind. Plato wrote in *Thaeatetus*, "we have intercourse with Becoming by means of the body through sense, whereas we have intercourse with Real Being by means of the soul through reflection." Real Being (i.e., the Forms) is Plato's attempt to account for the *recurrent* elements of our experience, as well as for such general ideas as justice, beauty, and equality. And, just as "Red" seems to have a sort of independent subsistence, so do the *relations* between particular things. When we say that Athens is larger than Sparta, or that New York is between Boston and Washington, the relations of *being larger than* or *being between* are not directly encountered by us; all that we can find are Athens, Sparta, New York, Boston, and Washington. Those relations are exemplified by the instances mentioned, but the relations are not identical with the instances. The relations are instantiated, or illustrated, but they are not exhausted by these examples, nor by any finite set of examples.

Thus, what our senses perceive are particular things existing at specific times and places; but in order for us to have knowledge of them, we require universals, such as colors, species, types, qualities, general ideas, properties, classes, and relations. These universals are independent of perception and cannot be located in space and time. When the farmer at the zoo first saw a giraffe, and complained, "There ain't no such animal!" he was denying the existence of the particular thing he saw because it wasn't an instance of a "such," that is, of a type or universal. When Adam first opened his eyes he didn't see "daisies" or "plants" but only blobs of color. A wit once thus commented on the plight of primitive man:

> The unrefined and sluggish mind
>   of *Homo javanensis*
> Could only treat of things concrete
>   and present to the senses.

The status of universals is one of the oldest and most persistent problems in philosophy. Plato considers them part of the built-in furniture of the world, prior to and independent of the particular things that imitate them or participate in them. But for Aristotle universals are no more than the properties that particular things have in common. "Nominalists" and "conceptualists" hold universals to be only words, or concepts. Russell omitted universals from his metaphysics of logical atomism. The proper approach is, I think, the pragmatic one: universals (or types, or classes) are not part of the world, but part of a human framework of concepts. They are suggested by what there is, but not in any necessarily unique way. They are devised by us to organize our experience most effectively. We recognize things as similar (that is, we abstract as a class) whatever best suits our purposes. (The Eskimos have words for the different kinds of snow but no single word for snow.) Any one thing resembles every other thing in the world in *some* way; Humpty Dumpty described a "tove" as "something like a badger, and something like a lizard, and something like a corkscrew." Aristotle divided animals into those which were red-blooded and those which were not; today we classify animals as vertebrate and invertebrate; but the individual existing creatures couldn't care less. In the nineteenth century biologists decided to replace the class of "quadrupeds" by the class of "mammals," to eliminate the class of "raptores," and to reclassify sponges as animals rather than plants, and whales as mammals rather than fish. Only man's need to impose order is constant.

("Man" or "humanity" is a universal: only individual persons exist, and no two of them are ever exactly alike. Beware, then, of any generalization about "what is the good for man" or what "man's duty" is. It is possible that human disagreements or ethical conflicts may not even in theory be rationally soluble.)

The "Truth" of Metaphysics

We have glanced at a large number of metaphysical theories: which of them is true? Any one, or all. Their function is not so much to describe a universe "out there" as to contrive a scaffolding of concepts that will implement man's need to understand and organize his experience. It is therefore inappropriate to call these theories true, but rather clarifying, or enlightening, or helpful. We must avoid here two complementary errors: on the one hand, that the world has a unique intrinsic preexisting structure awaiting our grasp; and on the other hand, that the world is an utter chaos. The first error is that of the student who marveled at how the astronomers could find out the true names of the distant constellations. The second error is that of Lewis Carroll's Walrus, who grouped shoes with ships and sealing-wax, and cabbages with kings (as if all classifications were equally useful). The world fits the mind only loosely. Nature is not a fixed datum. Its control over us is flexible; it does not fully constrain us. Metaphysical speculation, although sometimes wildly imaginative and uncontrolled, has often foreshadowed or anticipated scientific theories.[1] The metaphysicians, in their attempts to answer the question, "what in the world is there?" have been close to the poets as well as to the scientists.

---

[1] For example, atomism may be found in Democritus; evolution in Aristotle; "antimatter" and right-left parity in Pythagoras; and continental drift in Thales, who said that the earth floats on the ocean.

2

The Basis of Knowledge

IT IS CONVENIENT to pin the "problem of knowledge" on Plato, for he regarded knowledge as a mysterious kind of union between a knower and the known. Contemplation for Plato was a kind of love; and, just as the lover physically grasps his beloved, so does the knower spiritually apprehend the eternal Forms. The metaphor, of course, is older than Plato, for it was Adam who "knew Eve his wife," and the suggestive phrase "carnal knowledge" still recalls that ancient tradition. But if we take the metaphor too literally—if we ask how knowing involves grasping the immaterial—if we assume that Plato's Forms are quietly waiting out there to be seized—then we have allowed a poetic usage to create a philosophic problem. When a man gets to know something (as John Dewey remarks), the process is no more mysterious than when he gets to eat something. Man's curiosity is as natural to him as his hunger. But philosophers have usually been more puzzled by epistemology than by digestion.

Knowledge by Acquaintance and Knowledge by Description

Of course "knowledge" is not all that simple. We may begin here with Bertrand Russell's distinction between "knowledge by ac-

The Basis of Knowledge

quaintance" and "knowledge by description." Acquaintance is direct and immediate; it consists of "raw feels." We are acquainted with a person, or with a place, or with a food. Russell calls it "the kind of knowledge a dog-lover has of his dog." We may have degrees of acquaintance, but acquaintance as such is neither true nor false; that is, although I may be wrong in saying that that man across the street is my friend Bert, it is my inference that is erroneous, and not the acquaintance. Acquaintance is indeed the sort of knowledge a lover often has, or a teacher, or a physician, or an animal trainer. Martin Buber claims he knows God by direct acquaintance. But acquaintance is knowledge only in a preliminary or inarticulate sense. Organized scientific and philosophic knowledge, by contrast, is knowing *that* such and such is the case: it is descriptive of fact; it is couched in propositions.[1]

Knowing That and Knowing How

Second, knowing that, which is propositional, must also be distinguished from knowing how. One may know how to swim, for example, or how to tie a bowtie, without being able to describe exactly how one does these things. This is often true of skills and crafts, of wine tasting and puzzle solving, of being able to identify a literary style and to compose a melody. Most of us know how to recognize a face, for example, or an accent, without being fully able to state that knowledge in propositions. Michael Polanyi points out that to know how to balance on a bicycle does not entail knowing that "for a given angle of unbalance, the curvature of each winding is inversely proportional to the square of the speed."

Can *knowing how* theoretically always be reduced to *knowing that*? Knowing how to play tic-tac-toe can be articulated precisely in propositions, and formulated as a computer program. It remains a serious open question, however, whether or not, for example, the diagnosis of disease by a physician, or the translation

---

[1] The English word *know* blurs the distinction between having descriptive knowledge of a fact and being acquainted with a person: compare, though, the Latin *scire* and *cognoscere*, the French *savoir* and *connaître*, the Spanish *saber* and *conocer*, the German *wissen* and *kennen*.

of natural languages, or the taxonomy of animal and plant species, or the recognition of patterns, can be computerized. *Knowing how* to do these things perhaps cannot be fully specified in propositional *knowing that*.

We see in Chapter 19 how this distinction bears on some problems of language. It is apparently not possible to state fully the rules for some ordinary English usages which we all know how to employ, such as the order of adjectives. We say "it is a long metal rod," not "a metal long rod." The substitutability of *very* for *highly* is similarly complex. Something may be "very difficult" or "highly difficult"; but not "very hard" or "highly hard."

Knowledge and Experience

Some philosophers (Henri Bergson, for example) belittle science because science cannot capture the peculiarly ineffable quality of so many of our experiences. William James makes this point well in *The Varieties of Religious Experience*:

> Something forever exceeds, escapes from statement, withdraws from definition, must be glimpsed and felt, not told. No one knows this like your genuine professor of philosophy. For what glimmers and twinkles like a bird's wing in the sunshine it is his business to snatch and fix. . . .
>
> Life defies our phrases . . . it is .infinitely continuous and subtle and shaded, whilst our verbal terms are discrete, rude, and few . . . there is something in life . . . entirely unparalleled by anything in verbal thought. . . .

Can you describe the aroma of coffee? or the taste of cold water? No one can quarrel with Louis Armstrong's reply upon being asked what jazz is: "Man, if you gotta ask what it is, you ain't never gonna get to know." Nor with the Zen Buddhist nun Ryo-Nen, who thus describes the experience of silence:

> Sixty-six times have these eyes beheld the changing scenes
> of Autumn.
> I have said enough about moonlight,
> Ask me no more.
> Only listen to the voices of pines and cedars, when no wind
> stirs.

But there is no problem here unless one confuses two very different concepts: *experience* and propositional *knowledge*. Experience is a very wide philosophical term: it includes everything we do and everything that happens to us; it encompasses sensations and emotions and pains and aesthetic experiences and mystical transports. None of these should be confounded with propositional knowledge. It is not the function of knowledge to duplicate experience, but to describe it; not to reproduce what occurs, but to explain it. *Knowing* what anger is, for example, is not the same as *being* angry. To have tasted wine is not to know its chemical composition. In its specificity and concreteness, life often has qualitative aspects that defy representation in general descriptive terms. Not every encounter with the world results in knowledge. "Fact is richer than diction," said J. L Austin; but they are not competitors. Experience may be an incentive to acquiring knowledge, or it may be evidence for some kinds of knowledge, or it may become the object of knowledge; but experience is not itself knowledge. We should never confuse the description with what is being described, nor the explanation with what is being explained, nor the knowledge with the experience. The physician who has himself had an operation is likely to be more sympathetic to the patient with a ruptured appendix, but the physician does not thereby *know* any more *about* appendicitis. The male obstetrician does not ipso facto know less about menstruation and childbirth than the female doctor does. Experience and knowledge by acquaintance are of enormous intrinsic significance, but they are never a substitute for, nor a rival to, descriptive knowledge.

A conversation with Albert Einstein, reported by Rudolf Carnap, is revealing:

> Once Einstein said that the problem of the Now worried him. He explained that the experience of the Now means something special for man, something essentially different from past and future, but that this important difference does not and cannot occur within physics. . . . I remarked that all that occurs objectively can be described in science . . . the temporal sequence of events in physics; and . . . the peculiarities of man's experience with respect to time, including his different attitudes toward past, present, and future can be . . . in principle explained in psychology. But Einstein thought . . . there is something essential about the Now

which is just outside the realm of science. We agreed that this was not a defect for which science could be blamed, as Bergson thought.

The experiences of *now* and *here* ("indexical particulars") are known to us by acquaintance; they are what our propositional knowledge describes.

(We examine in Chapter 21 the claim of poetry and art to communicate knowledge. It is often the hallmark of the great literary artist that he finds the words to describe what the rest of us have inarticulately experienced or felt.)

Propositional Knowledge

Disputes about the nature of knowledge have frequently turned on whether "knowledge" must be propositional. On one side of the debate are Carnap ("Science in principle can say all that can be said"); Hans Reichenbach ("What we know can be said, and what cannot be said cannot be known") ; and the early Wittgenstein ("Whatever can be said at all can be said clearly . . . . Whereof one cannot speak, thereof must one be silent"). On the other side are Polanyi ("We know more than we can tell"); and those who assert that a baby knows that fire is hot; or that "a dog knows the difference between being stumbled over and being kicked" (O. W. Holmes) ; or that a plant knows down from up. The first group of philosophers has been accused of legislating conformity to their rigorous standard (in the manner of Benjamin Jowett, the master of Balliol, who allegedly proclaimed, "I am master of this college/What I don't know isn't knowledge"). The second group has been charged with excessively diluting the term "knowledge."

The solution seems to me to make it clear that propositional knowledge is different from (but neither better than, nor worse than) knowledge by acquaintance; and likewise different from knowing how, and from feeling, and from sensing, and from other sorts of experience. I will certainly not depreciate the importance of these: it may well be a matter of life and death sometimes to know how water tastes!

But it is propositional knowledge that is my concern here. The paradigm of such knowledge is "I know that p," where p stands for any proposition, that is, any statement that is either true or false, such as "Today is Tuesday" or "Eisenhower succeeded Truman." (We analyze the proposition as the unit of knowledge in Chapters 6 and 7.) Analysis of what is entailed by the assertion "I know that p" shows that four conditions are required:

1. That p be true. Thus, if I were to say "I know that $2 + 2 = 5$," you would object, "You can't know that, because it isn't true." "Only what is true can be known," said Plato.

2. That I believe that p. Belief is an attitude or act of the mind, so to speak (we study belief in Chapter 8, and its influence on perception in Chapter 4). Belief is not a kind of knowledge, but a requirement for knowledge. I might say, "I believe that p, but I don't know it"; however, I could never seriously assert, "I know that p, but I don't believe it." Thus, belief is a necessary condition for knowledge, but not a sufficient one. That is, one can believe wholeheartedly without knowing, but one cannot know without believing.

3. That I have good reasons, or sufficient evidence, for my belief that p; my belief must be justified. A. J. Ayer terms this "the right to be sure"; Dewey's phrase is "warranted assertability." This condition is required in order to distinguish knowledge from a lucky guess. If I were to say that there are at this moment 6,485 people visiting the Louvre, and this figure turns out upon investigation to be correct, you would be quite reluctant to concede that I knew it. You would demand to know how I knew it, or what my evidence was. In the play *Three Men on a Horse*, the hero regularly predicts the winners of horse races; but, regardless of his successful guesses, he does not *know* the winners. Similarly, the claims of astrology are not knowledge.

(Note that this condition for knowledge, like the second condition, does not operate inversely: I may sometimes have sufficient evidence, yet not succeed in knowing. When I finish reading a detective story, I may say, "I should have known!" When the cause of cancer is discovered, some scientists will undoubtedly feel that the answer was staring them right in the face all the time and that they "should have known." Thus, evidence is a necessary, but not a sufficient, condition for knowledge. This also raises the interesting question of whether knowledge can ever be unconscious. In order to know that p, must you also know that you know it? Do you know which shoe you always put on first? Or what the radio is playing while you read? Freud, in *The Interpretation of Dreams,* offers an interesting example of "unconscious knowing":

> It is a very common event for a dream to give evidence of knowledge and memories which the waking subject is unaware of possessing. One of my patients dreamt . . . that he had ordered a "Kontuszówka" while he was in a cafe. After telling me this, he asked me what a "Kontuszówka" was, as if he had never heard the name. I was able to tell him in reply that it was a Polish liqueur, and that he could not have invented the name. . . . At first he would not believe me; but some days later . . . he noticed the name on a billboard at a street corner which he must have gone past at least twice a day for several months.)

4. That I have no other evidence that might undermine my belief. Thus, I say correctly "I know that it is now 8:17 P.M." because my accurate watch reads 8:17. However, suppose that my watch had stopped this morning at exactly 8:17 A.M. Had I known that, the evidence for my true belief would have been destroyed. (We return to the analysis of these mental operations in Chapters 18, 19, and 20.)

Good Reasons

Epistemology is largely concerned with the third requirement of propositional knowledge, that is, with appraising the kinds of evidence or good reasons which are the basis of knowledge. Let us list them:

1. I know that grass is green, because I can see it. *Sense perception* is the evidence for our knowledge about the world (we examine sense perception in Chapters 3 and 4).

2. I know that the sum of any two odd numbers is always an even number, because I can prove it. *Logic* is the basis of our analytic knowledge (we examine logic in Chapters 5 and 6).

3. I know that it is wicked to torture a person, because my *intuition* tells me so. Knowledge of right and wrong is often based on such inner convictions of certainty. "Yet I doubt not through the ages one increasing purpose runs," writes Tennyson. Mystics and transcendentalists rely on this sort of reason. (We appraise the claim of intuition in Chapter 19—I fear it will not prove a very reliable basis of knowledge.)

4. I know that I have a headache, because I feel it. *Self-awareness,* or introspection, is the basis for knowing one's own "self-presenting" states. If I were to say to you, I wish it would rain; or, I feel drowsy, you would not ask me, how do you know? One's wishes, feelings, thoughts, hopes, and so on seem to be self-evident; they do not have to be inferred from something else in order to be known. But there are some problems (we explore them in Chapters 18 and 20).

5. I know that I walked home yesterday, because I remember it. Knowledge of the past begins on the basis of *memory*. But memory is of course no guarantee of truth. David Hume long preceded Sigmund Freud in claiming that remembered events differ from imagined events only in being more vivid. To verify a memory, one can compare it only with another memory: the past event cannot be hauled forth and compared with the present recollection. So there is no way to avoid a certain skepticism. Descartes said that our memories may all have been breathed into us by a malicious demon; and Russell, in a well-known passage in *The Analysis of Mind,* asserts:

> Everything constituting a memory-belief is happening now. . . . It is not logically necessary . . . that the event remembered should have occurred, or even that the past should have existed at all. There is no logical impossibility in the hypothesis that the world sprang into being five minutes ago, exactly as it then was, with a population that "remembered" a wholly unreal past . . . nothing that is happening now . . . can disprove [that] hypothesis. . . .

But a *totally* delusive memory is not what is meant by memory at all; just as there can be no "counterfeit coins" unless at least some coins are genuine, so a memory can be "erroneous" only if at least some memories are truthful. Undoubtedly we do in fact recall our past selectively; under hypnosis we recover forgotten experiences; we edit our memories, more or less deliberately. But all empirical knowledge (as we see in Chapters 9 and 10) is likewise selected and edited. Indeed, what is meant by "the present"? Literally, it is a dimensionless mathematical point, constantly vanishing. James called it "specious" and estimated that one can actually attend to a "present" time span of about twelve seconds. In this phenomenological sense, one may perceive as a unit a sentence, or a melody, or a chain of reasoning. A work of art (Chapter 21) likewise focuses the observer's attention on an extensive complex of sights or sounds so composed that it is experienced in a timeless present. (We return to the problems of memory in Chapters 17 and 18.)

6. I know that the velocity of light is 186,000 miles per second, because the physicists say so. We often rely on _authority_ (Bacon's "idols of the theatre"). Of course, we should accept someone as an authority only if he can himself produce other types of good reasons, which we all can in principle examine. Authority as a justification for knowledge is worthless if it cannot be dissolved into its ingredients.

7. I know that the number thirteen is unlucky, because everybody says so. Before we discard the justification of knowledge by _consensus gentium_ we must examine Peirce's criterion of truth (Chapter 8).

8. Joan of Arc knew that she would lead the French army, because God revealed this to her. _Revelation_ as a justification for knowledge seems to me (unless I receive one) unverifiable and unreliable.

9. St. Thomas knew that he would be resurrected after his death, because he had faith. Let no one make the disastrous error of confusing _faith_ with knowledge, or relying upon faith as a reason for knowledge. The attitude of belief, as I have said, is necessary for knowledge, but not sufficient; belief is a requisite for knowledge, but not a guarantee of it. To call belief "faith" does not improve it, whether that faith be in God, or in Jupiter, or in Destiny, or in human nature.

To recapitulate this chapter: descriptive knowledge (as contrasted with experience, knowledge by acquaintance, and knowing how) consists of propositions believed to be true for uncontroverted adequate reasons. Five of these reasons warrant further careful examination: sense perception, logic, intuition, self-awareness, and memory. It seems to me safe to deny the thoroughgoing skepticism of Gorgias, who argued that nothing existed; and if it did, it could not be apprehended; and if it could be apprehended, that apprehension could not be communicated. If he could tell us all that, how can knowledge not be communicated?

3

Our Knowledge of the External World

"I KNOW that grass is green, because I can see it." Surely nothing is simpler than that! But sense perception as a basis for knowledge needs to be examined closely.

Perceptual Knowledge

What exactly are the senses? They are usually specified as sight, sound, touch, taste, and smell. *Senses* are avenues by which what is going on outside of me can, in different ways, come in to me—either mechanically (as in sound or touch), or chemically (taste, smell), or photically (sight). There are also other, less clearly defined, pathways. I have a "proprioceptive," or kinesthetic, sense (which tells me where my foot is, without my looking), and senses of motion, of pressure, of temperature, and of pain. Recent studies of so-called visceral learning suggest that there may be other "interoceptive," or internal, senses. We might be able in time to sense our blood pressure, for example. A blind man develops an obstacle sense, which may be based on auditory echoes. Sometimes we are unaware of which sense is supplying us with information, or even of having received information; this phenomenon may explain "extra-sensory" perception.

Sense awareness varies among species. Some animals have sensory avenues that human beings lack, such as sensitivity to radio waves and to magnetic fields. Certain fish emit electrical impulses and sense their surroundings by the deformation of electric fields. Some birds sense changes in barometric pressure and polarized light. Thus <u>every organism lives in the world shaped for it by its sensory apparatus.</u>

The kind of information available to each creature is determined not only by its senses, but also by the range of stimuli. Human beings can hear sounds ranging from about 16 to 20,000 cycles per second, but some moths can hear up to 200,000 cycles. Human sensitivity to odors is minimal, but salmon can smell their way home through countless miles of trackless water. We can see a spectrum of colors ranging from violet to red, but this relatively small range of visible light lies within a vast continuous range of similar electromagnetic waves not visible to us. And individuals differ of course in the range of their sensory acuity: professional tea-tasters, for example, are said to be able to distinguish some 1,500 varieties of tea.

Certain characteristics of sensory perception as a basis for knowledge raise problems. Thus, it is troublesomely *subjective* and relative; it varies with many conditions which are extrinsic to the object perceived. As Sextus Empiricus put it,

> the vestibule of the bath house warms those who enter from the street and chills those leaving the baths . . . the same wine seems sour to those who have eaten dates and sweet to those who have eaten nuts.

Grass is green, but is it green on a cloudy day? or under a microscope? Is it green to a person who is color-blind? or who is high on drugs? or who comes out of a room illuminated by colored lights? None of these incidentals has anything to do with grass.

Perception is sometimes downright *deceptive*. There is that notorious oar in the water which has served philosophers faithfully for millennia by looking bent or broken. There are also mirages, hallucinations (Macbeth's dagger), illusions (the prestidigitator), phantom pain in amputated limbs, ambiguous after-images, and distortions caused by context, perspective, expectations, and conventions. These are part of the task of perception (discussed in Chapter 4); they also bear on our determination of "the facts" (Chapter 9).

Visual perception is *discontinuous*. Seeing consists physically of separate glances, each lasting about a quarter of a second. (The world might disappear in the intervals, and we would never know it.) The brain pieces together these distinct stimuli to construct an image of a stable and continuous world.

And there is a *time lag* in all sense perception. Light travels at a finite speed, as Roemer discovered in 1675. The sun we see "now" is actually as it was when the light left it about eight minutes ago. Some stars that we see now may in fact no longer exist. Sound, of course, travels much more slowly than light. Moreover, when a stimulus reaches the eye or ear or other sense organ, it takes time to pass through the nervous system to the brain. Thus, what we see or hear at any given instant is a delayed report by a dilatory messenger.

In sum, our perceptual knowledge of the world is shaped for us by a sensory apparatus of a particular kind, with a limited range. Our perceptions are subjective, somewhat deceptive, discontinuous, and outdated. But of course the cure for the shortcomings of our senses is not to stop using them, but to use them critically and to be aware of these shortcomings. Errors in perception are corrected by more discriminating perception. Still, we can never claim certainty or universality for empirical knowledge based on sense perception.

Primary and Secondary Qualities

Philosophers have long been puzzled by the relation between the grass outside me and the sense perception of green inside me. Democritus said, "Sweet and bitter, cold and warm, as well as the colors—all these things exist but in opinion, and not in reality." But if such qualities are only "secondary," or psychological, are there then "primary" qualities which are real? If I prick my finger with a pin, or burn my hand, the pain is surely *in me*; why then should I say that the sharpness is *in the pin,* and the heat *in the fire,* rather than in me? John Locke regarded such qualities of objects as shape, extension, solidity, and motion as primary, that is, as existing in the objects and not merely "in opinion." Leibniz, however, thought them only "apparent." Berkeley argued that *all* my sense perceptions occur only within me; whatever qualities are primary are never encountered apart from secondary qualities. *Esse est percipi,* he wrote: to be is to be perceived.

The issue of whether there are primary and secondary qualities is the kind of problem that has been dissolved: scientifically, by the realization that even size, shape, and velocity are relational properties; and philosophically, by G. E. Moore's analysis of Berkeley's claims. Moore showed that Berkeley confused awareness with the object of awareness, by mistaking a sensation of green for a green sensation. Our knowledge of external things is indeed based on internal sensations, but it is idle to try to classify sensations and qualities as primary or secondary.

Sense Data and Things

If we examine a perceptual experience carefully, we can usually analyze it into a sensory core, or sense datum (for example, a particular sound or color), and an act of inference or interpretation. That noise, we say, is the train; that light is a star. But the inference may be erroneous: that noise may actually have been thunder; that light may be an airplane. There is also reason to question whether perceptual experience can always be properly separated into a sensory core and an inference. If I say, "That blue thing is my pen," did I really first see a blue patch and then infer that it was my pen? (There is an analogous question in the philosophy of art: can what is *presented* on a colored canvas be distinguished from what is *represented* thereby?)

In the attempt, however, to establish empirical knowledge on as secure a basis as possible, let us take sense datum reports as the foundation. The simplest statement of a perception of a sense datum, devoid of inference (e.g., "blue here now"), is called a *protocol.* This is the indispensable minimum of what we can rely on; this is what is *"given"* to us, if anything at all ever is. There is nothing in the world between me and my seeing "blue here now." Sense data are immediately present to our consciousness, instantly revealed, directly apprehended. We cannot say that protocols are certainly true, as we have just noted, but protocols as such are not corrigible; there is no other test by means of which we may verify them. We can never get any closer to the world than our sense data.

(As infants grow up, they learn how to infer the existence of permanent objects from their fleeting sense data. It takes time for the infant to acquire habits of association and generalization. Gradually these habits become well established, but it is quite a while before children reach the age at which their perception is sophisticated enough so that they can enjoy being deceived by a magician.)

Robinson Crusoe saw certain marks on the sand and inferred that they were the footprints of another man on his island. Can we similarly construct the concept of "physical object" out of sense data? Mach, Russell, Goodman, and other philosophers have proposed this sort of construction; Carnap's *Der Logische Aufbau der Welt* is an outstanding attempt. John Stuart Mill defined *thing* (in a classic phrase) as the "permanent possibility of sensation." "Phenomenalism" is the position that to say that a material object has a physical property is to say that certain phenomena (i.e., sense data) are occurring. The "selective realists" assert that "things" are real groups of "sensibilia"—possibilities that become sense data whenever a mind becomes aware of them. But James snorted, "A permanently existing 'idea' or *Vorstellung* which makes its appearance before the footlights of consciousness at periodic intervals, is as mythological an entity as the Jack of Spades."

No one has as yet succeeded in specifying the particular sense data out of which any given thing could be constructed. W. V. Quine declares that the entire enterprise of constructing science out of sense datum reports plus logic has failed.

There are other nagging complexities in the notion of sense datum. Can I sense the same datum twice? If I blink at my pen, do I have two sense data of blue, or one repeated? If the second is not exactly like the first, which (if either one) is wrong? (That is why a protocol isn't corrigible.) Or is a sense datum never wrong, but always just what it seems to be? Does a sense datum take time? and if so, can it change? If you and I both look at my blue pen, do we share a single sense datum? Is the sense datum an event, or a thing? mental, or physical? or both? or neither? What sorts of data can be sensed? It is clear that "this looks blue" is a sense datum report, but what about "this looks stale"? or "he looks untrustworthy"? Are not these other qualities also simple, instantaneous, unmediated, and incorrigible? None of these irritating questions has been satisfactorily resolved.

Thus, the road that leads from my sense perceptions to my knowledge of a world outside myself is full of gaps, brambles, and obscurities. But it is the only road I have; if I refused to travel on it because of its risks, I would not ever get outside of me. It is true that inference to the independent existence of external objects cannot be demonstrated. Russell says flatly, "Belief in the existence of things outside my own biography . . . must be regarded as a prejudice." But our justification of such a belief is pragmatic: we survive and act successfully in the world by assuming it. I agree with Peirce, "Let us not pretend to doubt in philosophy what we do not doubt in our hearts."

4

The Task of Perception

WHEN I SPOKE in Chapter 3 of the infant learning how to see—
that is, learning how to associate certain sense data with objects
—I intended to introduce the subject of this chapter. Perception
is indeed a task to be accomplished and a problem to be solved.
Perception is active inquiry, not passive reception. The scientist
as well as the baby must learn how to see, that is, how to grapple
with the flux of sensation and make it amenable to our purposes.
The observer is not the spectator of a self-revealing ordered
universe. The painter Constable shrewdly remarked, "the art of
seeing nature is almost as much to be acquired as the art of reading Egyptian hieroglyphs."

Seeing-as

I mentioned the difficulty of separating sense data from the accompanying inference or interpretation. Did I really first see a
blue patch and then infer that it was my pen? Aside from protocols ("blue here now"), all acts of perception would seem to be
acts of perceiving *as* something. Think back to the first time you

saw an X ray, or an aerial photograph, or the man in the moon, or the face of a clock, or a musical score. Have you ever watched a cricket match, or a ballet, and wondered what the audience was applauding? Why did astronomers not know for years whether or not they were seeing canals on Mars? Because in every case, there is more to seeing than meets the eye! All seeing is *seeing-as,* and we must learn how to do this.

What enters the eye is not really seen until it is organized by the brain. To see *what is the case* requires context, inference, concepts, experience, interpretation. This is the basis of the Rohrschach test, which elicits a variety of "seeings-as" in response to a neutral inkblot. Hamlet got Polonius to agree that a cloud looked like a camel, a weasel, and a whale. Two people will stumble over a bit of hard clay, but only one of them will see it as a fragment of a Greek vase. A painter will see his model as a Venus, or as a Madonna, or as his mother. We see a Vermeer kitchen as cheerful and inviting, a Chirico landscape as menacing and ominous. The physicist "sees" the electron as a wave, and electricity as a current. The astronomer "sees" light from the sun as coming in individual rays. William James "saw" consciousness as a stream. Freud "saw" the libido as a reservoir. In the early seventeenth century, the orbit of Mars was seen as a circle (what other path could a heavenly body possibly take?); any deviations therefrom were seen as "librations" (the oscillations of the pans in a scale balance before they come to rest) ; but Kepler saw the orbit as an ellipse.

There is no "innocent eye." Nietzsche called this "the fallacy of the immaculate perception." In order for you to perceive something, you must add to your sense datum; you must furnish an element of projection. No single act of seeing-as is therefore necessarily the only one or the correct one. Moreover, any one interpretation excludes all others. The psychologist Joseph Jastrow used a well-known drawing to illustrate this point—it is a figure that can be seen as either a duck or a rabbit, and it shifts from one to the other as you look at it; it can never be seen as both, and neither interpretation is "correct." Likewise, if in looking at a painting you concentrate on the brush strokes, you will not see what the painting depicts, and vice versa. In addition, the figure and the ground in a picture may be reversible (M. C. Esch-

er and Salvador Dali are among the painters who make use of
this feature of perception). Perception is "multistable." The ambiguity, or available choices, are not always evident in an image,
and cannot always be isolated. There is therefore no sharp line
dividing perception from illusion.

Perception as the Solution of a Problem

The *selective* nature of perception is also a consequence of the
fact that the number of sensory stimuli, or possible messages from
outside, is greater than we can receive and process. The channels
of communication to us are crowded and noisy; we must filter
stimuli. What we receive is usually what we expect, or want, or
believe, or are used to. Our eyes and brains coordinate how objects look at different distances, from different directions, and
under different light, and show us an object to which we attribute a constant size, shape, and color. To perceive is to *solve
a problem*. Our capacity "to find strands of permanence in the
tumult of changing appearances" (Polanyi) has survival value.
Gestalt psychologists stress how we tend to perceive well-defined
patterns and wholes which are not really there, by integrating
heterogeneous cues and filling in contours. Michael Polanyi explains, in *Personal Knowledge*:

> Perception is manifestly an activity which seeks to satisfy stan-
> dards which it sets to itself. The muscles of the eye adjust the
> thickness of its lens, so as to produce the sharpest possible retinal
> image. . . . But sharpness of contour does not always predominate
> in the shaping of what we see . . . when a ball set against a fea-
> tureless background is inflated, it is seen as if it retained its size
> and was coming nearer. . . . The rule that we follow . . . is one
> that we taught ourselves as babies, when we first experimented
> with approaching a rattle to our eyes and moving it away again.

Influence of Convention

In addition to these physical, physiological, and psychological
considerations, social conditioning is important in determining
how things "naturally look." The term "realism" in art is used

to describe the conventions that are familiar to us; but "flat" Japanese painting, and the Bayeux tapestries, and ancient Egyptian painting are equally "realistic." Each society relies on its own visual schemata; it takes for granted its own "distortions" and "abstractions." Picasso's *Demoiselles d'Avignon* shows the nose in profile, and the eye in front view; twentieth-century Europe found this a revolutionary distortion, but that is how the ancient Egyptians "naturally" painted. *Trompe l'oeil* seldom deceives an infant, or another culture, or a later generation. That is why the history of art is not just a history of artists, but also of styles and conventions.

A striking example of the *persistence of convention* is reported by Meyer Schapiro. In Géricault's *Horse Race* (*c.* 1820), the galloping horses are shown with all four feet off the ground and pointed in opposite directions (*le galop volante*). No horse can do this naturally; the Lippizaner horses of Vienna perform it after years of intensive training. But Géricault was unconsciously copying certain English hunting prints, which had copied the engravings of Charles Cochin (*c.* 1750), who had been influenced by the introduction from China into France of porcelain, prints, and *chinoiserie*. In China, the *galop volante* is found as far back as the Han dynasty (206 B.C.–A.D. 220); the Chinese borrowed it from the nomadic Iranian tribes, who borrowed it from the Mycenaeans, who got it from Paleolithic man. And in all these centuries no horse ever did it!

The story of Dürer's rhinoceros also illustrates the overwhelming weight of tradition in determining representation, even when an actual model is before the artist's eyes. Dürer (who died in 1528) had never seen that famous exotic beast, the "dragon with an armored body." Nevertheless he made a woodcut of one, relying on second-hand evidence and his imagination. For centuries thereafter, natural history books used his half-invented creature as a model. When James Bruce visited Africa in 1790 and saw a rhinoceros, he called attention to how "wonderfully ill-executed" Dürer's woodcut was. Yet Bruce's own illustration, drawn from life, was so strongly influenced by his idea of what a rhinoceros ought to look like (i.e., like Dürer's woodcut) that no zoologist can identify what Bruce actually saw! (E. H. Gombrich tells this story in his *Art and Illusion* to show the persistent influence of convention.)

The influence of convention—or lack thereof—may be seen in how primitive people look at a photograph. Melville Herskovits writes,

> More than one ethnographer has reported the experience of showing a clear photograph of a house, a person, a familiar landscape, to people living in a culture innocent of any knowledge of photography, and to have the picture held at all possible angles, or turned over for an inspection of its blank back, as the native tried to interpret this meaningless arrangement of varying shades of grey on a piece of paper.

African audiences are at first baffled by our movies; it is not at all clear to them what is going on.

Perspective drawing is also conventional. The frescoes painted in Florence by Paolo Uccello (1397–1475) were apparently the first successful solution to the problem of showing three-dimensional space on the two dimensions of a wall or a canvas. (There were some earlier, tentative efforts; in this, as in everything else, it seems that nothing was ever done for the first time!) The laws of optics and geometry do not entail our conventional manner of showing distance, nor did it occur to earlier generations, nor to other cultures. We draw railroad tracks as if meeting in the distance; but we do not draw vertical telephone poles or the sides of a skyscraper as if converging at the top (although this may be because the psychological preference for seeing things in their most stable aspect overrules the convention of perspective). The painter Jehudo Epstein came to Germany in 1929 from a tiny orthodox Jewish community in Poland which prohibited "graven images"; he found that he could not draw a castle on a hill until someone lent him a book on perspective. Chinese painting employs a radically different convention: more distant objects are typically shown less distinctly or with less intense colors, rather than drawn smaller; and the painter may rely on a moving focus rather than on a fixed point of view; thus, a mountain might be shown from above and from below, or at different times. (But the fact that depth can be represented by various conventions does not help to answer a question with which it is sometimes confused, whether a newborn baby perceives spatial depth, nor whether a man who is born blind and acquires sight in maturity can distinguish a cube from a sphere by looking at them from a distance, since all his experience up to that point has been from the sense of touch. So far as I can find out, there is no hard evidence on either of these issues.)

Influence of Belief

The influence of belief, or hypothesis, on perception is so striking that one might almost say, not that seeing is believing, but that believing is seeing. There is abundant experimental evidence that what people report about their own afterimage depends on what they are told to expect. "Stooges" can get subjects in experiments to agree that they see unequal lines as equal, or that a fixed candlelight in a dark room is moving (the "autokinetic phenomenon") ; these erroneous perceptions persist even after those who have been misleading the subjects have left the room! Experiments have also shown that the unconscious bias of researchers in the social sciences affects their finding.

The witches of Salem and Loudun swore that they had seen, heard, and touched the devil; some even gave details of sexual intercourse. Nietzsche described the powerful influence of myths on the excitable ancient Greeks, who "saw" the goddess Athena in the marketplace and "heard" the tree-nymphs speaking. Hundreds of sober citizens today swear that they have seen flying saucers.

The history of science, too, is full of accounts that illustrate the influence of belief on perception. Scientists, like everyone else, tend to rely upon entrenched paradigms which may predetermine their choice of data. In 1846 James Challis, an astronomer at Cambridge, set out reluctantly to verify the hypothesis proposed by Leverrier and Adams that there existed a planet then unknown (Neptune); he had no confidence in their hypothesis and did not realize until afterward that he had actually unwittingly sighted the planet on four different occasions. Later in the nineteenth century, on the other hand, many astronomical observers reported that they had seen the supposed (but actually nonexistent) planet Vulcan, presumed to lie between the sun

and Mercury. The actuality of hypnotic phenomena was denied
for a century; Mesmer (1733–1815) was denounced as an impostor; a Dr. Esdaile (1808–1859) performed some three hundred
major operations in India by hypnosis, but no medical journal
would print his account (editors said the Indians had simply
wanted to please Esdaile and liked to be operated on!). Kelvin
declared X rays to be a hoax.

A most revealing account of the influence of belief on perception has been given by a curator of the Metropolitan Museum
of Art about a famous ancient Greek statue of a horse:

> For some years, every day or two I would walk through the Greek
> bronze gallery. I'd look at the horse, from a different angle every
> time. One day, in July 1961, I did a double-take. For the first time
> I paid attention to a line—it can be seen in all the photos in all
> the books—that runs from the top of the mane down to the tip of
> his nose. I examined it through the glass showcase. . . . I knew as
> sure as I was standing there that the piece was a fraud. I had seen
> the piece a thousand times before and the line had not registered.
> This time the line did. . . .

Hearing-as

My examples in this chapter have been concerned mostly with
seeing, but similar considerations apply to other senses. It comes
as no surprise that we hear a wide variety of different sounds as
the one we expect. If you are told, "Bert was sleepy, so he went
to bed," almost any consonant can be substituted for the *b* in
bed, with no change in what the brain reports. A phoneme can
sometimes be excised from a tape and replaced by, say, a cough,
and its absence will not be noticed. (Let court reporters and
psychoanalysts be warned!) The psychologist A. M. Liberman
declares, "the sounds of speech are a special . . . code on the phonemic structure of language, not a cipher or alphabet." And,
according to William James:

> How little we actually hear, when we listen to speech, we realize
> when we go to a foreign theatre; for there what troubles us
> is not so much that we cannot understand what the actors say as

that we cannot hear their words . . . we hear quite as little under similar conditions at home, only our mind, being fuller of English verbal associations, supplies the requisite material for comprehension upon a much slighter auditory hint.

In fact, how a given vowel is pronounced varies considerably from speaker to speaker. We possess a kind of mental map of a language, into which each of us fits the sounds we hear. This is one reason for the persistence of a regional or foreign accent: the speaker thinks he is reproducing just what he hears. It is also the reason why typewriters and telephone dials constructed so as to be activated by the sound of the human voice can be set for a single speaker only.

Music offers additional evidence of hearing-as. If you are told that a passage of Beethoven's Fifth Symphony is the "elephant roll" or that a certain composition is called the *Moonlight Sonata* or *Rain-drop Prelude,* your hearing of those sounds becomes irrevocably hearing-as. I cannot myself ever hear the beginning of Mendelssohn's A Major Symphony without forming the words, "It*a*lian, It*a*lian, *Sym*pho-o-ny."

Onomatopoeia, too, is conventional. Speakers of different languages "hear" certain common sounds quite distinctly. American cats say *meow*; French cats say *ron-ron*; German, *schnurr-schnurr*; Japanese, *niago*. Our dogs say *bow-wow* or *arf-arf*; in France dogs say *gnaf-gnaf*; in Spain, *guau-guau;* in Japan, *wung-wung;* in Africa, *kpei-kpei.* In France the rain drops as *plouf-plouf*; in Japan, *zaa-zaa.* A baby's cry in Japan is *ogya-ogya.*

Thus, sensory perception is not passive reception, but active inquiry. It is a task to be accomplished. What is seen, says Sartre, is possessed; to see is to deflower. In my own metaphor, we must cook the raw sensation before we can digest it. We must place sensations in a context, draw inferences, use concepts, project, select, learn, impose structure; in doing this, we rely on convention, on tradition, on accepted paradigms, hypotheses, beliefs, and social pressures. If we succeed in our task, our perception will disclose a world somewhat more amenable to human goals.

5

When Do We Attain Certainty?

IN CHAPTERS 3 AND 4 we discussed the kind of knowledge of the world that we acquire through sense perception. Philosophers, in their search for certainty, have often contrasted this knowledge with the knowledge to be attained by reason. Leibniz, for example, spoke of *vérités de fait* and *vérités de raison*; and Hume distinguished "experimental reasoning concerning matter of fact and existence" from "abstract reasoning concerning quantity and number."

Analytic and Synthetic Propositions

Let us specify some kinds of propositions that seem to be quite certainly true:

1. Statements of identity. "Bert is Bertrand"; "St. Anne is the mother of Mary."
2. Statements asserting the inclusion of a subclass within a class. "All black cats are cats"; "all cats are animals"; "all squares are rectangles" (i.e., all rectangles with equal sides are rectangles).

3. Definitions. "A bachelor is an unmarried man"; "a triangle has three angles"; "a yard is three feet."

4. Stipulations. "A proposition is either true or false."

5. Statements making implicit meanings explicit. "Every wife has a husband"; "if Bert is a younger son, then Bert is a brother"; "a positive integer is even or uneven."

The propositions in these overlapping groups are true by virtue of the meanings of their terms, or by their form alone, or by the explication of symbols, or by convention. Such propositions are called *analytic*. Denial of an analytic proposition is self-contradictory. If you claimed to have found an exception—a wife without a husband, or a four-angled triangle, or a black cat that was not a cat—it would be clear that you did not understand the meanings of the words that make up the proposition. Someone may indeed ask, what if we decided to call all women over the age of twenty "wives"?—or to write the number three as "4"? Only chaos results from such arbitrariness. Words possess established meanings and uses. If we do not maintain some fixity of meaning during discourse, communication (even with ourselves) becomes impossible. Abraham Lincoln once asked a friend, if you call a dog's tail a leg, how many legs would he have? When his friend answered five, Lincoln said he was wrong, because calling a dog's tail a leg doesn't make it one.

Analytic propositions, then, are certain. They are immune from revision on the basis of empirical evidence. We know them to be true a priori, that is, in advance of any experience, regardless of what happens, independently of fact. They are true "in all possible worlds." However, let us be clear about what sort of information they provide, and why Mill called analytic propositions "verbal" rather than " real." The price of their certainty is that they have no factual content; they do not restrict the frame of empirical possibility. As Wittgenstein says, " 'It will either rain or not rain' tells you nothing about the weather." The proposition "All politicians are liars, or some are not" is certainly true, but it merely exemplifies how such terms as *all, some, or,* and *not* are used; it supplies no information. (A motto suitable to a University chapel might be, "The Divine is rightly so-called.")

An illustration may clarify this point. If I say now that it will rain in Times Square at noon on July 4, 1980, I am offering very specific information, but the probability of my being correct is slight. If I say it will rain somewhere in New York City sometime during July 1980, I am providing less specific information, but the probability of my being correct is greater. If I say it will rain somewhere in America sometime during the twenty-first century, I am providing almost no information, but I have a correspondingly greater chance of being correct. The analytic proposition "It will either rain or not rain" carries this process to infinity, so to speak. It is the limiting case: it gives zero information, with 100% probability. Since an analytic proposition gives no information, nothing can disprove it: it is not falsifiable.

All propositions that are not analytic (that is, true by their meanings alone) are *synthetic*. Synthetic propositions contain information and require factual or empirical evidence to demonstrate their truth. Sometimes a statement may be ambiguous. Consider the proposition "A good man keeps his promises." Suppose that Bert, who is in every other way a good man, breaks a trivial promise. If you then say that Bert is no longer a good man, you are treating the proposition as a definition of "good man" and therefore analytic. But if you say that Bert is still a good man, and there may be exceptions to the rule, then you are treating the proposition as falsifiable and therefore synthetic.

Similarly ambiguous propositions are "No true American would strike a lady," Yogi Berra's "You can observe a lot, just by watching," and "Study philosophy long enough, and you will understand it perfectly" (how long would it take to falsify that?). Ambiguity may of course be intentional. Seneca said to the bloody emperor Nero, "However many people you slaughter, you cannot kill your successor." But any ambiguity between the analytic and the synthetic may always be removed by making explicit what is intended.

Let us now examine the distinction more closely. Kant thought that the predicate of an analytic proposition is "contained" in the subject and adds nothing to the subject, but rather breaks it up into its constituents, whereas in a synthetic proposition you add "to the concept of the subject a predicate which has not been in any wise thought in it, and which no analysis could possibly extract from it." For that reason he declared "7 + 5 = 12" to be synthetic, since when you think of "7 + 5" you do not actually have "12" in your mind; you therefore add something to the subject. But Kant seems on shaky ground here. To distinguish between analytic and synthetic propositions by referring to what you may or may not have thought is to introduce a dubious psychological element. The basis of the analytic must rather be found in logic, by examining what "the concept of the subject" objectively entails. Such propositions as "7 + 5 = 12" are held by Russell and many others to be analytic. They are explications of symbols, and the symbol "12" is logically equivalent to the symbols "7 + 5".

However, in determining analyticity, we cannot disregard the relevance of what we happen to know at a particular time, and what classifications prove to be suitable. Kant considered "all bodies are extended" as analytic, and "all bodies have weight" as synthetic. That is, he regarded "occupying space" (but not "having weight") as contained in the meaning of "body." Contemporary analysis of the concept of "body" (or "matter") now makes this distinction quite doubtful.

But if analytic propositions are subject to revision as knowledge accumulates, how can we say they are certainly true? "All whales are mammals" is analytically true (inclusion of a subclass within a class), but a century ago whales were classified as fish. Biologists now find it more useful to classify whales not on the basis of habitat, but rather according to the fact that they are warm-blooded, air-breathing, and viviparous. It is not the whales that have changed, but the suitability of our classifications. When Harold Urey in 1932 discovered deuterium, or heavy hydrogen, he referred to it as a new isotope of hydrogen, although it could be separated chemically; but isotopes had always been defined as chemically inseparable! What these examples show is the utility of a change in the use of a term or the application of a concept. When we decide that a proposition is analytic, we treat it as timelessly true, but our decision need not therefore be eternally useful. Classifications are often abandoned (as we noted in the discussion of universals in metaphysics, Chapter 1).

Philosophers as far back as Hobbes have said that it is the rules of language which determine what is analytic. In other words, they maintain that an analytic proposition reveals the (perhaps unsuspected) implications of linguistic usage. Schlick thus asserts that "we would never have any use" for such a sentence as "the child is naked and dressed at the same time." Ayer declares that it is grammar which rules out saying that something is red and green at the same time. But this explanation seems to me inadequate. Language and grammar are just too changeable, trivial, superficial, parochial, and imprecise. They fix only the outer limits of approved usage. (This problem is discussed more fully in Chapter 19.)

Recent Attacks

The clarity of the analytic-synthetic distinction has come under attack in recent years. I have said that "A bachelor is an unmarried man" is analytic. What about "A bachelor is an unhappy man"? The latter proposition, you might exclaim, is not even true, let alone analytic. But consider: what do we mean by "unhappy"? Suppose another Freud or Einstein appears and reveals an illuminating new theoretical framework for analyzing the concept of happiness, so that—just as whales became mammals—and chemically separable deuterium became a hydrogen isotope —we come to realize that a requisite to happiness is the stable monogamy which the bachelor eschews. Morton White sees this as the ancient problem of "essential predication," that is, of determining what predicates or qualities are of the essence of a subject. "Brothers are male siblings" is analytic. What about "Brothers show sibling rivalry"? Is rivalry an essential predicate of siblings? Do dictionary definitions have any authority over and above common usage? What about the overtones of words: may synonyms always be substituted for one another? (cf. *sophisticated, disingenuous,* and *uncandid*; and wouldn't you laugh at *The Male Siblings Karamazov*? See Chapter 19). If you cannot imagine ever saying "this is red and green," or if you react with aversion to "the child is naked and dressed," remember that some people cannot imagine, or react with aversion, to putting salt on ice cream. Thus any behavioral criterion alone (that is, a distinction based on what people actually say and do) might be insufficient. If you were to say that the difference between the analytic and the synthetic represents a difference in kind rather than a difference in degree, Herbert Feigl has cleverly asked whether the difference between differences of degree and differences in kind is itself a difference of degree or a difference in kind. Quine declares that the analytic and the synthetic form a continuum, rather than separate classes, and that "our analyticity intuition grades off." Carl Hempel now denies that "analysis of meaning" can be made at all clear.

Pragmatic Justification

I would argue, however, that the analytic-synthetic distinction is much too useful to be discarded. (Abel's Razor: *theoria non delenda praeter necessitatem*: razors should not be thrown away as long as they give a fairly decent shave, even if they do not reach all the whiskers, until you have a better one.)

The proper approach is to clarify how the distinction introduces order into our experience. There is no extrinsic criterion for the analytic: it is *we* who decide what cannot be denied without self-contradiction, and we who will not permit exceptions to an analytic proposition (does a good man keep his promises?). The situation is similar in physics, which retains such principles as the conservation of energy, regardless of what seems to be contrary evidence. Thus in the 1930s when energy was being "lost" from the nucleus of a radioactive atom in beta decay, Pauli said that this energy must be escaping in the form of some unknown particle. It required over fifteen years to detect the neutrino, but the physicist's confidence in the conservation of energy was justified. (When deuterium was discovered, on the other hand, the physicists deemed it better to change their concept of the isotope.) If we decide someday that rivalry is to be part of the meaning of "sibling," it will be in order to improve our description of psychological phenomena. The decision is pragmatic; it is based on our need to understand, predict, and control, not on any extrahuman structure of meanings. The analytic-synthetic distinction serves to regulate our inquiries and to organize our knowledge. It is man who is the measure.

No Synthetic A Priori

I have said that it is only analytic propositions which are certainly true; but there are contrary opinions. Here are some examples of propositions that are asserted to be synthetic a priori; that is, it is claimed that they are known in advance of any experience to be certainly true, although they do not merely analyze meanings, but provide genuine information about the world:

1. The whole is equal to the sum of all its parts.
2. Whatever is colored must be extended.
3. Whatever has shape has size.
4. Every sound has pitch and volume.
5. I see with my eyes.
6. A man must be some age or other.
7. Everything that exists might have been different from what it is.
8. Every cube has twelve edges.
9. If an event A precedes an event B, and B precedes an event C, then A precedes C.

Rationalist philosophers have thought that these truths are inherent in the objective structure of the world and that we recognize them by our "natural light of reason," or by immediate intuition of essences (the phenomenological *Wesensschau*). Such claims seem questionable. The examples given, if carefully examined, will be found to be either actually analytic (1, 3, 4, and 8), or not a priori (2 has been doubted by Fichte and Moore), or too ambiguous, vague, or loosely phrased to permit analysis (5, 6, 7, and 9). More intractable examples, in my opinion, however, are:

10. Nothing is both red and green all over and at the same time.
11. Pink is more like red than black.

Examples 10 and 11 seem quite clearly a priori—nothing (not even a pointillist subterfuge) would make me doubt them—yet it is not immediately apparent that they are analytic. However, colors are what they are because they constitute a *formal* order. Why is it analytic that nothing can be at once two feet long and three feet long? Because it is part of the meaning of something being a certain size that it cannot simultaneously be any other size. This is not a fact about the world (where everything, of course, may be constantly changing in size), but rather a determination to use "size" in a certain way. The perception of color is causally associated with electromagnetic waves, which have a certain length (size) and therefore do not at the same time have any other length. Although I admit I am not thoroughly satisfied with this analysis, I do not think there is a case to be made for synthetic a priori propositions.

I have used examples from logic and mathematics throughout this chapter; they are the best examples of the analytic. They require, however, a separate chapter, because of the important claim that in their universality and clarity they disclose the eternal structure of the world.

6

Logic, Mathematics, and Metaphysics

IN CHAPTER 5 I asked, when do we attain certainty? and I answered that only analytic propositions are certain, or known to be true a priori; they explicate meanings and contain no factual information. Once you learn that "bachelor" means "unmarried man," you know a priori and for certain that any bachelor you meet is unmarried; but all that you know is the meaning of a term.

Let us now examine the second example of knowledge I offered in Chapter 2, in which the justification given is reason, or proof: "I know that the sum of any two odd numbers is always an even number, because I can prove it." If this proposition is analytic, how can it provide genuine information? And what does it mean to prove it? What is the nature of implication?

Aristotelian Logic

Logic is Aristotle's great achievement. He first showed that the ways in which to make a valid inference from one proposition to another are purely formal; in other words, validity consists of following rules, regardless of what the propositions are about. Thus, "all *x* is *y*" is contradicted by "some *x* is not *y*" (if either is true the other is false, and if either is false the other is true) whether the propositions containing *x* and *y* are about politicians being liars, or cats being animals, or anything else. The forms of valid inference apply universally.

The proposition is the basic unit of knowledge. It asserts a connection between a *subject* and a *predicate* by a *copula* (the verb *is* or *are*). Since a proposition may be either affirmative or negative, and since it may refer to all, or only to some, of the subject, there are four basic propositional forms (called *A, E, I,* and *O*). These may be converted and combined in specified valid procedures. (All of the detailed valid operations were not finally sorted out until A.D. 1276 by Peter of Spain, who shortly thereafter became Pope John XXI. Logicians for a thousand years memorized the rules of syllogism; when Pippa in Browning's poem passed the university she heard the students droning the ancient mnemonic *Barbara Celarent Darii* . . . in which the vowels indicated the propositional forms) .

Laws of Thought

The Aristotelian logicians said that there were three basic "laws of thought." These laws are:

1. *Identity.* Everything is what it is and not something else (*x* is *x*).

2. *Contradiction.* The same attribute cannot both belong and not belong to the same subject at the same time and in the same respect (*x* is not both *y* and not-*y*); or, a proposition cannot be both true and false.

3. *Excluded middle.* An attribute either does or does not belong to a subject (*x* either is *y* or is not *y*); or, a proposition is either true or it is false. Any middle ground between truth and falsity is excluded.

The Aristotelians considered these three laws as absolute principles from which any demonstration must begin; and they were held to be more than rules for valid inference. As Spinoza put it, "The order and connection of ideas is the order and connection of things." The laws were thus deemed to be laws of being as well as laws of thought, to be constitutive principles of metaphysics as well as of logic. The proposition connects a subject with a predicate because the world consists of substances that have attributes. This was a stunning insight; we will shortly see whether it can be maintained.

Criticism of Traditional Logic

Kant wrote in 1787 that logic, since Aristotle, "has not been able to advance a single step, and is to all appearances a closed and completed body of doctrine." But soon thereafter, in a remarkable intellectual explosion, the two-thousand-year-old structure of logic was torn apart by such men as Boole, DeMorgan, Frege, Peano, Peirce, Schiller, Russell, and Whitehead. There were three major lines of critical analysis.

I. Essentially, Aristotle's view of propositional form was found to be insufficiently precise. He treated alike all propositions of the form "all x is y," although this form may actually cloak some sharply different kinds of assertion. Some examples are:

1. "All bachelors are unmarried men." Definition.
2. "All whales are mammals." Analytic inclusion of a subclass within a class.
3. "All cabinet members are Republicans." Inductive inclusion of a subclass within a class (based on the enumeration of a finite class—in this case the class of cabinet members).
4. "All politicians are liars." Synthetic inductive generalization based on a sample, believed probably correct.
5. "All full professors are Ph.D.'s." Statement of a requirement, or resolution: in order to be a full professor, one must possess a Ph.D.
6. "All citizens of authoritarian dictatorships who openly oppose the regime are brave." Hypothetical statement that if indeed

there are any such citizens, they would be brave; but there may be none.

Note also the variety of meanings that may be contained in the copula *is*:

1. "St. Anne is the mother of Mary." Identification.
2. "The raven is black." Ascription of an attribute to a subject.
3. "Ted Kennedy is a senator." Assertion of membership in a class (in this case, the class of senators).
4. "To strive is to succeed." Assertion of entailment: if you strive, then you will succeed.
5. "God is." Assertion of existence.
6. "This spoon is silver." Description of composition: the spoon is *made up of* silver.

(Russell called the ambiguity of *is* "a disgrace to the human race." That ambiguity is the reason why metaphysical references to "Being" are often profoundly confused.)

Aristotle's propositional forms were thus found to be less satisfactory for the organization of knowledge than had been supposed (although the validity of his logic is not thereby denied).

II. A second deficiency of traditional logic is its failure to elucidate some important aspects of inference, especially the logic of relations and the sentence connectives. Thus:

1. Such propositions as "Socrates is the teacher of Plato" do not lend themselves to the connection of a subject with a predicate by the copula *is*; rather, the terms "Socrates" and "Plato" are connected by the relation "is the teacher of." The proposition "New York is between Boston and Washington" connects three terms by the relation of "betweenness."
2. *Sentence connectives* are such terms as *and, or, not,* and *if . . . then . . .* Consider the ambiguity of *and* in "I love apples *and* oranges" and "I love peaches *and* cream." Or consider the implicit temporality in "They got married *and* had children" and "They had children *and* got married." The word *and* operates differently in these examples. Consider the ambiguity of *or* in "Take a raincoat *or* an umbrella" and "This

medicine will cure you *or* it will kill you." The former (inclusive) *or* permits both alternatives; the latter (exclusive) *or* does not. (When G. E. Moore's wife gave birth, a student asked, "Professor Moore, is it a boy or a girl?" Moore chortled, "Yes!") Relations and sentence connectives are clarified in modern logic.

III. A third line of criticism centered upon the three "laws of thought." What kind of laws are they, exactly? And what is it that gives them their special character, their aura of absolute undeniability? Are they based on how people actually think? But many prominent citizens seem to have no difficulty in thinking self-contradictory thoughts. And, in any event, to say that the laws of thought reflect thinking processes would be to confuse empirical descriptive psychology with logic, which is normative, and which considers not the process of thinking but the propositions that result from this process. (Schiller made this mistake.) If the laws of thought, then, are rules that prescribe how people *ought* to reason, why ought they do so? To say that someone ought to do something implies that he might not do so; for instance, if you tell me that I ought to tell the truth, it is because I might lie; but how could I possibly violate the law of identity?

Are the three laws perhaps based on the requirements of language, as some philosophers have asserted, so that all that logic reveals is grammar or syntax? But language and grammar have been found to be mutable and diverse in ways that distinguish them clearly from logic. Are the three laws learned from experience, just as we learn the most general laws of science? (Mill argued for this empiricist interpretation.) But there is no evidence at all for such learning, and, unlike the laws of science, there is no sense in which the laws of thought can be found false.

Are the three laws all that are needed for valid inference, which might account for their special status? No, the more thoroughgoing analysis of modern logic indicates that there are other rules that require explicit statement; for example, *permutation* (if p and q are propositions, then "p or q" is equivalent to "q or p"), and *modus ponens*, or detachment (if p is true, and p implies q, then q is true) .

Most perplexing, perhaps, is the question of whether and how the three laws can be laws of being as well as laws of logic. The term "being" is, at best, misleading and bewildering; at worst, almost meaningless. The pervasive ambiguity of the verb "to be" and the confusions involved in what has been called "the onto-logical commitment of the copula" (even though many lang-uages—Hebrew, for example—have no word for *is*) have yielded some staggering metaphysics and theology. In addition, what could it mean to say that the laws of identity, excluded middle, and contradiction apply to the world: is the world in fact the kind of place in which things always are unchanging and retain their identity? or in which everything is unambiguously either wet or not wet? and never both wet and not wet?

The New Logic

The new logic is motivated by the desire for greater clarity, pre-cision, completeness, generality, and utility. It is expressed in symbols, and embodied in systems which state explicitly what is assumed, and what is inferred, and how. The triumphant climax of the revolution in logic was the *Principia Mathematica* of Whitehead and Russell, the first volume of which appeared in 1910. They employed two "primitive" connectives, the curl ∼ (for *not*) and the wedge ∨ (for *or;* it permits the truth of either or both alternatives). By means of these two primitives, White-head and Russell defined the three symbols for *if . . . then . . .* (the horseshoe ⊃), *and* (the dot •) , and equivalence (three lines ≡). They specified two rules of inference or derivation (substitution, and *modus ponens*) and five primitive (i.e., un-proved) propositions: permutation, tautology, addition, associa-tion, and summation. (The symbolic apparatus was later simpli-fied: all the connectives, for example, were found to be reducible to a single primitive—Scheffer's stroke function for alternative denial; and all the five primitive propositions to one; but these are technicalities.) Whitehead and Russell's system is so explicit and exhaustive that the proposition "$1 + 1 = 2$" is not proved until well into the second volume.

One consequence of this new insight is the divorce of logic from metaphysics. Logic is now seen as a set of rules, or calculus, by which propositions are transformed into, or inferred from, other propositions. Nothing, no new item of knowledge, is added thereby. Logic operates like a meat grinder or juice extractor: the output differs from the input, but contains nothing new. In this extensional, or *truth-functional,* view of logic, the truth of any complex or inferred proposition depends only on the truth of its ingredients, or premises. Logic is not concerned with meanings, or with facts, or with Being, but only with validity of inference. Logic uses "meaningless" symbols in order to concentrate on form alone: it sets norms only because it exposes forms; that is, it tells you what the consequences are of using symbols in certain ways. Logic is autonomous. It elucidates what a proof is. The virtue of the symbolism is its perspicuity; that is, that you can see through it clearly. There is no "objective correlate" or "residual essence" to the symbols used for the transformation of propositions; nothing in the world is controlled by the rules of *modus ponens* or equivalence or negation. Gilbert Ryle makes this point forcefully:

> The world neither observes nor flouts the rules of inference any more than it flouts the rules of bridge, prosody, or viticulture. The stars in their courses do not commit or avoid fallacies any more than they revoke or follow suit.

Logic is "true in all possible worlds" because it shows what is meant by the term "possible": a world in which "$2 + 2 = 5$" is not a possible world.[1]

It is important to realize that the horseshoe symbolizes *material implication,* not necessity. The proposition "if p, then q" or "$p \supset q$" is equivalent to the proposition "either p is false or q is true" and to the proposition "it is not the case that p is true and q is false." If the proposition "$p \supset q$" is true, it is because of the truth values of p and q separately; that is, the truth of the complex proposition is a function of the truth of the simple propositions which it combines. As we noted in our discussion of causality in Chapter 1, philosophers since Hume have doubted whether there is any necessary connection between two events which are described as cause and effect. There is no logical necessity that

---

[1] An old riddle asks, how far can a dog run into a forest? The answer is, halfway, because after that he's running out of the forest. This is not a truth about the world, but about the terms *into, out of,* and *halfway,* which we have devised.

the sun rise tomorrow, nor that stones fall. The new truth-functional, or extensional, logic thus dissolves necessary implication into material implication.

Inference and Implication

If logic is a meat grinder, and produces nothing that was not in the premises, do we then never acquire new knowledge from it? Learning is indeed temporal, although logic is not. We acquire knowledge by making inferences; this is psychological, and takes time. But if the inference is valid, it is because it accords with logical implications, and these are not new but timeless. Nevertheless, in pursuing logical analysis our discoveries may in fact be rather startling. John Aubrey describes how Thomas Hobbes first came by chance upon a copy of Euclid, lying open at the page containing Pythagoras' theorem.

> He read the proposition. "By God," sayd he, "this is impossible." So he reads the demonstration of it, which referred him back to such a proposition; which proposition he read. That referred him back to another, which he also read . . . at last he was convinced. . . . This made him in love with geometry.

In another elegant proof, Euclid showed that there is no greatest prime number.[2] This may be new knowledge to you, even though it is timelessly true.

In a recent Broadway play, a guest at a party asks a Catholic priest, "Don't you sometimes hear embarrassing things in confession?" "Oh, yes," he replies, "in fact when I was just starting out as a young priest, the first man who came to me for con-

---

[2] A prime number is not divisible by any number except by itself and 1. If you were to try to list all the prime numbers, you would find that the higher you go, the farther apart they are, since the more numbers you pass, the more frequent become their multiples. It seems plausible, then, that eventually there might be a last or greatest. But Euclid proved that the notion of a greatest prime number is self-contradictory: whatever prime number n you might assert to be the greatest, if you were to multiply it by every number smaller than itself, and then add 1, you would then get a number $(n!+1)$, which would of course be greater than n. If this new number is prime, then n cannot be the greatest prime; and if this new number is not prime, then its prime factors (if it has any) must be greater than n, since it is not divisible by n or by any number smaller than n, because you added 1 to your product.

fession told me he had committed a murder." Later on in the play, a newcomer joins the party, and, on being introduced to the priest, says, "I met you long ago, Father; in fact I was the first man to come to you for confession." The audience gasps, suddenly realizing that the man is a murderer. But that inference to new knowledge is timelessly implied by the logic of the premises.

An ancient rationalist tradition in philosophy seeks to discover the "first principles" of nature and then to arrive by reason alone —as Euclid's geometry did—at precise, intersubjective, eternally true propositions about the world. Pythagoras sought these first principles in numbers as the substructure of reality; Plato and Aristotle relied on intellectual intuition to arrive at them; Plotinus on mystical ecstasy; Descartes on clear and distinct ideas. Indeed, many impressive advances in knowledge have come about by attempting to "reason out" the structure of things. Thus, Mendeleev in 1869 sorted out the sixty-three then known chemical elements into a "Periodic Table" according to their atomic weights and chemical properties. In order to make the pattern of his Table "come out right" Mendeleev had to adjust some of the weights and leave some gaps, yet he predicted that the gaps would be filled by elements whose existence was then unsuspected; and indeed those elements have since been found. Bode's Law (about 1770) predicted correctly the discovery of unknown planets in our solar system, based on the mathematical relations of their orbits.

But alas for the view that reason alone can provide knowledge of the world! Let me cite merely two of many rationalist proofs that misfire. One Francesco Sizzi, arguing against Galileo's discovery of the satellites of Jupiter, pointed out that

> There are seven windows in the head, two nostrils, two eyes, two ears, and a mouth; so in the heavens there are two favorable stars, two unpropitious, two luminaries, and Mercury alone undecided and indifferent. From which and many other similar phenomena in Nature, such as the seven metals, etc., which it were tedious to enumerate, we gather that the number of planets is necessarily seven.

And the great Kepler in 1596 insisted that

> God in creating the universe and laying out the heavens had in view the five regular solids of geometry, celebrated since the time

of Pythagoras and Plato, and that it was in accordance with their properties that he fixed the number of the heavens, their proportions, and the ratio of their movements.

It now seems quite clear that logic and mathematics deal, as Peirce says, with "hypothetical states of things" and "assert no matter of fact whatever." Or Einstein: "in so far as mathematics is about reality, it is not certain, and in so far as it is certain, it is not about reality." Or Russell: "Mathematics may be defined as the subject in which we never know what we are talking about, nor whether what we are saying is true."

Logic as a Regulative Calculus

There were three baseball umpires, calling balls and strikes. The first one said, I call them as I see them. The second one said, I call them as they are. But the third one declared, until I call them, they ain't nothing. The first umpire is a sense datum subjectivist: nothing will persuade him that he may have made a mistake. The second is a rationalist: he declares that he is describing the objective structure of the world. Only the third realizes that sorting out pitched baseballs is a man-made ordering; nothing in the world is objectively a "ball" or a "strike" without an umpire's decision.

But even though the rules of logic do not describe the world, this does not mean that they are conventional, like the rules of baseball or bridge. Conventions (such as driving on the right side of the road) may always be altered; but there is no alternative to logic. If we changed the postulates of *Principia Mathematica,* we would produce not a different logic, but either another version of the same logic, or no logic at all. Postulates and theorems may in fact often be interchanged; but "the deviant logician's predicament," says Quine, is that "when he tries to deny the doctrine, he only changes the subject." There are indeed different kinds of logic—multi-valued logics and modal logics (which deal with possibility and necessity). But these are not alternatives: they merely add to logic certain undefined terms. There is no alternative to logic, as there is to baseball or to bridge, because logic uniquely serves the human need to understand and cope with the world. Ernest Nagel advises us, in his essay "Logic Without Ontology," to

> reject the conception of "*the* objective structure of *the* system of fact" capable of being known without the mediation of any selective symbolic system. . . . Structures cannot be known independently of activities of symbolization . . . the precise manner in which our theories are formulated is controlled by specifically human postulates no less than by experimental findings. The attempt to justify logical principles in terms of their supposed conformity to an absolute structure of facts thus completely overlooks their actual function of formulating and regulating the pursuit of human ideals.

Man's goal is the best possible organization of knowledge. Logic accomplishes this purpose by directing and regulating human inquiry. The more the world then becomes a cosmos, rather than a chaos, the more successful is man; but it is man who is the measure.

Arithmetic and Geometry

I have glossed over some problems in this chapter, in order to develop my theme.

To begin with, in speaking of mathematics as analytic, I have not differentiated arithmetic from pure geometry, in which, once certain axioms are assumed, then certain theorems are logically implied. Russell held them both to be analytic, and I have followed him; but there are other opinions. Poincaré regarded geometry as analytic, but arithmetic as synthetic; Frege, on the contrary, viewed arithmetic to be analytic, but geometry synthetic. (Kant considered both arithmetic and geometry as synthetic and a priori.) I cannot here do justice to the views of Poincaré and Frege, but I show in Chapter 12 how geometry although analytic may be applied to the world.

I have also taken it for granted that mathematics (including arithmetic and geometry) is not to be distinguished from logic. Both deal with the drawing of necessary conclusions. This is also the view of Russell, and it, too, is controversial. He challenged anyone to point out where in the three volumes of *Principia*

Mathematica logic stopped and mathematics began; he succeeded in reducing all mathematical concepts (such as number) to strictly logical concepts (such as class).[3]

The Limits of Logic

One problem here concerns the completeness of arithmetic. Although there are unsolved problems in arithmetic, it is natural to assume that they will eventually be solved. Thus, Goldbach's "theorem" (that every even number is the sum of two prime numbers) has been verified with no exceptions for thousands of numbers, but it has not been proven, and no one knows whether it is true or not. Fermat's "last theorem" (that $x^n + y^n = z^n$ cannot be satisfied by integral values when n is greater than 2) is likewise unproven, although Fermat noted two hundred years ago that he had solved it, without saying what the solution was. But no one thinks that these problems are inherently insoluble. (The "continuum problem" posed by Cantor in 1871 also remains unsolved, although somewhat clarified in 1963 by Paul Cohen.)

Quite another kind of problem, however, was raised by Brouwer. Since pi, the ratio of the circumference to the diameter of a circle, is a transcendental number with no repetitive period (3.14159 . . .), it is logically impossible, given our number system, to write it down completely. Therefore, we may never be able to know, for example, whether a given sequence of digits (say 7777777) ever appears in it. This is not a matter of probabilities, since every place in that endless series is *now* timelessly determined; no element of chance is involved. Thus, the proposition that that sequence of digits exists cannot be called either true or false. Brouwer accordingly argued that the law of the excluded middle does not apply in dealing with infinite sets.

But there is a more pervasive difficulty, which involves *self-reference*. Epimenides of Crete is said to have irritated most of the ancient world by declaring, "All Cretans are liars." If his

[3] Russell's view, called *logistic,* is opposed by Hilbert's *formalism* and by Brouwer's *intuitionism.* Quine points out that mathematics reduces only to *set theory*; and he questions whether this is properly a part of logic. Mathematics also requires the concept of infinity, which is not part of logic.

statement is true, then it is false. This paradox can of course be readily cleared up, but the difficulty reappears within the foundations of modern logic. Here is an illustration: a certain British Army regiment decided to engage a barber; but, since there were more men in the regiment than he could take care of, and since some of the men did not mind shaving themselves, the commanding officer declared that the barber "was to shave all those men who do not shave themselves." This seemed quite clear; but what about the barber himself? If he does shave himself, then he is not to shave himself; and if he does not shave himself, then he is to shave himself. A second example is Grelling's paradox: classify adjectives on the basis of whether they describe themselves (e.g., *English, polysyllabic, old, unhyphenated*) or do not describe themselves (e.g., *French, monosyllabic, obsolete, obscene, long*). Call adjectives that describe themselves "autological" and those that do not describe themselves "heterological." Now, what about the adjective *heterological* itself? If it does describe itself, that is, if it is autological, then it is heterological; and if it does not describe itself, that is, if it is heterological, then it is autological. These examples may appear to be jocular or trivial (like the little old lady who kept a box marked "string too small to save") but the problem of clarifying self-reference is important. Philosophy after all is a reflexive activity; it consists of thinking about thoughts, speaking about words, arguing about reasons. And *number* (surely a basic concept) is defined in *Principia Mathematica* in terms of "class of classes." The question arose whether a class could be a member of itself. (The class of chairs, for example, is not itself a chair. But the class of concepts *is* a concept; thus, it includes itself.) Russell adopted a "Theory of Types," which requires that whatever involves all of a collection must not itself be a member of that collection; thus, the theory rules out as meaningless the assertion that a class either is or is not a member of itself. There is a deeper question here as to whether a language may be used without contradiction to analyze itself fully (i.e., whether the syntax of a language can be entirely formulated within its own syntactical system). Wittgenstein argues that some things about a language can only be shown, and not said. Russell's Theory of Types does avoid the paradoxes of self-reference, although it is not intuitively obvious. When Poincaré, who disagreed with Russell, learned about this, he snorted wickedly, *"La Logistique n'est plus stérile; elle engendre la contradiction!"* (Logic is no longer barren; it gives birth to contradiction.)

An even more profound peculiarity, however, was brought to light in 1931 by Kurt Gödel. He showed that there are inherent limitations on *Principia Mathematica,* indeed on any deductive system powerful enough to generate arithmetic: namely, given any consistent set of axioms, there are always true arithmetical statements that cannot be derived from that set. Gödel could construct a sentence of elementary number theory that would be true if and only if it could not be proved; he could prove, for example, the sentence "this sentence cannot be proved." Thus, it is impossible to construct a consistent system of postulates that contains all the true propositions of arithmetic. No system of arithmetic can be both consistent and complete, and this peculiarity is inherent and incurable. Although this limitation is relative to specific rules of inference, it has been a shattering discovery. There have been other disconcerting findings in mathematics, of course, such as that the ratio between the circumference of a circle and its diameter is the transcendental number pi, which cannot be stated precisely; or that the diagonal of a square is likewise incommensurable with the side (which so agitated Pythagoras); but whether Gödel's discovery is or is not more significant than these, or whether it bears more profoundly on the comparison of minds with machines, is unresolved (Chapters 18, 19, and 20 touch on this question).

What must be brought out, however, is a new awareness of the essential limits of logic. Hao Wang writes:

> We can formalize without residue neither the fundamental intuitive notions of positive integers nor the basic notion of sets or classes. . . .

> There is no way to formalize in an ordinary logistic system our intuition that 1, 2, . . . are the only integers. . . .

> There is no axiom system in which we can get *all* the real numbers or the classes of positive integers.

This is another facet of the "loose fit" between the human mind and the world, of the disparity between the categories of knowledge and experience.

7

Meaning and Naming: How Language Bites on to the World

In discussing the Theory of Types in Chapter 6, I explained why Russell declared it meaningless to say that a class either is or is not a member of itself. I believe this was the first time that "meaningless" was so used: aren't the words themselves clearly meaningful? Common sense would agree with Mill and Frege that the meaning of a sentence ought to depend only on the meaning of the words that constitute it; but Russell showed that there may be grammatical sentences, and thus apparently meaningful sentences, without meaning. For this reason, the distinction between the truth and falsity of a proposition is less basic than the distinction between a significant (true or false) sentence and a meaningless series of words; before considering whether a statement is true, one must first determine if it is meaningful.

The Meanings of "Meaning"

What does *meaning* mean? At least eight senses may be distinguished:

1. *Indication.* "These black clouds mean rain."
2. *Cause.* "What do these footprints in the sand mean?"
3. *Effect.* "This means war!"
4. *Intention.* "I meant to stay home and study."
5. *Explanation.* "What does this phrase in *Finnegans Wake* mean?" (This sense is developed in Chapter 10)
6. *Purpose.* "Violence by terrorists is meaningless."
7. *Implication.* "If it rains, that means we won't go."
8. *Significance.* "Does human life have any meaning?"

But this listing does not help us to determine whether a sentence is meaningful or meaningless. The problem is ancient. Socrates jested about whether or not triangles were virtuous; Mill about "abracadabra is a second intention"; Russell about "quadruplicity drinks procrastination"; a whimsical generation at Oxford about "Saturday is in bed." Carnap wanted to rule out as meaningless "This stone is thinking about Vienna," declaring it no better than "New York is between." Wittgenstein posed this series to illustrate the subtlety of a decline into nonsense: "a new-born baby has no teeth; a goose has no teeth; a blade of grass has no teeth." Where in the following sequence would you say that we cross the border into meaninglessness: the priest hopes for a life after death; so does the boy; the baby; the dog; the clam; the flower; the rock; the inflationary pressures?

The decision clearly involves not logic and language alone, but also science and metaphysics. We can talk meaningfully about the world only if we take into account what the world is like. Aristotle appreciated this problem, and stipulated the following set of categories as defining the range of applicability of a term, or, in other words, as the *only* ways in which predicates may be meaningfully attributed to any subject:

1. *Substance.* "Socrates is a man."
2. *Quantity.* "He is six feet tall."
3. *Quality.* "He is wise."
4. *Relation.* "He is the teacher of Plato."
5. *Place.* "He is in the marketplace at Athens."
6. *Time.* "He is there in midsummer."

7. *Action.* "He is talking."

8. *Passion.* "He is being attacked."

9. *Situation or position.* "He is surrounded by his disciples."

10. *State or condition.* "He is barefoot."

The last two categories are omitted in some versions; Aristotle must have decided they were not ultimate and could be analyzed into the others.

Names and Descriptions; Sense and Reference

The basic problem is to clarify the relation of words to things. It is only under certain circumstances that sounds or marks on paper acquire meaning, or refer. *Reference* is how language bites on to the world. It is a distinctively human activity, and, unlike thinking, it is public. The most elementary way in which to refer is to name. *Naming* is the direct application of a word to a thing.

(How many mysterious overtones there are to this linkage between a thing and its name—in mythology, folklore, literature, and our everyday habits. Think of magical spells based on names; the story of Rumpelstiltskin; the unutterable secret name of God; the Holy Name Society; the Sphinx compelling Oedipus to reveal his name; the angel changing Jacob's name to Israel; a tribe taking the name of its totem; a religious convert assuming a new name. Orthodox Jews will not name a child after any living relative. In an Australian myth, plants and animals did not exist until they were named. We give names to some domestic animals (usually pets) but not to others (usually not chickens). A convict or army recruit is identified by a serial number, not by name. *Moby Dick* begins, "Call me Ishmael"—the outcast and wanderer! Kafka's *The Trial* is about a man who is being deprived of his humanity: he is called only Joseph K. An old commentary on Genesis 2:19-20 points out that Adam's naming of the animals was his first action after being created, and it was uniquely human—the angels couldn't do it! In Plato's *Cratylus*, Socrates remarks, "Cratylus is right in saying that names belong to things by nature" and "it is not for every man to give names, but for . . . the name-maker, . . . of all artisans among men the rarest." Think of the term "proper name!")

Nothing stands between a thing and its name. That linkage is logically primitive. Like pointing to a thing ("ostensive definition"; see Chapter 19), naming cannot be reduced to, or explained by, a simpler activity. But naming is not the only means by which we can refer to things; we can also use *descriptions*. A name identifies; it is a tag (Mill compared it with the chalk mark made on the door by the *Arabian Nights* robbers); it does not describe. However, I can refer to "the dog that woke me last night by its barking" without knowing which dog it was; and to "the heavenly body farthest from the earth" without being able to identify it otherwise. We can use different descriptive phrases to refer to the same entity. Benjamin Franklin, for example, can be referred to as "the first Postmaster General of the United States" or as "the inventor of bifocal spectacles." The planet Venus is called both "the evening star" and "the morning star."

Thus, there are two distinct aspects of meaning: the *sense* of the words (called *Sinn* by Frege) and the *reference*, which is what the words point to, or designate (which he called *Bedeutung*). A name (e.g., "Bert") has no sense, only reference; whereas a description (e.g., "the heavenly body farthest from the earth") may have no known reference, but only sense. Terms such as *I, this, now, here* have a fixed sense and a constantly changing reference. Such terms are called "indexical" or "egocentric particulars" by Russell, and "token-reflexives" by Reichenbach.

> "The rule is, jam tomorrow, and jam yesterday—but never jam *today*."
> "It must come sometimes to 'jam today,'" Alice objected.
> "No, it can't," said the Queen. "It's jam every *other* day: today isn't any other day, you know."

These two aspects of meaning, sense and reference, are roughly parallel to the connotation and denotation of a term (in logical, not literary, usage) and to the intension and extension of a class. The *connotation* of "bachelor," for example, is "adult unmarried man"; it is what anything would have to be in order to be a bachelor. The *denotation* of "bachelor" is all the actual persons you can so designate. Thus, "ghost" has connotation, but no denotation. The connotation of "cordates" is "all creatures with a heart"; the connotation of "renates" is "all creatures with a kidney"; but in fact all creatures with a heart have a kidney, and vice versa, so that both terms have the same denotation. Similarly, the *intension* of the class of bachelors is the definition, or "what you have in mind" by the term; whereas the *extension* is all the actual bachelors in the world.

Those philosophers who are suspicious of unobservable psychic processes, or unverifiable mental events, or hypostatized meanings subsisting apart from words, question whether there are such things as intensions; that is, whether the phrase "what you have in mind" denotes anything at all. (Intensions are called "guardian angels" by Richard Martin.) Some of these rigorous philosophers are also reluctant to speak of *propositions* (which are mental entities); they prefer *sentences* (which are physical—they can be seen and heard). I agree that it makes no sense to speak of propositions that are not embodied in sentences. However, I think we require the term "proposition" to denote what is presupposed by, or common to, different utterances of the same sentence, and different sentences having the same meaning (e.g., "the king is dead," "dead is the king," "*le roi est mort*"). The proposition would, then, be loosely the sense of a sentence. I am *not* asserting that "meanings" are entities subsisting apart from words (which is what Platonism may assert), nor that meanings may be designated in any way other than by words (or other symbols). But though meanings require words, they are not identical to words (Chapter 19). Therefore, the perennial argument as to whether words refer to things (as Mill claimed) or to our thoughts about things (Locke's position) may be dissolved thus: words refer to both thoughts and things, because words have both sense and reference.

Problems of Naming and Meaning

Of course there are problems in this account of naming and meaning. Some problems are relatively trivial. Not everything actually has a unique name, and not every name in fact denotes a unique thing. There are two different writers both named Samuel Butler, and there is one writer named both Samuel Clemens and Mark Twain. What happens when one uses a name in fiction (Mr. Pickwick) or in mythology (Pegasus) or in folklore (Santa Claus)? Do these names refer to beings having some kind of putative existence, or hazy reality? No; it is a mistake to think that if a word purports to be a name, then something must exist which it names; these are names in only a Pickwickian or metaphorical sense. Naming and describing may overlap when one uses a name as a description (calling a ruthless conniver "another Stalin") or a description as a name ("El Greco" or "Holy Roman Empire"). Many names did in fact originate as descriptions, and creative writers often coin names in this way ("Oedipus," "Shallow," "Adam Verver"). Sometimes a name and a description practically coalesce, for example, in the case of the painter known to us only as "the Master of the 'Adoration' at Avignon." We know almost nothing about the person named Homer except that he is the author of the Homeric poems. Such issues present no profound problems for logical analysis. The circularity of names and descriptions is not vicious. It is, like the constant process by which dictionary definitions derive from actual usage and in turn influence actual usage, one of the ongoing procedures of using linguistic symbols to organize experience.

A more serious problem is *referential opacity*. There are certain linguistic contexts in which you cannot substitute one name for another name, or one description for another description, even though they refer to the same particular thing. This constraint would seem to play havoc with accepted logical rules. Three of these "opaque" or "oblique" contexts may be illustrated:

I. In the following pair of propositions the first is true, the second false:

 1. Samuel Clemens adopted the pen name "Mark Twain" to conceal his identity.
 2. Mark Twain adopted the pen name "Mark Twain" to conceal his identity.

II. Propositions involving "modal" contexts (e.g., possibility, impossibility, necessity) are opaque, and cause confusion. Thus, propositions 3 and 4 are true, but 5 is false:

 3. The number of states in the United States is fifty.

 4. Fifty is necessarily less than fifty-one.

 5. The number of states in the United States is necessarily less than fifty-one.

III. Propositions involving such "intentional" or "psychological" attitudes as believing, hoping, doubting, etc., are referentially opaque. Thus, propositions 6 and 7 are true, but 8 is false:

6. Bert thinks the capital of Oregon is Sacramento.

7. Sacramento is in California.

8. Bert thinks the capital of Oregon is in California.

Or, to take another example, propositions 9 and 10 are true, but 11 is false:

9. Oedipus wanted to marry Jocasta.

10. Jocasta was Oedipus' mother.

11. Oedipus wanted to marry his mother.

In the preceding three referentially opaque contexts, error or confusion results from substitution of one term for another even though both have the same reference.

Also puzzling is the question of reference if you deny that a certain thing exists; for example, if you say that there is no Loch Ness monster, or that there is no such thing as a perpetual motion machine. Since you must refer to it or think of it in order to deny it, does it not then in some way become a "subsistent entity"? Meinong argued that if we say there is no such thing as a golden mountain, then there is something to which we do refer. One can even make true or false statements regarding this thing; for example, it would be true to say that "it" is golden and false that "it" is silver. But how untidy it would be to clutter up the universe with such dubious reifications! We have noted how metaphysics must avoid this trap (Chapter 1). We are misled here by grammar, just as we would be if we were to take an "imaginary uncle" to be, like a "rich uncle," a kind of uncle. (Other examples of how language may mislead us are presented in Chapter 19.)

Russell's *Theory of Descriptions* dissolved problems arising from this kind of ambiguity, by distinguishing between descriptive phrases and names. "The golden mountain" is a descriptive phrase which has no denotation. "The present Queen of England" and "the present Queen of France" are formally identical phrases; nevertheless, the first has a denotation and the second has not. In a famous example, Russell analyzed the proposition "Scott is the author of *Waverley*" as the conjoint assertion of these three propositions:

1. At least one person wrote *Waverley* (i.e., there is such a book).
2. At most one person wrote *Waverley* (i.e., we may indicate someone as being *the* author).
3. There is nobody who both wrote *Waverley* and is not identical with Scott (i.e., Scott is the only one who wrote *Waverley*).

Thus, the original proposition is not about a person named Scott (as it would be in "Scott is tall"), but rather about the property (having written *Waverley*) which in fact Scott happens to have (he is the one who wrote that book).

I have said that naming and describing are two ways in which language bites on to the world. Note that this distinction corresponds generally to knowledge by acquaintance and knowledge by description. You must have direct acquaintance with something in order to pin a name on it, or the name would fail of its purpose. If God had said, after Adam named the cats, dogs, and cows, "There is another animal over at the far end of the garden—what name would you give it?" Adam would no doubt have replied petulantly, "How can I give it a name when I can't even see it?" If you would now like to have a great-grandchild named "Bert," you may indeed reserve that *word,* but it does not *name* anything until the child is born. "Neptune" did not become the name of the planet that was presumed to cause the perturbations in the orbit of Uranus until it was actually spotted; "Vulcan," in a supposedly analogous situation, never did become the name of a planet.

Names and descriptions are of course both words, and a word is a device by which one thing can signify something else. Words are conventional *symbols* used for the purpose of reference. They are not, of course, the only conventional symbols. There are also the gestures used and understood by auctioneers, football referees, and dancers; handshakes and other customary greetings; Churchill's "V"; traffic lights; elevator buzzers; such artifacts as the flag, the Crown, and the Cross; the lion as a symbol of courage; Moby Dick as a symbol of evil. Art may be loosely regarded as a symbolic language (Chapter 21) .

There are, in addition to words and other conventional symbols, certain signs that are not purely conventional, but stimulate habits of response in other ways. Peirce includes in his general theory of signs what he calls the icon and the index. The *icon* refers to something by *looking* a little like it. Thus, a photograph, a waxwork, and a road map are icons. The *index* is *causally* connected with what it refers to. Thus, smoke is a sign of fire; clouds are a sign of rain; a boulder on a hill is a sign of a glacier; a scar is a sign of an injury; footprints are the sign of an animal.

Contemporary Theories of Meaning

A major impetus in twentieth-century philosophy has been linguistic: to clarify thought by clarifying language. How many hopeless tangles result from the careless or wanton use of words! What can F. H. Bradley possibly have meant by "the Absolute enters into, but is itself incapable of, evolution and progress"? or Hegel by "Being and nothing are one and the same"? or Heidegger by "the Nothing is prior to the Not and the Negation . . . the Nothing itself nothings"?

Philosophers, however, are not the only offenders. Scientists speak of the *élan vital,* of absolute space, of the libido, of the racial unconscious, and of the group mind. These concepts purport to explain various phenomena; but the terms have no clear denotation or extension; no way appears whereby to correlate them unambiguously with what can be observed. Ernst Mach was suspicious of even such terms in physics as atom, ether, and magnetic field.

There has been a widespread disinclination to regard a term as meaningful unless one could specify exactly what facts it entailed, or what actions would verify its use. In Dewey's phrase, "the application of symbols to things is the cashing of promissory notes." Peirce, in a famous definition, prescribed a long list of operations that

> tells you what the word "lithium" denotes by prescribing what you are to *do* in order to gain a perceptual acquaintance with the object of the word . . . what a thing means is simply what habits it involves . . . there is no distinction of meaning so fine as to consist in anything but a possible difference in practice.

P. W. Bridgman, startled by Relativity Theory to discover that the phrase "two simultaneous events" is literally without meaning, argued for operationalism; that is, that the meaning of a term is a set of operations. F. C. S. Schiller held that the meaning of a term is not a mental entity, but rather the ways in which it is used. Schlick set the program for the logical empiricists and positivists:

> Whenever we ask about a sentence, "what does it mean?", what we expect is instruction as to the circumstances in which the sentence is to be used . . . the conditions under which the sentence will form a *true* proposition, and of those which will make it *false*. . . . The meaning of a proposition is the method of its verification.

But, alas, the attempts by operationalists, empiricists, positivists, and pragmatists to connect meanings securely with actions cannot be deemed successful. Just as meanings are not the same things as words, so meanings are not the same things as operations or methods or uses. Schlick's identification of meaning with verification also goes too far. There is no way to verify certain kinds of propositions, such as those concerning the remote past ("It snowed in Manhattan on January 6, 1092"—there are no records), or the remote future ("Stars will continue to shine after all life is extinct"—who will do the verifying?), or types ("The lion is fierce"—you may study any number of individual lions, but not "the lion"), or some kinds of feelings ("She secretly loves him"—if the loving is secret, it cannot be verified), or things that do not yet exist ("Inventions nobody has thought of might solve the energy crisis"). But do these propositions then have no meaning?

Nevertheless, the philosophical legacy, or residue, of these twentieth-century empiricist movements, despite their partial failure, is a caution which must never be disregarded. We reach out to cope with the world in many and complex ways: in names and descriptions, in sense and reference, in signs, symbols, words, and gestures, in thinking and in acting. All of these modes bear on the concept of "meaning." And no future philosopher will ever be free to ignore such demands as, What exactly do you mean? How, precisely, do you know? What conceivable turn of events would verify what you say or be incompatible with it?

8

Truth and Belief

"WHAT IS TRUTH?" asked jesting Pilate; had he stayed for an answer, he would still be waiting. For, while we all speak of truth easily enough, the term has no entirely satisfactory definition. The problem is to clarify the nature of truth, rather than to provide criteria for it; in other words, to explicate *how* or in what way a true proposition differs from a false one, rather than to identify *when* a proposition is true (which refers to the adequacy of the reasons for believing it, or the basis of knowledge; see Chapter 2).

Theories of Truth

There are three major theories of truth:

1. A proposition is true if it *corresponds* to a *fact*. Aside from the complexities of the term "fact" (Chapter 9), nothing seems simpler: the proposition "Snow is white" is true if and only if in fact snow is white. But how can you ever compare such different entities as a proposition and a fact? How can you con-

front a "state of mind" with a "state of affairs" to see if they correspond? They do not resemble each other any more than the word "snow" looks or feels or sounds like snow. Many true propositions (for example, counterfactual hypotheticals such as "If I were twenty-one, I would join the Peace Corps") have no corresponding fact at all. Moreover, as Austin contends, to require that a proposition either correspond or not correspond to a fact is like saying that a map must be either accurate or inaccurate. Wittgenstein at first held that the true proposition was a picture of a state of affairs, but he later found this position untenable.

2. Hegel and his followers avoid comparing dissimilar entities by defining the truth of a proposition as its *coherence* with other *propositions*. Thus, if you deny that an apparent sense perception is truthful (e.g., that the oar in the water is broken, or that the sleight-of-hand magician has made a rabbit disappear), you do so on the ground that if the proposition is true it is inconsistent with other true propositions. The coherence theory permits of degrees of truth (although no single proposition by itself can be true or false); the ideal is the perfectly integrated system in which each proposition implies, and is implied by, all others. But the fatal defect of the coherence theory of truth is that there is no way to relate a coherent system of propositions to reality. Astrology constitutes a coherent system; so do hypothetical n-dimensional geometries; so do Grimm's fairy tales; and so do the delusions of the psychotic; but we do not take them to be true. Moreover, the growth of science often shatters an existing coherent system: Darwinian evolution, Einsteinian relativity, and quantum mechanics all overthrew established systems. And the very concept of a completely coherent system is now seen, since Gödel's Theorem, to need radical modification (Chapter 6). Thus, although we may take coherence as a requirement for truth (we trust our memories more when they are mutually reinforcing and consistent), coherence does not suffice as a definition of truth.

3. *Pragmatic* theories define truth in various ways. The true proposition is one which will solve a problem, or render experience more congruous, or transform a doubtful situation into a determinate one, or advance the purpose of inquiry, or

"work," or be useful, or generally "prove itself to be good in the way of belief" (James). The common core in these loose formulations is emphasis on the human activity of verifying: *making* true. A proposition is not intrinsically true because it corresponds to an extrinsic reality, nor because it is coherent with other propositions. It *becomes* true only when acted upon. Many of the pragmatists' terms are vague: "useful" for what? "satisfactory" to whom? "work" how? Russell, who held to a form of correspondence theory, exclaimed, "The pragmatist theory of truth is to be condemned on the grounds that it does not work!" Nonetheless, the imprecise pragmatic theory best associates truth with the satisfaction of the human need to understand, predict, and control phenomena. For this reason it best explains what is meant by the truth of natural laws or scientific theories.

Pragmatism and Science

Ever since Hume's analysis of causation, it has been clear that events in the world are not connected by necessity. "Laws of nature" are descriptive, not legislative. They are devised by man for the purpose of organizing his experience. Einstein wrote:

> Science is the attempt to make the chaotic diversity of our sense-experience correspond to a logically uniform system of thought. . . . The sense-experiences are the given subject-matter. But the theory that shall interpret them is man-made. . . . hypothetical, never completely final, always subject to question and doubt.

Any two points on a graph may be connected by more than one curve; any finite sequence of observations may be described by a "law." If predictions by extrapolation are verified, the law becomes true. The observed facts seldom determine a scientific theory fully or unequivocally. The astronomy of Ptolemy can be used to predict celestial phenomena; it did not fail to explain observed facts, but was merely more complicated than that of Copernicus. The hypothesis that light is carried by a universal fluid called "ether" was not abandoned overnight; indeed, it has adherents today. The phenomena of quantum mechanics can be described in more than one theoretical framework; some formulations are more "indeterministic" than others. These examples are striking, but scientific theories seldom satisfy all our demands. It is as if a wealthy man were to say to an automobile designer: make me the best possible car and spare no expense. But the attributes of "the best possible car" are mutually inconsistent: speed may conflict with safety, comfort with maneuverability, beauty with ease of repairs, and so forth. Any actual car, like any hypothesis of science, is an adjustment among various desiderata. Thus, in contemporary science, the electron is regarded sometimes as a particle and sometimes as a wave. It does not have a fixed location. Light is considered to be both a stream of photons and a wave. In acoustic theory, a gas is described as a continuous medium, but in other branches of physics a gas consists of molecules. The universe is said to be both finite and unbounded. These instances of the "loose fit" between mind and the world strike us as leaving much to be desired. However, in the metaphor of James,

> It seems *a priori* improbable that the truth should be so nicely adjusted to our needs and powers. . . .In the great boarding-house of nature, the cakes and the butter and the syrup seldom come out so even and leave the plates so clean.

If a scientific theory makes successful predictions, and if it does not conflict with other well-established theories, and if it makes no false predictions, then, whatever its shortcomings, it is true.

This is not really a new insight. When Copernicus first asserted that the earth goes around the sun, in his *De Revolutionibus,* the preface contained this remark by the theologian Osiander:

> There is no need for these hypotheses to be true, or even to be at all like the truth; rather, one thing is sufficient for them—that they should yield calculations which agree with the observations.

If only Galileo would have said that! The Church then would not have objected.

Peirce thought that that "loose fit" would be temporary. He defined the truth as that opinion "to which the community ultimately settles down . . . sufficient investigation would cause one opinion to be universally received and all others to be rejected." I wish I could share his faith in a final *consensus gentium!* (This is one of the justifications for knowledge—the seventh "good reason" mentioned in Chapter 2.) I think it more plausible that experience would continue to overflow even our best-entrenched doctrines. Think of the challenge posed to established scientific theories in recent years by extrasensory perception, visceral learning, and acupuncture! I believe we ought to be both skeptical and open-minded in such situations. James leaned over backward in his attempts not to foreclose what could occur; he was consequently taken in by unscrupulous practitioners of spiritualism and psychical research. He described this area of endeavor as

> a field in which the sources of deception are extremely numerous. But I believe there is no source of deception in the investigation of nature which can compare with a fixed belief that certain kinds of phenomena are *impossible*.

There is an important difference between *truth* and *knowledge*. Knowledge must be justified by evidence or good reasons (Chapter 2), which is why the true predictions of the horse-player in *Three Men on a Horse* do not constitute knowledge. It is conceivable that the oracle at Delphi, or the vision of the mystic, or the tea leaves of the fortune-teller, or dreams, or revelation might yield successful predictions. The superiority of certain sorts of justification is not a priori, but pragmatic.

Belief

One of the difficulties that pragmatic theories of truth face is the danger of the fallacious conversion of "the true is useful" to "the useful is true." You might as well say that I breathe when I sleep is the same as I sleep when I breathe! Politicians often find it useful to tell lies to the voters. Diplomats probably could not successfully carry out any assignment without deception. It might benefit a sick person to be told a lie. But clearly all these useful beliefs continue to be false.

What actually is belief? In the analysis of knowledge, "I believe that p" is taken as a necessary condition for "I know that p." And there is a sense in which the truth ought to command one's belief. So it is important to clarify what belief is, although it proves to be a recalcitrant concept. Philosophers refer to belief as a "propositional attitude" or as an inner state of mind which is directly evident through introspection. St. Augustine defined it as "thinking with assent." Hume thought it was a kind of feeling. But there is good reason to insist that belief be more than a mental state. Bain, for example, said that a man believes that upon which he is prepared to act. Schiller defined belief as "a spiritual attitude of welcome which we assume towards what we take to be a truth. . . an affair of our whole nature, and not of mere intellect." And Peirce said that "different beliefs are distinguished by the different modes of action to which they give rise."

The view that belief must be associated with action has considerable force. After all, how would you know whether someone (or, indeed, you yourself) really believed something if, in an appropriate situation, he (or you) did not act? Do you believe that our legal system ought to be strengthened if you always avoid serving on a jury? Sometimes you discover the existence of an unconscious belief or prejudice—even in yourself—only when an occasion arises that calls for action (I did not think I had any sexist prejudice until I found I had used as an example of the problem of self-reference, the little old lady who kept a box marked "string too small to save.") The requirement of action, however, does not apply to all cases of belief. You might, for example, believe that death is like a profound sleep; this belief could scarcely issue in action. And sometimes it might be foolish to act upon a belief. Thus, even if I believed very strongly that a certain horse would win a race, it would not be prudent to bet my life's savings on him. Or, if I were on a sinking ship three miles from shore, and I believed I could not swim more than a quarter of a mile, it would nevertheless be foolish not to try to swim to land. In short, the connection between belief and overt action is complex and tenuous.

Nor is it clear whether belief is a voluntary state of mind, that is, within our power to give or to withhold. We tend to believe our own rationalizations: is our belief then connected with our desire? Coleridge asked for the "willing suspension of disbelief." If you are commanded to "believe, and you will be saved," can you do it? Pascal (long before brainwashing!) advised that if your faith is weak, you ought to behave as if you believed: "Use holy water and order masses to be said . . . this will naturally make you believe, and make you dopey" (cela vous abêtira). Can the soldier in battle get himself to believe in fatalism? Can your belief be controlled by posthypnotic suggestion?

> "There's no use trying," said Alice: "one can't believe impossible things."
> "I dare say you haven't had much practice," said the Queen. "When I was your age I always did it for half an hour a day. Why sometimes I've believed as many as six impossible things before breakfast."

Descartes thought belief could be controlled by the will; Spinoza thought not; St. Thomas Aquinas thought that belief on matters of faith was voluntary, since it was not compelled by the facts and, therefore, was deserving of praise.

If belief is voluntary, can it also ever be obligatory? Are you obliged to believe every analytic proposition? Does "the evidence is complete" mean "you ought to believe"? Conversely, are you obliged to withhold belief in cases where the evidence is incomplete? (Consider: "No matter what you show me, I can't believe my husband is unfaithful!" "I know I will die someday, but I can't believe it!") There is an interesting issue here of what might almost be called life style. W. K. Clifford said, "It is wrong always, everywhere, and for everyone, to believe anything upon insufficient evidence"; and Brentano maintained that we ought to believe only what is true. James, however, insisted that a policy of suspending judgment on momentous issues would result in impoverishing life:

> Our passional nature not only lawfully may, but must, decide . . . between propositions, whenever it is a genuine option that cannot by its nature be decided on intellectual grounds. . . . I have also a horror of being duped; but I can believe that worse things than being duped may happen to a man in this world.

But Santayana ironically declared that "James did not really believe: he merely believed in the right of believing that you might be right if you believed."

9

Science, Facts, and Hypotheses

"SCIENCE SEEKS TO DISCOVER and formulate in general terms the conditions under which events occur," writes Ernest Nagel. Note that there is no limit on the kinds of events scientists investigate, nor on what procedures are essentially scientific, nor on the scope of science. It is convenient to divide science into branches, which are differentiated by their methods and focus of interest. The branches may encounter different problems: the astronomer cannot experiment; the geneticist can predict only probabilities; the atomic physicist must postulate entities he can never observe; the scientific psychologist can sometimes find nothing to measure; the political scientist may have to examine his own motives in explaining other people's actions; the sociologist finds that his predictions may be self-fulfilling or self-defeating; the anthropologist may be unwittingly altering the phenomena he is investigating. But none of these peculiarities makes astronomy, genetics, atomic physics, psychology, political science, sociology, or anthropology inherently unreliable, nor excludes them from the realm of science. We should forget the stereotype of the scientist as the man in a white coat mixing chemicals in test tubes. There is no single scientific method other than the unremitting criticism of evidence and reasoning in every way possible.

Let us also note that scientists are human beings. That means that their judgment may be biased, their selection of problems may be whimsical, their assessment of the evidence may be faulty, their determination of the facts may be subjective, their motivations may be suspect, and their observations may be distorted by their values. But these factors may all be made explicit, and controlled. Science is a social and self-corrective enterprise.

But science is entirely a human enterprise. The objectives of science are to describe, explain, understand, investigate, predict, and control, and these are characteristically human goals. The ideals of science are reliability, definiteness, precision, objectivity or intersubjectivity, testability, self-correctiveness, comprehensiveness or universality, and systematic coherence. Human welfare is not as such an objective of science; for this reason, science needs to be supplemented by philosophy. The functions of a scientific theory may be variously stated: to inform ("All men by nature desire to know"—Aristotle); to predict ("*Savoir c'est prévoir*"—Comte); to control (Bacon, James, Dewey); to summarize the data economically (Mach). Wittgenstein calls a scientific theory a system of coordinates, not itself either true or false (since it makes no substantial assertions about the world), but more like a mesh used to cover a surface; a coarse square mesh might cover more than a fine triangular mesh, and vice versa. (Beware the fisherman who uses a net with two-inch openings and declares that all the fish in the ocean are larger than two inches!) But Nagel makes it clear, in *The Structure of Science*, that disputes over whether a theory should be said to be literally true or false, or rather to be a logical instrument for organizing experience, or a compendious summary of data are only conflicts over preferred modes of speech.

Selection of a Theory

According to Whitehead, science tries "to see what is general in what is particular." But there's the rub! The particular thing always has more than one general aspect or property. Gomperz offers the following descriptions of the flight of a sparrow:

There goes a sparrow.
This bird is flying.
Here is an animal.
Something here is moving.
Energy here is being transformed.
This is not a case of perpetual motion.
The poor thing is frightened.

No description can succeed in telling all that can be told about a particular thing or event; "fact is richer than diction" (Chapter 2). When human actions are being characterized, varying descriptions will result in different imputations of responsibility (Chapter 20). A theory, like a description, is not mechanically dictated by the facts, but is selected in order to advance our objectives. It is the product of human ingenuity and creativity. A theory is arrived at neither by automatic induction, nor by generalization, nor by observation of obvious regularities, but by a leap of the imagination to a new unifying idea. All the facts of biological evolution—variation, natural selection, the struggle for existence—were known before Darwin and Wallace, but it was they who proposed a theory of open-ended natural selection (Chapter 13). As Einstein put it:

> Given to us are merely the data of our consciousness. . . . There is only one way from [them] to "reality," to wit, the way of conscious or unconscious intellectual construction, which proceeds completely free and arbitrarily. . . . We are free to choose which elements we wish to apply in the construction of physical reality. The justification of our choice lies exclusively in our success.

Facts

I began this chapter by indicating that different areas of scientific inquiry run into varying problems in getting at the facts. There is no one criterion for scientific methodology, and there are at least six constituents which enter into the determination of what is a fact:

1. The *human organism*. In discussing our knowledge of the external world (Chapter 3), I showed how the human sensory apparatus determines the range of facts. Note also the rele-

vance of the human life span. Would a race of intelligent animals that live for only an hour be likely ever to discover that glaciers drift? or that a melody is being played on a phonograph record revolving once a century?

2. The scientific *instruments* available. "Fact" is relative to the methods and conditions of observation—to the accuracy of thermometers, yardsticks, and clocks. Operationalism emphasizes that things do not have a "size" which is independent of the instruments used to measure it. (And of course instruments cannot dispense with the human observer; even a computer print-out must be read at some point by a person.)

3. *Memory.* One can be aware of repetition or of generality only if one now has a sense of what has occurred in the past.

4. The *personality,* aims, and bias of the individual scientist. This factor is usually (perhaps not always?) corrected for by other scientists.

5. *Language.* The observer can describe the world only in the language available to him. "Fact" has a linguistic constituent. As B. L. Whorf has shown, speakers of languages that do not have a word for "wave" will see not waves but only changing undulating surfaces. The Navahos use one word for blue and green, whereas the Bororó of Brazil have no single word for parrot. In Arabic a wind may be described as *sarsar,* which means both *cold* and *whistling.* The language of Tierra del Fuego has a useful word, *mamihlapinatapai;* it means, roughly, the state of mind in which two people regard each other when both want a certain thing to be done but neither wants to be the first to do it. How many lovely facts are available to them! Of course La Rochefoucauld said a long time ago, *"Il y a des gens qui n'auraient jamais été amoureux, s'ils n'avaient jamais entendu parler d'amour"* (There are people who would never have fallen in love if they had not heard love spoken about). Cassirer and Sapir argue that the forms of language predetermine the modes of observation and interpretation; Wittgenstein said that "if we spoke a different language, we would perceive a somewhat different world." Waismann's metaphor is "language is the knife with which we cut out facts." There is no "fact of the matter" outside language.

6. Most significantly, fact is relative to *hypothesis.* There are no

"raw facts." The human eye is not a camera, unfocused, automatically and unselectively recording impressions. Facts are not found haphazardly, nor in isolation. The scientist is not a passive observer of a self-evident structure (as we saw in Chapter 4). Malinowski tells of the young anthropologist who went out in the field to record a certain tribal ritual. He dutifully photographed everything in sight, only to realize later that the significant part of the ceremony was taking place somewhere else. The scientist must know what to look for (aren't the "facts" of cancer all there?). He must select; he must evaluate; he works from an implicit paradigm which determines what he will consider as a relevant fact. Consider whether the following propositions are statements of fact: a glass of water has the same temperature all over; the universe is expanding; nothing can get colder than $-273°C$.; the unemployment rate has dropped; Bert is accident-prone; a Christian Scientist feels no pain; Henry Moore's sculptural forms draw on the racial unconscious; perception is possible outside the senses; Bert saw a UFO. To decide whether these statements report facts requires not observation alone, but clarification of a hypothesis. James said, "Animal magnetism wasn't a fact until the theory of hypnosis permitted it." Kant put it, "Knowledge of the world demands more than just seeing the world. One must know what to look for in foreign countries." According to Poincaré, "Science is built up of facts, as a house is built up of stones; but an accumulation of facts is no more a science than a heap of stones is a house." Eddington paradoxically remarked, "Never accept a fact until it is verified by a theory!" But of course Aristotle knew this when he said that all knowledge arises out of previous knowledge. To ask for "nothing but the facts!" is to demand a map drawn to no particular scale.

Hypotheses

It is the hypothesis, which guides us in the determination of the facts, that is of the essence. In order to be of maximum usefulness in acquiring and organizing knowledge, a hypothesis must meet eight conditions:

1. It must be *falsifiable*; that is, it cannot be an analytic statement (which will remain true regardless of what occurs). Molière satirized the doctors who postulated a "dormitive power" in certain drugs to explain why they make you sleepy. But we continue to be offered similarly circular hypotheses: dogs bury bones because they have a bone-burying instinct; human beings fight because they have a pugnacious tendency; a cable snaps because its load exceeds its tensile strength. These allegedly explanatory hypotheses merely restate that which is to be explained. They are not falsifiable; they are devoid of empirical content. If a hypothesis refers to such entities as bone-burying instincts, which are not manifested in any way other than in the burying of bones (that is, entities which so far as we can tell exist only in the phenomena they allegedly explain), then it is ad hoc and can never be put to the test. If a hypothesis does no more than summarize what is already known, it cannot be disproved.

2. The explanatory hypothesis must of course be *true*. I have read that "lost persons travel in circles because spiral movement is a property of all living matter in motion."

   "Please, would you tell me," said Alice, "why your cat grins like that?"
   "It's a Cheshire cat," said the Duchess, "and that's why."

3. The hypothesis must be *simple* "even if," as Nagel maintains, "the simplicity tacitly demanded cannot be articulated precisely, may be almost entirely a psychological matter, and is likely to change as mathematical techniques . . . improve." Simplicity is always relative to a conceptual scheme (compare figuring a 10% tip in American dollars and in English pounds, shillings, and pence). Even in mathematics, simplicity cannot be defined; it may depend on conventional or cultural factors. The simplicity may be in the concepts employed, or in the laws in which they are used. It may be linguistic (in structure or in notation), or ontological (that is, in the extralinguistic entities postulated). Is Copernicus' heliocentrism simpler than Ptolemy's geocentrism, if Copernicus requires that the earth move? The decision was not easy to make. Is a corpuscular

theory of light simpler than a wave theory? If the simpler (or more parsimonious) hypothesis is the one with the fewer parameters, then it will automatically also be more probable since a wider range of subsequent findings will be considered as confirming evidence. The requirement of simplicity is explained by Nelson Goodman thus:

> [The world] is neither simple nor complex except relative to—as organised under—a given system. The world has many different degrees of complexity, as it has many different structures; and it has as many different structures as there are different true ways of describing it. Without science, or some other mode of organisation, there is no simplicity or complexity. . . .
>
> We must not ignore the facts; but truth and simplicity often contend with one another, and truth cannot always win . . . simplicity not only functions as a test of truth but sometimes outweighs truth.

4. The hypothesis must be elegant, or *beautiful*. The physicist Dirac says, "it is more important to have beauty in one's equations than to have them fit the experiment . . . fundamental physical laws are described in terms of mathematical theory of great beauty and power." Sometimes the criterion of beauty takes the form of a demand for *symmetry;* it is for this reason that physicists first postulated the existence of so-called antimatter.

5. The hypothesis must be as *general* as possible; it must avoid names and arbitrary or unreasonable restrictions of time and place. Other things being equal, the wider the scope of the hypothesis, and the greater its *range* and *variety* of predictive power, the better. Yet generality and simplicity may sometimes conflict. In economics, for example, "perfect competition" is more simple as an explanatory hypothesis, but "imperfect competition" is more general.

6. The hypothesis, if possible, ought not to be purely *statistical* or probabilistic. There are some areas of science, however, quantum mechanics, for example (Chapter 12), and genetics, in which only probabilities can be predicted. No one can state when the next alpha particle will be emitted, but only how many particles on the average will be emitted in a given time interval; no one can state whether the next baby born in a

given family will be blue-eyed or brown-eyed, but only what the probabilities are in a large number of births. This is the basis for the dissatisfaction of some physicists with present-day quantum theory, and their search for what they call "hidden parameters." Einstein summarized his opposition to purely statistical hypotheses in a famous remark, "God does not play dice with the universe." In the social sciences, explanatory hypotheses are usually probabilistic. We may explain that there was a riot in Attica prison because confinement and frustration tend to breed aggression, but this hypothesis does not permit us to predict the time and place of the next prison riot.

7. The hypothesis should bring out *analogies* where possible. The scientist may use a model for this purpose (for example, of the atom or of the solar system). The model of course is never an exact replica; it is either much larger or much smaller than, and omits certain features of, whatever it represents. If the scientist offers a hypothesis that electricity "flows along a wire like water in a pipe," or that molecules interact "like billiard balls colliding," this aids us in grasping the hypothesis, as does a diagram drawn to prove theorems in geometry; but the model must not be confused with the hypothesis itself.

8. The hypothesis should, finally, satisfy certain criteria that can best be described as *metaphysical*: that there is no infinite regress of explanatory causes; that there is continuity in the world ("Nature makes no leaps," said Leibniz); that the world be regarded as stable; even that the world be properly anthropomorphic. Max Planck said of the "Principle of Least Action" (which is, loosely, that a physical system undergoing change chooses the process for which the action will turn out to be a minimum) that it "creates the impression in every unbiased mind that Nature is ruled by a rational purposive will."

Perhaps an example will clarify some of the variety of considerations in selecting a hypothesis. In economics, the business cycle has been explained by at least six theories, each citing different factors: monetary changes, such as the contraction and expansion of bank credit (Friedman); technological innovations and inventions, such as railroads (Schumpeter, Hansen); psychological attitudes and expectations (Pigou, Bagehot) ; variations in consumption and savings (Hobson, Sweezy); variations in investment (Hayek, Mises); and sunspots and the weather (Jevons). Each of these hypotheses will uniquely determine the facts.

Scientific Explanation

We have discussed in Chapter 9 how facts are selected, marshaled, and organized by a scientific hypothesis. This hypothesis, when it has been verified (and can be called a theory or law), also serves the function of explaining those facts.

Varieties of Explanation

There are of course many kinds of explanation; they are the answers to many kinds of question. Some examples follow:

1. What is photosynthesis? What is an ombudsman? What is heuristics? Here the explanation would be a *definition* of these terms.
2. What does this fire insurance policy mean? Can you explain *Finnegans Wake*? Here the explanation would be a *paraphrase* of these documents, which would restate the sense in simpler or more familiar words.
3. Will you explain chess to me? The explanation here would be to state the *rules* of the game.

4. Why is there no greatest prime number? Why is the sum of the interior angles of a Euclidean triangle 180°? Here the explanation would be the *analysis* of what is logically entailed by certain postulates of logic and mathematics (Chapter 6).

5. How do you fly a kite? How do you ski? The explanation here would be a practical *demonstration* of a skill or a technique; it might not require language.

6. Why did Brutus stab Caesar? This explanation would provide Brutus' *reasons*, motives, and beliefs (Chapter 20).

7. Why are snow and milk alike? The explanation here would require reference to the metaphysical *universal* "whiteness" in which both substances participate (Chapter 1).

Thus, there are various ways in which an explanation may be given. One of my favorites appears in a story by Ring Lardner: " 'Why are we going in there again, daddy?' 'Shut up,' his father explained."

All of these explanations contain a core of what Mill called "considerations for the intellect to give its assent." The explanation releases the tension that provoked the question. It evokes the "aha!" response: oh, so Brutus thought Caesar wanted to be emperor! so the Trojan horse was full of soldiers! so Miss Prism was the nurse! so there was sabotage on the plane! If the puzzlement is not in fact eliminated, the explanation is not accepted. Byron wrote, of Coleridge

> Explaining metaphysics to the nation—
> I wish he would explain his explanation.

This psychological aspect of explanation varies with the person, and with his degree of bewilderment and sophistication; however, the explanations which science provides, by means of logical inference from a law, are independent of persons.

How Science Explains

Science explains a fact, ideally, by embedding it within a general law from which, along with the particular conditions involved, the fact to be explained may be logically deduced. Thus:

1. Why did the pond freeze? Because the temperature dropped below 32°F., and water freezes at 32°F.

2. Why did the pipe rust? Because it is made of iron, and iron combines chemically with the oxygen in the air.

3. Why did the water pipes burst last winter? Because water expands when it freezes.

4. Why did Bert catch malaria? Because he was bitten by the anopheles mosquito, which is the carrier of that disease.

5. Why was there an eclipse of the sun? Because of the laws of gravitation and the orbits of the planets.

In each case, the particular fact is explained by being comprehended under, and derived from, a general law. The scientist explains what happens by devising *concepts* (e.g., temperature, oxidation, and gravitation) to describe particular experiences, and by supplying a framework of covering *laws* from which, in conjunction with the specific conditions involved, we may make inferences about what it is that we want to have explained.[1]

Misconceptions About How Science Explains

We must be wary of some common misconceptions about scientific explanation:

1. It is sometimes said that science describes, rather than explains. This point is usually raised by those who would prefer to explain that Bert caught malaria because he deceived his wife, or that the pond froze so that the children could skate. On November 1, 1755, an earthquake in Lisbon killed some fifteeen thousand people within six minutes and demolished thirty churches and a thousand homes. The quake was explained by the theologian John Wesley in a sermon on "The Cause and Cure of Earthquake" as the result of sin, which he said "is the moral cause of earthquakes, whatever their natural cause may be . . . they are the effect of that curse which was brought upon the earth by the original transgres-

---

[1] This is a simplified account of the "deductive-nomological" explanation of events. It disregards such difficulties as that of defining "law."

sion" of Adam and Eve. Actually, no sharp line can be drawn between description and explanation. If the scientific explanations of why the pond froze and why there was an eclipse are really only descriptions, what, then, would an explanation be? How else would you explain these events?

2. It is sometimes said that science explains the strange by the familiar; but typically the reverse is the case. Such familiar phenomena as rust, sunrise, tides, illness, family resemblance, and so on, are explained by such unfamiliar concepts as oxidation, gravitational attraction, invisible germs, and genes.

3. Scientific explanation is not the same as "understanding" in the sense in which it is said, for example, that D. H. Lawrence understood women, or that T. E. Lawrence understood the Arab mentality, or that an experienced nurse understands children. Such understanding is more like knowledge by acquaintance or like knowing how (Chapter 2) than like science.

4. A scientific explanation need not be a causal law. It may be a law of simultaneous existence rather than of succession. Boyle's Law, for example, associates the pressure of a gas with its volume, but pressure and volume are not cause and effect.

Increase in Generality

Just as a fact is explained by a law, so a law in turn may be explained by another law of wider scope; the greater the generality, the better the explanation. Indeed, the development of physics exemplifies this point. Galileo's laws explained how bodies fall; and Kepler's laws of planetary motion explained why the sun rises and sets. But it took Newton to explain both Galileo's and Kepler's laws (as well as other laws dealing with the tides) by embedding them all within his more general laws of gravitation, from which the laws of Galileo and Kepler could be deduced. The laws of gravitation describe the motion of all matter. Newton's laws were in turn explained by Einstein, who subsumed gravitation, along with the laws of the motion of light, within the even more general framework of Relativity Theory. Can relativity in turn be explained? Einstein and others have proposed a unified field theory to incorporate both relativity and quantum mechanics (quantum mechanics in its turn explains atomic phenomena and electromagnetism). But no such unified field theory has as yet been clearly stated.

In any event, does it follow from this pattern of explanation by greater scope or generality that scientific explanation will (or perhaps has!) come to an end? No part of the universe would escape a unified field theory—neither matter nor energy, neither the remote past nor the endless future, neither the "infinitely large" nor the "infinitely small." Such a theory might of course be found inaccurate or inadequate, and it might be discarded like so many other seemingly indubitable theories; yet, it is hard to imagine a wider or more general context under which it might be subsumed. On the other hand, there is no reason to suppose that man's doubts will ever be entirely allayed. Explanation is always relative to a given knowledge situation; you must stop somewhere. Take an analogous question, that of location: if you ask, Where is the Empire State Building? or where is seat J6 (in a theater)? or Madagascar? or the star Alpha Centauri? you would in each case be answered by a locating of the object within a system of coordinates—streets and avenues in Manhattan, or rows and files in a theater, or latitude and longitude on the earth or in the skies. But if you ask, Where is the universe? no answer can be given, not because there is some bit of knowledge we do not have, but because of the form of the question. It is logically incoherent. Who made God? and how high is up? likewise involve category mistakes, and do not allow an answer.

Explanation by Reduction

The growth of science toward increasing comprehensiveness depends in part on the ability to transfer information gained in one area into other areas, by reducing one concept to another. When sound was reduced to a wave in the air, all that was previously known about water waves could be applied to sound waves. Lightning has been reduced to electricity, heat to molecular motion, magnetism to molecular alignment, chemistry (largely) to physics, Mendelian heredity to molecular genetics (although the job is far from complete, as any thoughtful geneticist will admit). It is essential to bear in mind that these explanatory reductions are not ontological, but conceptual or linguistic; that is, they do not eliminate entities, processes, or events from the world, but are economical ways of describing phenomena. (In Chapter 1 we discussed the metaphysics of reduction and the reductive fallacy.) Heat is as real and as hot as it ever was, although the kinetic theory of gases relieves us of the need to consider it as an entity apart from molecules. Plants "breathe" through their leaves as vigorously as ever, and really absorb energy from the sun, even though scientific connecting principles now permit the reduction of cellular respiration and photosynthesis to more general physicochemical laws. I stress this point because a good deal of needless emotion is stirred up when someone speaks of reducing mental states to physical brain states, or living organisms to complex physicochemical systems, or psychology to neurophysiology, or cognition to stimulus and response, or social phenomena to compounds of individual behavior. (These issues are discussed in subsequent chapters.) Whether any of these reductions will ever be completely carried out is not known, but there is no logical reason why all these phenomena may not be described and explained in a more economical vocabulary.

System

Scientific explanation may sometimes require the concept of system. The nerves of animals, for example, consist of neurons, which are composed of the chemicals DNA, RNA, and certain proteins. Any questions about what nerves do may be answered in terms of these molecules; however, the operation of the nervous system cannot be described by merely adding up the properties of individual molecules or neurons—to do so would be to commit the reductive fallacy. A system differs from a machine in that, whereas a machine is a sum (or aggregate) of parts, a system is a whole which determines the operation of its parts. A system (unlike a machine) is essentially invariant to changes in its parts or elements. But "system" has not been clearly defined, and we should use the term with care. We should never foreclose further analysis of any alleged system. As Nagel shows,

> Although the occurrence of systems possessing distinctive structures of interdependent parts is undeniable, no general criterion has yet been proposed which makes it possible to identify . . . systems that are "genuinely functional" . . . from systems that are "merely summative [i.e., machines]."
>
> The mere fact that a system [e.g., a living organism] is a structure of dynamically interrelated parts does not suffice, by itself, to prove that the laws of such a system cannot be reduced to some theory developed initially for certain assumed constituents of the system.

Emergence

The theory of emergence is sometimes proposed to remedy the inability of the metaphysics of mechanism (Chapter 1) to explain how anything new can come into the world. If you have two stones, one of which weighs three pounds and the other four pounds, you can predict that their combined weight will be seven pounds. Weight thus is one of the many properties that are summative, or additive, or resultant. A machine likewise is a sum of parts: if a dismantled clock were spread out before you on a table, you could in time figure out how to put it together even if you had never seen a clock and were unaware of its purpose. However, some properties of some aggregates *cannot* be predicted solely from the properties of the parts; for example, the salty taste of sodium chloride; the smell of a perfume made up of chemicals never before combined; the particular musical quality of a chord consisting of notes not previously sounded together; the wetness of water (its constituent parts are the gases hydrogen and oxygen) .

A Chinese proverb tells us, "the cart and the horse are three." Unpredictable or "emergent" properties, unlike predictable resultant ones, may be the properties of organized systems. Proponents of this theory explain life as an emergent property of the chemical constituents of living creatures; thus life could never be reduced to any ingredient parts. But is it clear that this is so?

Although it is true that at any single stage in our intellectual growth we may be unable to predict the emergent properties of some aggregate, there seems no reason why there must be logically unpredictable qualities, that is, qualities which are absolutely (rather than relatively) emergent.

Interdependence of Theory and Observation

In the growth of science toward greater generality and comprehensiveness, the new theory (such as Newton's gravitation of all matter) is said to incorporate the older one (such as Galileo's laws of falling bodies). But this is not strictly accurate. The growth of knowledge is not simply cumulative, and the new theory may in fact contradict the old. In this instance, for example, Galileo regarded the acceleration of a freely falling body as constant, but Newton said that acceleration decreased (although imperceptibly) the farther one moved from the center of the earth. Another aspect of the growth of science is the change in such conceptions as mass. For Newton, it was essentially the "quantity of matter, arising from its density and bulk"; for Einstein, however, mass increases with velocity; inertial mass is defined as equivalent to gravitational mass.

These changes in conceptual structure pose a serious problem. Since, as we have seen, there is an intimate connection between concepts and the facts which they select and reveal; since no knowledge is ever clearly given to us without concepts; and since seeing is "seeing-as" and "seeing-what-is-the-case" (Chapter 4), it might happen that two different scientific theories could never be confronted with each other. Kepler believed that the earth travels around the sun, and Tycho Brahe that the sun moves around the earth; surely they could not settle their disagreement by getting up early some morning to watch the sun rise. One might argue that they saw different things since theories interact with the observations on which they are based. In the long run, however, all theories function within, and cope with, the same realm of possible human experience. At some point, therefore, they must either touch, or be limiting conditions of each other (as Newtonian "mass" at rest is the limiting condition of Einsteinian "mass" in motion).

The interdependence of theory and observation is clear in the use by scientists of explanatory unobservables. In distinguishing science from metaphysics, I said that the scientist relies on observation. However, he refers freely to electrons, gravitational fields, and probability waves, which are theoretical constructs with only indirect links to what can be seen. Are they then "parts of the world"? It is always risky to talk in science about something one can never observe. A similar problem concerns "dispositions," that is, properties not immediately evident to perception, but which can be encountered only if certain appropriate actions are taken (e.g., solubility, brittleness, elasticity, etc.). What does it mean to say that this bit of chalk in my hand is "soluble in water" if it is never actually immersed? If I say that my car has a disposition to stall, or that my record player has a disposition to jump, I can isolate the defective wire or needle; but a disposition to dissolve cannot be so simply examined. How can science cope with such nonobservable aspects, either of observable chalk, or of nonobservable electrons? By coordinating what cannot be seen with something that *can* be seen, for example, the electron with certain tracks in a cloud chamber. Whatever questions one may ask about the electron are answered by reference to the tracks. The invisible solubility of chalk is coordinated with procedures that are visible.

Such coordinating definitions, or reduction sentences, or operational rules, or epistemic correlations (as various philosophers call them) are not analytic; although they serve as partial definitions, they also have factual content; no finite number of them suffices for a full determination of such "open concepts" as dispositions. But that is the nature of our empirical knowledge: the whole fabric of theory and observation is mutually reinforcing.

Moreover, as Pierre Duhem argues,

> The physicist can never subject an isolated hypothesis to experimental test, but only a whole group of hypotheses; when the experiment is in disagreement with his predictions, what he learns is that at least one . . . is unacceptable and ought to be modified; but the experiment does not designate which one should be changed.

Physics is not a machine which lets itself be taken apart; we cannot try each piece in isolation.

In Otto Neurath's vivid metaphor, scientists are sailors who must repair and rebuild their ship while remaining at sea. Every plank may be replaced in the course of time, but at every stage in the process, *some* planks must be left untouched. Karl Popper has a similar view in *The Logic of Scientific Discovery*:

> The empirical basis of objective science has thus nothing "absolute" about it. Science does not rest upon rock bottom. The bold structure of its theories rises, as it were, above a swamp. It is like a building erected on piles . . . driven down from above into the swamp, but not down to any natural or "given" base; and when we cease our attempts to drive our piles into a deeper layer, it is not because we have reached firm ground. We simply stop when we are satisfied that they are firm enough to carry the structure, at least for the time being.

Thus, in Quine's striking figure of speech, "our statements about the external world face the tribunal of sense experience not individually but only as a corporate body."

Explanation and Prediction

Explanation in science is often said to be theoretically identical to (logically isomorphic with) prediction: you have explained the last eclipse satisfactorily only if you can predict the next one accurately. However, some philosophers argue that a good explanation need not require prediction. Thus, you can explain that you could not fall asleep last night because of the coffee you drank, although you cannot predict that coffee will keep you awake tonight. You can explain that Bert died because he was stung by a wasp, even though not every wasp sting causes death. Darwinian evolution is cited as an outstanding example of a theory that does not make predictions. "Nothing in biology is less predictable than the future course of evolution," Ernst Mayr has written. Independent parallel lines of development, when subjected to the same selection pressure, may respond differently;

biological survival in the past can be explained (or "retro-dicted") from information that does not suffice to support predic-tion of the future (Chapter 13). There is an asymmetry here be-tween past and future because the explanatory scientific law is statistical or probabilistic, rather than universal. But there is a further important question: is coffee by itself a fully adequate explanation of insomnia, or a wasp sting of death, in view of the very fact that we cannot always predict these results? It would therefore seem preferable to say that these explanations allay our doubts only partially: we need a better hypothesis. An ideal or adequate explanation would specify and isolate the particular factors involved, so as to enable us to predict.

It is sometimes asserted that this analysis of scientific explana-tion (as inference from general laws) will not suffice to explain human actions (which are not so much caused, as motivated by reasons); or the activities of living creatures (which require ref-erence to purposes or goals) ; or the events of history (which are unique). These three areas are separately examined in subsequent chapters; they will be seen to demand only slight modifications of the schema of scientific explanation.

How Science Grows

The growth of science is not a clear-cut, straightforward pro-gression toward a unique, all-inclusive final truth. Many adven-titious factors influence the course of science and becloud so simple and sanguine a prospect. First, the *choice of problems* on which the scientist decides to work depends on such considera-tions as political and social pressures (e.g., for pollution control and population control, and against investigating genetic factors in intelligence) ; financial rewards (e.g., what the government will subsidize or industry support); ethical incentives (e.g., "it is better to do biology than physics") ; expediency or the state of the discipline (e.g., the availability of computers and other equipment); the urgency of the problem compared with its diffi-culty (biologists, for example, are now facing the decision as to whether it is worthwhile attempting to complete the taxonomy of living creatures) .[2]

Second, there are fortuitous, or *chance,* elements in scientific progress; some famous discoveries have been accidental (Fleming and penicillin, Büchner and enzymes, Becquerel and the radioactive emission from uranium). There are fashions in ideas; ecology is now "in"; Mendel's paper was ignored for decades. There are, moreover, accidents of personality (in scientific ability, in who makes up the scientific establishment) .

Third, how the scientist hits on a new hypothesis is a mystery ("like a flash . . . an act of insight"—Peirce; "by intuition, based upon *Einfühlung*"—Einstein) . What has been called the *logic of discovery* is obscure, perhaps below the level of conscious awareness, perhaps similar to the creativity of the artist. Even the designing of an experiment "becomes an art" (Kelvin) . Dalton arrived at his atomic theory despite (or because of?) incorrect assumptions and experimental error. The scientist is not ipso facto the best judge of his own mental processes, any more than anyone else is.

Fourth, there are *extrascientific influences,* not merely on the choice of problems by the scientist, but on the conclusions at which he arrives: religion (against Darwinian evolution) ; politics (for Lysenko and the transmission of acquired characteristics, in the Soviet Union); philosophy (toward deterministic or indeterministic interpretations of quantum mechanics) ; social policy (the French Academy denied for a long time that there were any such things as meteorites, because they feared that an ignorant peasantry might consider them to be supernatural).

What Needs to Be Explained?

Finally, there is the question of what situations are seen by scientists as requiring explanation. I said earlier that puzzlement may vary with the person and the context. Are there situations that

2 There exist some five million species of animals never described, each species unique; every year perhaps hundreds of them become extinct, irreversibly gone; if taxonomists throughout the world now describe annually about ten thousand species, the task would require another five hundred years!

are intrinsically puzzling? or that objectively require an explanation? There are always implicit assumptions of what may obviously be taken for granted, or of what is "natural"; these paradigms are seldom made explicit, however. Aristotle regarded all bodies as "naturally" at rest, so that some push or force would be needed to move a thing and keep it moving; thus, a rocket flying through space, a ship at sea, or anything else in motion would have to be explained. Galileo and Newton, on the other hand, thought that uniform motion in a straight line was just as "natural" as rest; therefore, only a *change* in motion required explanation, or had to be accounted for.

Let me recall some exemplary episodes to illustrate differing opinions as to what is considered obvious and what is puzzling and demands explanation:

1. The ancient Greeks did not think that how the world began had to be explained.

2. Galileo refused to accept the influence of the moon on the tides: that was obviously astrology!

3. Francis Bacon opposed both Aristotle and Copernicus, since it seemed to him obviously wrong to group the earth, which is motionless and dark, with the planets, which move and shine.

4. Kepler was puzzled as to why the planets are at their particular distances from the sun; since Newton, however, this question is regarded as of merely historical interest.

5. When Bentley asked Newton why our solar system consists of many planets traveling about one sun, Newton replied, "Why is there one body in our system qualified to give light and heat to all the rest, I know no reason, but because the author of the system thought it convenient."

6. Neither Huygens nor Leibniz accepted Newton's concept of gravitational attraction: although the inverse square law could be used to predict phenomena, it did not provide an explanation, that is, allay doubt. Leibniz wrote that the concept that bodies were attracted to each other by "gravitation" would be "just as if there were watches able to tell the time by some 'horodeictic faculty' without the need of wheels, or

mills able to crush grain by a 'fractive faculty' without the need of anything in the nature of millstones."

7. Kelvin thought in 1900 that the basic general outline of physics was pretty much complete, and that there were no important questions left to be answered. Berthelot wrote in 1885, "The world is now without mysteries." Both were great physicists.

8. X rays were discovered in 1895 when Roentgen wondered why a screen glowed unaccountably. But this glow had been observed by other scientists who did not think it needed explaining.

9. No one before Descartes regarded the relation of mind to body as a problem.

10. Why is the velocity of light a constant? Milič Čapek writes:

> Einstein regarded the negative result of all experiments establishing the constancy of the velocity of light as one of the ultimate and irreducible features of physical reality, while Lorentz and FitzGerald hoped to *explain* the constancy of light velocity as a kind of happy or unhappy coincidence which may be derived from the unchanged laws of classical mechanics.

11. After Pasteur proved in 1861 that bacteria could not arise spontaneously, but only from preexisting bacteria, Darwin wrote, "It is mere rubbish, thinking of the origin of life; one might as well think of the origin of matter."

12. In describing the revolutionary achievement of ancient Greek artists in depicting the visible world, Gombrich has pointed out that

> the "corrections" introduced by the Greek artist in order to "match" appearances are quite unique in the history of art. Far from being a natural procedure, they are the great exception. What is normal to man and child all over the globe is the reliance on schemata, on what is called "conceptual art." What needs explanation is the sudden departure from this habit. . . .

13. *Homo sapiens* is apparently the only species which makes war, that is, kills its conspecifics without a reason. Does this require an explanation?

14. Does it require an explanation that sentences in one lan-

guage can be translated into another language (see Chapter 19)?

15. Does the fact that space has three dimensions have to be explained? Kant and Poincaré tried to do so.

These examples seem to illustrate great variations in what people take to be obvious (or natural, or just brute fact), rather than puzzling or needing explanation. It is never entirely obvious what is obvious.

Some Contemporary Explanations

Let me now list some statements that are currently being accepted as explanations, in appropriate contexts. Do they provide "considerations for the intellect to give its assent"? Do they allay doubt?

1. The emission of an alpha particle is theoretically unpredictable.

2. Matter is being constantly created, at the rate of one hydrogen atom per liter volume every thousand million years, in order that the large-scale aspect of the universe remain constant.

3. "Two pieces of matter placed anywhere at all in an otherwise empty universe will necessarily influence one another in two ways, and . . . in two ways only: they will affect one another's motion, and they will affect one another's temperature"—Herbert Dingle.

4. "The 'constant' of gravitation is secularly increasing. . . . Planck's 'constant' h can be shown . . . to depend also secularly on the time"—E. A. Milne.

5. The radius of curvature of space is increasing with time—H. P. Robertson.

6. "It is an indispensable condition of quantum theory that all electrons, all protons, all neutrons, must be identical . . . the absolute identity of all electrons is a property they must have if they are to explain"—N. R. Hanson.

7. There is an absolute maximum velocity in the universe, namely, the speed of light.

8. "Electrons and protons have no exact position"—Henry Margenau.

9. "The postulate that the velocity of light is independent of the velocity of its source is indispensable to relativity theory" —P. W. Bridgman.

10. "Opposing and contradictory motions are the rule throughout the universe, and this is an essential aspect of the very mode of things . . ."—David Bohm.

11. A traveler returning to earth after a high-velocity round trip through space returns younger than his twin brother, who stayed at home.

The Anthropocentric Growth of Science

The human element in the progress of scientific explanation cannot be eliminated. The usual image of the scientist is misleading. He is not finding his way through a labyrinth which has one and only one pathway through it (there may be more than one, and there may be none). He is not putting together the pieces of a jigsaw puzzle (that is, pieces which can be correctly joined in one way only) . He is not solving a mathematical problem, nor a chess puzzle: both mathematics and chess presuppose specific postulates and rules of inference. Nature proffers no rules, no definitions, no stipulations, no guides, no Ariadne's thread. We make all these up ourselves. It is not nature which prevents our grouping cabbages with kings, but our own demands for order. And we have no reason to believe that our categories and discoveries and conclusions are the only ones possible.

Our perceptual knowledge is delimited by our characteristic biological capacities, and there are limits to the completeness of our theoretical structures. But our observations and our theories mutually reinforce each other. If we never trusted some sort of evidence, nothing whatever could ever be tested. The structure of our science is pragmatically justified; it is the most reliable knowledge there is; it is in every sense objective.

But it is *our* science; it alleviates *our* puzzlement; it supplies the answers to the questions *we* have asked. Nature answers—if she answers at all!—only those questions which we put to her. Man is nature becoming aware of herself, but she might have other children! If there should exist intelligent creatures elsewhere in the universe, will their "science" inevitably be the same as ours? At the court of Louis XIV there was an ongoing debate as to whether two "perfect artists" painting the same scene would produce identical pictures. Would two "perfect scientists" working independently produce identical sciences? Both of these questions imply that regardless of how the problem is viewed, regardless of the human mind, there is only one correct solution. But there is no reason to believe that any such unique solution exists. There is an irreducibly anthropocentric surd in knowledge. No observation, no measurement, no thought process ever confirms a hypothesis with absolute precision. We can never be certain in an experiment that we have excluded all extraneous factors, nor what degree of error may be tolerated, nor what other explanations may be possible. Answers to questions have contexts, and presuppositions. We can no more explain everything at once than we can doubt everything at once (*pace* Descartes!). The decision as to when to accept an explanation and when to question it is ultimately and idiosyncratically human.

We are thus again referred back to the primal philosophic injunction: Know thyself. Man is the measure.

I I

The Social Sciences

I BEGAN Chapter 9 with the definition "Science seeks to discover and formulate in general terms the conditions under which events occur," and I was being deliberately provocative when I included in the branches of science political science, sociology, and anthropology. It is important to realize that despite differences of method, interest, technique, subject matter, and degree, *all* scientific knowledge must be confirmed or verified; all must be justified by evidence or good reasons. The criteria for a good hypothesis (that it be falsifiable, simple, beautiful, general, etc.) apply equally. So do the ideals of science (reliability, precision, objectivity, testability, comprehensiveness, etc.), and the requirement that the justification for a claim be unremittingly criticized. Not every scientific explanation satisfies all of these goals equally well, but the goals are the same for all of our organized empirical knowledge.

However, not all philosophers agree with this ideal of unified science. They argue that the actions of human beings comprise a unique and ultimate category of events, and that therefore such fields as social psychology, sociology, anthropology, economics, and political science cannot be studied by the methods of the natural sciences (by which they usually mean physics). This is an issue fraught with emotion, and usually fought by polemic. In part they fear the possible results of the scientific knowledge of human behavior; in part they oppose what they regard as scientific imperialism; in part they are sensitive to Poincaré's jeer, "Physicists have a subject matter, but sociologists study only methods." Still, they make a substantial point, which must be considered on its merits, and that is, that there is a radical difference between the scientific understanding of why a leaf flies in the wind and why a man flies from a mob; if the scientist did not himself know fear and hate, he would miss the point of the latter event entirely. Human actions, it is argued, are charged with meanings. The behaviorist observer, who is limited to what he can see, and who ignores the "inwardness" of human actions, "denudes the world of meaning"; he sees the same overt action in the kiss of a lover, the kiss of a prostitute, and the kiss of Judas. What would he report, it is asked, about what was going on, if he were a visitor from Mars who landed in New York at 11:00 A.M. on Armistice Day, and saw everyone standing around silently?

The term *Verstehen* ("to understand") denotes the position of those who claim that the social scientist can and must make use of his own inner experience. The student of human actions is part of his own subject matter. He must use the methods of *introspection* and *empathy*, which have nothing in common with the procedures of natural science. Thus, Isaiah Berlin claims that "a man who lacks common intelligence can be a physicist of genius, but not even a mediocre historian." Dilthey and Windelband distinguish the "nomothetic" natural sciences (which generalize) from the "idiographic" social sciences (which try to articulate individuality). This position must be seriously examined.

(Some philosophers argue that no generalization about human behavior is ever valid, since individuals have free will. This position, I believe, is quite untenable. Reliable predictions are made regularly about the number of automobile accidents that will happen over the weekend, and the number of parcels that will be lost at Grand Central, and the shift in political preference that accompanies a move by a family from the center of a city to the suburbs.)

Claims of the *Verstehen* Position

It will be useful to consider in detail twelve specific claims about the social sciences that might be interpreted as justifying the *Verstehen* position:

1. In the natural sciences, a hypothesis is verified by experiment, but the social sciences cannot experiment. The ability to experiment is essential to the testing of explanations in the natural sciences. However, physics need not be taken as the model for the natural sciences, and neither astronomy nor geology can experiment. Moreover, if the meaning of "experiment" is somewhat broadened to include an investigation for which there are controls, then the social sciences do experiment. Thus, a study in Canada of male hospital attendants found that those who had been shown a movie of a violent knife fight were more aggressively punitive toward their patients than a control group of attendants who were shown a "peaceful" movie. Other inquiries in the social sciences have investigated whether voters are influenced by a candidate's religion; and whether having a television set at home has any effect on how often the children go to church on Sunday.

2. The natural sciences can repeat experiments in order to verify their hypotheses, and can generalize their results. Any one cubic centimeter of pure water is exactly like any other; if you find out its weight, then you can predict the weight of every cubic centimeter of water. The social sciences, however, it is claimed, deal with situations that are not uniform: no two persons and no two social contexts are exactly alike. The events of the past have a specific time and place index; there is a uniqueness (or *Einmaligkeit*) to the French Revolution, for example, or to the rise of fascism, which makes it impossible to include it in any generalization. However, this claim for the *Verstehen* position cannot be upheld. It is only by an idealization that two actual cubic centimeters of water may be taken to be alike: they are never *exactly* alike, but the differences between them (in impurities, for example, or

temperature) may be irrelevant to a particular inquiry, just as the differences between two voters or two villages may be ignored in certain investigations. Certain of the natural sciences (such as geology) deal with unique past events; and every physical event is (under certain interpretations) uniquely dated by entropy. The uniqueness of past historical events does not prevent the discernment of patterns (for example, in all revolutions) or the pragmatic grouping of individual events into classes in order to point out functional interrelations (such as between war and inflation, or between frustration and aggression). Causal laws connect kinds of events by abstracting from those singularities which are held to be irrelevant to that inquiry (e.g., whether the hospital attendants in the previously cited study were blue-eyed or brown-eyed).

3. The natural scientist, it is claimed, can isolate what his hypothesis applies to, so that his predictions are not upset by outside variables. He may close off the solar system as if it were an aquarium, so to speak; celestial mechanics requires only mass, location, and velocity for a full description of phenomena. Social phenomena, on the other hand, are endlessly ramified; there is no way to cut them off clearly. Can anyone cope with the complexity of the factors relevant to an election? or to the fluctuations of the stock market? When it was suggested to James that psychology is the study of the knee jerk and related phenomena, he replied that *all* phenomena are related phenomena. How many variables are relevant to intelligence, for example—health? heredity? money? eye color? brain size? climate? And in social situations, there may be consequences that are unintended: if I decide to sell my shares of stock, the price will drop. But the reply to this claim is to point out that the tacit understanding, *other things being equal,* applies in all investigations, physical as well as social. Galileo's laws of falling bodies seem to be the essence of simplicity, but that is because they disregard the friction and resistance of the air—if they did not do so, they would have to take into account the shape and material of the falling body and be endlessly complex. Kepler's law that a planet travels in a simple elliptical orbit

abstracts from the complicated gravitational attraction exerted on each planet by every other body in the solar system. In fact I cannot move my finger without disturbing all the stars. In both the natural and social sciences, we always assume that we may disregard certain elements as irrelevant or trivial. Some areas of physics, such as cloud formation and hydrodynamic turbulence, seem to be as complex as any phenomena the social sciences study.

4. The astronomer may confidently predict the next solar eclipse, so that his hypotheses may be unequivocally verified; whereas, it is claimed by the *Verstehen* position, no social scientist can predict with any assurance. This charge is true, but it is a matter of degree. No physicist would dare to predict where a flying leaf will be ten minutes hence. No sociologist would hesitate to predict that no woman will be elected Pope in 1978.

5. The hypotheses of the natural scientist, it is claimed, can be stated with precision and universality because he operates with certain constants that hold true throughout the universe. Among these are the speed of light (c), Planck's constant of energy levels (h), the electric charge of the electron (e), the mass of the electron (m), and the gravitational constant (G). The social scientist has nothing to compare with these unchanging aspects of the physical world. However, it would be an exaggeration to claim that there are no constants in human actions; for instance, human mortality, perhaps sexual desire, and the law of diminishing returns.

6. The physical scientist, it is claimed, can verify his hypotheses by observation; he can see the eclipse and the falling apple; but the social scientist can see only the smallest part of "social reality." He relies on introspection and empathy to uncover the motives of human behavior, which are unobservable and inaccessible. If the anthropologist observes a primitive society, he has no way of finding out that it is their belief in witchcraft which motivates their behavior. He may be as mystified by their ritual as they would be if they saw him drop a letter into a mailbox after licking a stamp. If the social scientist is limited to what he can observe, what will he report when, for example, he sees that you don't vote (is

it because of laziness? or disgust? or rebelliousness? or a bribe?) or when you stand still on Armistice Day? When the physicist postulates unobservable entities, such as electrons, to explain phenomena, he introduces precise rules that co-ordinate those unobservable electrons with something that can be observed, namely, tracks in a Wilson cloud chamber; but he need not empathize with his electrons. The social scientist does not know what motive to coordinate with your not voting; he must refer to his own motives in order to formulate the conditions under which such events occur. Now, this may well be the source of explanatory hypotheses in the social sciences; introspection and empathy may be use-ful, perhaps even necessary; but what counts in science is not where the hypothesis comes from, but whether and how it is verified. The historian Guglielmo Ferrero writes:

> I am not one of those historians who must submerge themselves in masses of documents to form an opinion. As soon as I know the facts, I enter into the psychology of the men who were important to the events. . . . I read their works; I study their actions; then, . . . interpreting from experience, I try to form an opinion, and finally I work out an hypothesis which I verify by research.

But empathy may actually mislead you. When you bomb your enemy in wartime, do you predict his submission be-cause you empathize with the terror, or do you predict his resistance because you empathize with the challenge? Can you by *Verstehen* empathize with Lee Harvey Oswald? or with Hitler? or with believers in witchcraft? "Intuition pre-vents some people from imagining that anyone could pos-sibly dislike chocolate," says Karl Popper. The poet, too, uses empathy; in the "pathetic fallacy" he imputes human feelings to inanimate objects—the "angry" storm, the "brave" early crocus, nature's "lavish ingenuity." Prediction of human ac-tions *may* but *need not* speculate on motives or other unob-servable factors. If the social scientist correctly predicts voting behavior, that is, if his hypothesis is verified by what happens, then his empathy with presumed laziness or disgust or rebelliousness or whatever, is beside the point.

7. The raw material of the natural sciences can be measured with precision, but concepts in the social sciences (e.g., "army

morale," "equality of opportunity," "free enterprise," "national character") are inherently vague and qualitative (or intensive). You can measure a woman's height, but not her patriotism. You can put two people on a scale together to get a heavier weight, but you cannot add their I.Q.'s to get a genius. However, (*a*) some natural sciences (e.g., meteorology) are quite imprecise; and "it is never possible to predict a physical occurrence with unlimited precision," as Planck said. (*b*) The social sciences are increasingly relying on mathematics. Consider, for instance, anthropometry, cybernetics, theory of games and economic behavior, sampling and poll-taking, elaborate statistical analysis by computers, "cliometrics," the newest branch of history. In economics, the raw data of experience are already in numerical form. Some surprising facts have emerged from the use of mathematics in the social sciences: there is an isomorphism between the spread of rumors and the spread of disease (just as sounds have the same form as water waves); in sufficiently large aggregations there is a relation between the rank and the frequency of certain elements (Zipf's "law of least effort"—the second letter in order of frequency, *t*, appears half as often as the first, *e;* if the cities of a nation are ranked in order of population, then the largest city has twice the population of the next largest). (*c*) Although intensive qualities cannot be measured, they often can be scaled, or placed within some rank or order. The hardness of minerals, for example, is not measured, but expressed in terms of a scale from 1 (talc) to 10 (diamond); a new mineral might be described as being between 7 (quartz) and 8 (topaz). The pecking order of a group of barnyard fowl is also a scale. By careful analysis, it has been found possible to scale such intensive qualities as patriotism and race prejudice. (*d*) The "mystique of quality" is misguided; "the difference between the qualitative and the quantitative is not a difference in nature but a difference in our conceptual system—in our language," says Carnap. When you say that it is hot, and when you say that the temperature is 86°F., you are not denoting different things, but using different sets of symbols. To call a sound high-pitched and to identify its wavelength is to refer to the same "piece of the world" in different ways. Quality and quantity are not antithetical; any quantity is a quantity of a quality.

8. In the natural sciences, phenomena may be studied without regard to their past (an inclined plane is just what it is), whereas human beings and societies are only what they have come to be. This is a problem for the social sciences, which may find their predictions falsified because of unobservable and unverifiable past histories. Not everyone who dips a madeleine in tea will react as did Marcel Proust. Only the burnt child dreads the fire. Living creatures have memories, dispositions, and expectations. Behavior is altered by habits and conditioning. Thus, a person's past history influences his present reactions (Russell's "mnemic phenomena"); rocks do not remember. But this constraint does not preclude the search for generalizations about behavioral phenomena (for example, one might investigate whether all burnt children dread fire equally) and in physics the influence of the past is not always irrelevant (hysteresis is the lagging or retardation effect in viscosity and internal friction). Everything is what it has come to be. If you were to take someone's place in the middle of a chess game, you could determine your best move just by examining the position on the chess board at that time, but you could not similarly replace the bridge player in the middle of a hand without knowing the previous bids and cards played. Thus, the physicist can often make predictions on the basis of general laws and present conditions, whereas the sociologist may require, in addition, a temporal or historical perspective: knowledge of how things got to be the way they are. Sartre misses the point when he remarks that American "hyper-empiricism—which on principle neglects connections with the past—could arise only in a country whose History is relatively short." But that a social situation (or a man, or a bridge game) is what it has come to be does not prevent scientific inquiry—why should it?—any more than it does in historical geology. In evolutionary biology, every living species is what it is as the result of a long history of natural selection; but only the history which is incorporated into its present structure is of any scientific significance.

9. In the social sciences, explanatory hypotheses may become confused because there is an unavoidable interaction between the scientist and what he studies, between his statements and the people to whom he makes them. The astronomer's prediction of an eclipse has no effect on the eclipse; but the sociologist's predictions, when publicized, may be self-fulfilling ("there will be a run on the bank"; "prices on the stock market will go up"; "ghetto children are likely to become delinquents"; remember what happened to Macbeth when the witches predicted he would become king). The sociologist's predictions may also be self-defeating ("the commodity you manufacture will be overproduced"; "you'll have an accident if you drive home in this weather"; "Jones is the underdog in this election and can't possibly win"). This is the Cassandra paradox: a prediction *to* you *about* you may motivate you to defy the prediction. Moreover, as opinion researchers will confirm, a question may often be asked in such a way as to evoke a certain response. The poll-taker may unconsciously interfere with the situation being investigated; this criticism was made of the Kinsey report. The announcement of a new disease or syndrome, genuine or imaginary, will elicit some responses of "That's just what I have!" Thus, the physician (like other investigators) may induce by his manner or remarks an otherwise nonexistent pathological condition ("iatrogenic causation"). Different physicians using the same drugs on the same patients may get different results.

Interactions between social investigators and what is being investigated do occur, and they do present a problem for social science. But this complication is again a matter of degree. In physics, too, the insertion of a thermometer into a liquid alters its temperature; and in all intra-atomic measurements, the observing device interacts with what is being observed. However, there is no reason why all these interactions cannot be examined. The impact of self-fulfilling or self-defeating prophecies ("seldep") can be evaluated. There is no insurmountable difficulty in generalizing these behavior patterns.

Adolph Lowe has argued in *On Economic Knowledge* that economic theory does not unravel a tangle from outside, but is the means whereby a participant within the process consciously alters it:

> That knowledge should be inseparable from action, because that which is known may first have to be created in the image of a rationally conceived design, is probably the one characteristic that . . . separates the science of Society from the science of Nature.

But, as I argue throughout this book, neither in physics nor in human affairs is there a determinate, ordered "reality" which can be known by the passive reception of discrete sense impressions.

10. The natural scientist is indifferent to his subject matter, but the student of human affairs can scarcely be detached in investigating birth control, socialism, sexual freedom, crime, drugs, pornography, and so on. The social sciences, unlike the physical, are permeated with values. It was the hope of Auguste Comte that his newly founded "science of society" would eliminate values by distinguishing, for example, the question of whether to land a man on the moon from the question of how to do so; or whether to solve India's population problem by putting a sterilizing chemical into the water supply from how to do so. (These examples, of course, are not from Comte.)

The involvement of the social sciences with ethical or moral issues has various aspects. (*a*) As in the examples cited, the issues themselves may pose ethical considerations. But, obviously, issues in the natural sciences do so as well. Whether to develop new pesticides, or a new nerve gas; what kinds of experiments to perform on animals, fetuses, and prisoners, all involve moral questions. (*b*) The judgment of the social scientist may be affected by his interests: think of conservative and liberal analysts of unemployment and inflation, of Mao and Khrushchev on the inevitability of war, of labor and capitalist determinations as to whether wages or profits rose faster. But such bias occurs in the natural sciences as well: think of the Soviet advocacy of Lysenkoism, of Nazi opposition to relativity physics, of Oppenheimer versus Teller on the hydrogen bomb, of arguments about evolution and the age of the earth. Scientists may be biased; but this applies to the natural sciences and the social sciences equally. Theoretically, bias may be made explicit and compensated for; scientific procedures are self-corrective. (*c*) Some of the applications of social theories have been suspect: functionalism in anthropology has been denounced as a device for the imperialist management of primitive societies; but physical theories have of course also been used for ulterior purposes. (*d*) The social scientist may select his problems because he believes the results of his research will be socially valuable (e.g., to raise real wages); but so does the physicist. Both are human beings. (*e*) It is claimed that fact and value are in principle impossible to separate in the social sciences: can you describe a concentration camp factually without using the word "cruel"? But, as Ernest Nagel has shown, there is a sharp difference between *characterizing* and *appraising*, that is, between defining or clarifying a condition, and approving or condemning it. You might say that absinthe is the best way to drink yourself to death. An atheist is no less competent than a devout believer in distinguishing a truly religious person from one who is only going through the motions. A pro- or anti- attitude need not obfuscate a statement of the relation of means to ends. (*f*) Since no hypothesis is ever completely proven, there is often in the physical as well in the social sciences some problem that requires rational decision; for example, how high should we build a dam to prevent floods? what safety factor should we use for a bridge? when is a certain new drug safe to market? what percentage of toxic side effects may we ignore? when ought a new discovery be published? These decisions involve values; they must be made in both the natural and the social sciences.

11. In the natural sciences, it is claimed that the facts dealt with can be unambiguously isolated; whereas the social sciences face problems in establishing their hypotheses not only because the concepts used are qualitative and vague (which is claim #7), but also because social facts are *contextual* and holistic. They involve human actions, which are never without a setting. Thus, a "voter in the primary" is more than just a "person moving a lever"; a "banker certifying a check" is more than just a "person pushing a pen"; a piece of green

paper is money only if the people handling it believe it to be so; a man wearing a uniform is an army officer only if he is so regarded. Social data are never "brute facts." They require interpretation by concepts. These concepts, it is claimed, are unavoidably normative and can be properly understood only by the participants themselves "from the inside." No outsider can break into this interlocking set of meanings and values (the "hermeneutic circle"). But this argument for the *Verstehen* position transforms a practical difficulty into a theoretical impasse, and confuses experience with knowledge.

No special intuition or empathetic understanding is required to predict and describe what people do. If social facts are indeed contextual, and institutions are constituted by systems of rules, or "forms of life," they can be investigated just like any other phenomena, even if they are networks which are more than the individuals involved. An army, or a football team, or a square dance, or a revival meeting, or a philosophy class consists of persons who have mutual interactions and expectations. "One chimpanzee is no chimpanzee," said Yerkes, perceptively.

The thesis of *holism* takes the beehive as the model for human society: laws stating the properties of wholes or collectives are required in order to explain and predict social events; personality variables are irrelevant; individuals are the actors who just happen to play roles in a social scene. Tolstoy wondered in *War and Peace* how the army could want war when each soldier wanted peace; but, whether in a lynch mob, or a political convention, or a social club, or a Dutch tulip craze, persons will do in groups what they will not do acting alone. Every culture assumes some notion of order or hierarchy without which no description of social facts is complete. Marxist holism claims that what each of us thinks and how each of us acts are to be explained by how our class is related to the modes of production.

Three considerations, however, may be adduced to modulate the view that social science is distinctively holistic. (*a*) Natural science must also often take account of context (e.g., the critical level necessary for an atomic reaction; or in magnetism or ecology). (*b*) The astronomer can study the stars in the Big Dipper as a single constellation; the sociologist can study the behavior of a mob as a unity. Thus, microeconomics studies the observable actions of single individuals; macroeconomics deals with such abstractions as "balance of trade" and "Gross National Product." The "aggregation problem" in economics of inferring the total demand for consumer goods from the number of shirts that Bert buys presents no greater theoretical difficulties than the physicist faces in dealing with temperature as the property of a thermodynamic system rather than of a single molecule. (*c*) Most important, the thesis of *methodological individualism,* which is opposed to holism, argues that all social or collective terms can be analyzed exhaustively into the behavior and dispositions of individual persons. Accordingly, Adam Smith and Mill base social theories on individual propensities; Pareto claims that "psychology is at the base of all the social sciences"; and Erich Fromm uses the categories of psychoanalysis to explain politics and economics. John Maynard Keynes built his *General Theory* of economic activity on three psychological factors: a propensity to consume, an attitude to liquidity, and an expectation of future yield from capital assets. Lewis Namier contributed to historiography by his study of the eighteenth-century British political parties, in which he maintained that party decisions were motivated by the self-interest of individual party members. This sort of reduction of the social sciences to depth psychology, I believe, often teeters on the edge of the reductive fallacy. I doubt that the jury system in England can be accounted for by some Anglo-Saxon psychological trait or that it was the "authoritarian personality" that produced Nazism. I am not persuaded by Geoffrey Gorer's contention that the success of Bolshevism may be attributed to the Russian addiction to swaddling clothes. However, there are sufficient grounds to dispute the claim of holism that contextual social facts must be theoretically distinguished from physical facts.

12. Max Weber contends that no objective analysis of "social reality" can be made because "life, with its irrational reality and its store of possible meanings, is inexhaustible." We must

select, then, he says, what we consider to be the essential features of an event, and use meaningful categories to construct an "ideal type" which we then impute to the event. "Capitalist" is an example of such an accented construct; no living person actually spends all his time maximizing his profit. However, *all* the concepts of science (not only those of "social reality") are idealized; *all* descriptions are selective. The concept of "capitalism" is useful; so are the concepts of "frictionless engine" and "ideal gas," which are likewise arrived at by giving certain variables extreme values.

These twelve diverse and overlapping arguments for the *Verstehen* view do not impair the naturalist ideal of the unity of science. In different areas of inquiry, there are differences in subject matter, technique, and complexity, but any claim to knowledge must be validated, verified by evidence, and justified by reasons. There is no basis for excluding the investigation of human actions from the maximal organization of knowledge. Empathy is neither necessary nor sufficient for scientific explanation.

Sociology of Knowledge

There are two other interesting problems in the understanding of culture. One is the sociology of knowledge. Let me introduce this discussion by citing certain historical curiosities. At the battle of Adrianople (A.D. 378), the Roman cavalry was defeated by the Goths, who had recently discovered the stirrup and so had the advantage of being able to stand up while on horseback. But people had been riding horses for perhaps a thousand years before that: how is it that no one had previously invented that simple device? And why did the ancient Romans never discover the use of manure for fertilizer? The Japanese and Chinese had long fertilized their fields with manure. Why did the ancient Greeks never adopt the true arch in their buildings, despite its advantages, although older neighboring cultures had used it? Why was Euclid's parallel postulate not seriously questioned for some two thousand years? Why were Mendel's discoveries in genetics overlooked for years?

The sociology of knowledge tries to account for such anomalies by ascribing them to factors extrinsic to the knowledge itself, that is, to social and historical coefficients. On an elementary level, of course, such considerations as bias are obvious: an anthropologist who is a fascist is more likely to "prove" the inferiority of the colored races than one who is nonpolitical; experimenters working for tobacco growers are less likely to find a correlation between cigarette smoking and lung cancer than scientists employed by a consumers' organization. Scientists have their full quota of bias and prejudice, and we should never fail to take this into account. But we *can* take it into account. The procedures of science are self-corrective. (When the *nouveau-riche* lady came down to breakfast wearing diamonds, and was told that "it's vulgar to wear diamonds in the morning," she replied, "That's what I used to think before I had any.") The thesis of the sociology of knowledge remains trivial even in more impressive terminology: when Russell tried to explain the philosophy of pragmatism as the offshoot of American industrialism, commercialism, and admiration of power, Dewey countered that it would be just as sensible to explain English neorealist philosophy in terms of a landed aristocracy, or French dualism by the Frenchman's penchant for having both a wife and a mistress.

The sociology of knowledge does become significant, however, when it stresses how often a value judgment is mistaken for a fact. "We hold these truths to be self-evident," declare the Founding Fathers. But is self-evidence always self-evident? Can we be sure we are not being deluded by disguises, distortions, self-deception, self-concealment, unconscious influences? The term *ideology* was coined in France about 1810 to describe a "science of ideas" which could be used to produce social harmony (this view of the purpose of knowledge filters down through pragmatism). But Hegel used "ideology" to denote the "false consciousness" of persons who, because their thinking was only a partial and transitory stage in the dialectical development of the Absolute, could not know their own true position in history. Marx made the stronger point that all truth is "class truth" and that all ideas are an "ideological" defense of the status quo. Other thinkers who treat ideology as the consciousness of a particular epoch in time are Nietzsche, Weber, and Lukacs. Mannheim argued that the growth of knowledge does not proceed historically according to "imma-nent laws of development," but rather is so determined by non-theoretical or existential factors that one can always figure out *when* any statement was uttered. Thinking is done by individuals in specific social and historical settings; thus, the "historically changing nature of mind" enters into the form and substance of all knowledge. Mannheim made this point in *Ideology and Utopia:*

> It is impossible to conceive of absolute truth existing indepen-dently of the values and positions of the subject and unrelated to the social context. Even a god could not formulate a proposition on historical subjects like $2 + 2 = 4$, for what is intelligible in history can be formulated only with reference to problems and conceptual constructions which themselves arise in the flux of historical experience.
>
> The very principles, in the light of which knowledge is to be criticised, are themselves found to be socially and historically conditioned.

This thesis has had considerable impact; but I believe it to be mistaken, because it confuses the empirical question of how and why certain beliefs come to be held with the logical question of whether those beliefs are valid. The sociology of knowledge de-mands that, in appraising the truth of a proposition, we never disregard its genesis. The answer to this requirement is that there is indeed a relation between one's social-historical situation and the principles one uses to criticize knowledge—but this relation is factual, not logical. The observer may always be made aware of his perspective when he is confronted with other observers. This is an aspect of the self-corrective nature of the scientific process; it holds equally for natural science and for social history. And there is another objection: is not the thesis of the sociology of knowledge itself also an ideology, socially conditioned? What makes it immune? If it poses the problem of *irremediable* social subjectivism, then (like solipsism) it poses a pseudo-problem.

(My own contention in this book, that there is an irreducibly *human* dimension to knowledge [Chapter 10], is quite another claim: it is man who is the measure, and not any one form of society—*Homo sapiens,* and not capitalist America in 1975 or any other culture. We examine later some of the difficulties in determining whether there are any invariants in human nature. Nonetheless, the human is to be distinguished from the extra-human, or the superhuman, or the subhuman [whatever these terms may be taken to denote]. But—unless and until we find in-telligent creatures elsewhere in the universe—I cannot begin to suggest any operational meaning at all to the term "nonhuman knowledge." That would be like asking me to turn the light on fast enough to see what the dark looks like!)

Cultural Relativity of Conceptual Frameworks

A second, related problem is the thesis that no one can ever fully understand an alien culture. The anthropological observer se-lects data according to an implicit cultural framework. The "facts" never speak for themselves. You might, while traveling in Africa, describe an event you see as follows: "Bert got into his jeep and drove off." However, an African tribesman might de-scribe it very differently: "White man is sucked in by iron mon-ster and is carried away." Contained in what you take to be a simple neutral account of the facts, are all the ingredients of your tacit point of view: that people act freely; that they act inten-tionally; that machines are inanimate; that they can be made to move; that science differs from magic. When do these implicit presuppositions of yours ever become explicit? On what common ground can they ever be confronted by those of your African counterpart?

The difficulty in becoming aware of one's culturally bound assumptions may be illustrated by a charming anecdote told by Paul Bowles. He was visiting his friend Brooks in Thailand. A Thai named Yamyong has asked Bowles to explain the signifi-cance of the American necktie. Why are the ends not equal? Why is the wide end sometimes longer? Why is the narrow end some-times longer? Why does the necktie sometimes reach below the waist? Bowles finds it hard to give Yamyong an answer that will satisfy him. Later, as the following story reveals, Bowles is mysti-fied by one of Yamyong's explanations:

Brooks sat beside me on the bus going back to Bangkok. We spoke only now and then. After so many hours of resisting the heat, it was relaxing to sit and feel the relatively cool air that blew in from the rice fields. The driver of the bus was not a believer in cause and effect. He passed trucks with oncoming traffic in full view. I felt better with my eyes shut, and I might even have dozed off, had there not been in the back of the bus a man, obviously not in control, who was intent on making as much noise as possible. He began to shout, scream, and howl almost as soon as we had left Ayudhaya, and he did this consistently throughout the journey. Brooks and I laughed about it, conjecturing whether he were crazy or only drunk. The aisle was too crowded for me to be able to see him from where I sat. Occasionally I glanced at the other passengers. It was as though they were entirely unaware of the commotion behind them. As we drew closer to the city, the screams became louder and almost constant.

"God, why don't they throw him off?" Brooks was beginning to be annoyed.

"They don't even hear him," I said bitterly. People who can tolerate noise inspire me with envy and rage. Finally I leaned over and said to Yamyong: "That poor man back there! It's incredible!"

"Yes," he said over his shoulder. "He's very busy." This set me thinking what a civilized and tolerant people they were, and I marvelled at the sophistication of the word "busy" to describe what was going on in the back of the bus.

Finally we were in a taxi driving across Bangkok. I would be dropped at my hotel and Brooks would take the three bhikkus on to their *wat*. In my head I was still hearing the heartrending cries. What had the repeated word patterns meant?

I had not been able to give an acceptable answer to Yamyong in his bewilderment about the significance of the necktie, but perhaps he could satisfy my curiosity here.

"That man in the back of the bus, you know?"

Yamyong nodded. "He was working very hard, poor fellow. Sunday is a bad day."

I disregarded the nonsense. "What was he saying?"

"Oh, he was saying: 'Go into second gear,' or 'We are coming to a bridge,' or 'Be careful, people in the road.' Whatever he saw."

Since neither Brooks nor I appeared to have understood, he went on. "All the buses must have a driver's assistant. He watches the road and tells the driver how to drive. It is hard work because he must shout loud enough for the driver to hear him."

"But why doesn't he sit up in the front with the driver?"

"No, no. There must be one in the front and one in the back.
That way two men are responsible for the bus."
It was an unconvincing explanation . . . but to show him that
I believed him I said: "Aha! I see."

This anecdote illustrates the difficulty we have in becoming
aware of, and making manifest to ourselves, our own pervasive
latent conceptual frameworks. Thus, on an elementary level, an
American lawyer investigating methods of social control in primitive societies does not usually question his own implicit schemata
of crime, tort, and contract. An American anthropologist takes
it for granted that the kinship relation is either cognate (through
the mother) or agnate (through the father) or ceremonial
(through a ritual); and he tacitly imposes this format on to
situations which may be regarded quite differently by their African participants. One man's account of another depends on both
of them: what Peter tells about Paul reveals as much about Peter
as it does about Paul. (A similar problem exists for the historian;
see Chapter 15.) But the difficulty is more deep-seated. Thus,
Peter Winch, following Wittgenstein, writes,

> Where it is appropriate to speak of "understanding how things
> really are," it is a mistake to suppose that . . . methods of investi-
> gation are necessarily in competition with each other.

The primitive belief in magic is tied into a world view or conceptual structure which defines "reality" and "rationality" in its
own way. Primitive people are imprisoned, just as we are, in a
universe of discourse—a "language game" or "form of life"—
which, it is argued, cannot criticize itself because it provides the
only tools of criticism. Like trains on parallel tracks, disparate
conceptual structures of reality cover the same ground but never
intersect.

This view, however, like the sociology of knowledge, meta-
morphoses an empirical difficulty into a theoretical anomaly. It
ignores confrontation and *growth*. (A homely personal anecdote:
when as a boy I first set out for school, my mother warned me
solemnly against eating hamburgers in restaurants. They were
filled with leavings and sawdust, she explained, and were little
better than poison. I did not doubt her—why should I?—and
would to this day have continued to think so, were it not that I

saw other boys eat them and thrive. Does not knowledge grow in just this way?) If our ideas were never challenged—if we never saw that there were other tracks—if we did not grow, and learn, and travel—then our beliefs might in fact never change. Why should conceptual structures of reality and rationality differ in this respect from food taboos? To live a "form of life" is not ipso facto to exempt it from self-scrutiny.

Social self-awareness is as hard to come by as personal self-knowledge (see Chapter 18) ; and, just as the trained psychologist may be able to predict your own actions more accurately than you yourself can, so the anthropologist may reach a more thorough comprehension of the customs and mores of a society than the society's own members have. You need not, in order to state the rules, "know them from inside." Beware the mystique of empathy. Beware the confusion of experience with knowledge.

I cannot persuade the astrologer that his theory is nonsense (I have tried!) ; nor can he persuade me that it is scientific; but does this stand-off imply that his predictions are exempt from scrutiny? or cannot be appraised on their merits? The Jehovah's Witness and I do not appreciate each other's strong opinion about blood transfusions; but is there then no objective science of medicine? The metaphor of parallel tracks is false. It assumes what is not the case, namely, that it is possible to traverse the *same* ground with tracks that *never* make contact. For all descriptions of human experience must eventually come to grips with, and be tested in, that same realm of human experience. The "facts" are indeed dependent on language and on hypothesis, but we can and do learn other languages and strange hypotheses; "seeing" is indeed seeing-as and seeing-what-is-the-case, but we can and do examine each other's interpretations. If there should exist essentially neutral data which can be conceptually accounted for in more than one way, and if these conceptual formulations have no observable differences between them, and are equally satisfactory in predicting and controlling events, then any differences between them would be purely terminological; that is, their Jamesian "cash value" would be the same. There is no logical obstacle to an objective science, natural or social, provided that human beings continue to grow and to experience and to inquire; that is, that they continue to become human.

There are problems in my ability to understand other cultures; but those problems are not different in kind from the problems in my ability to understand my own culture; or indeed my own family; or even myself. These problems are not insurmountable. I started this chapter by referring to the claims of the *Verstehen* theorists that there is a difference between understanding why a leaf flies in the wind and why a man flies from a mob; and that, therefore, you can't study men as you do leaves. Of course that is true; but it is a truism. For you can't study ancient men as you do contemporary men; or primitive men as you do civilized men; or men as you do women; or men as you do children; or men as you do apes; or men as you do leaves; or other men as you do yourself. But the requirement of the *justification* and optimum organization of knowledge remains constant.

Space, Time, and Matter

OUR UNDERSTANDING of these three fundamental constituents of
the world has been revolutionized in this century.

Matter

The traditional and commonsense view of matter, essentially un-
altered from earliest times to the nineteenth century, is that if you
keep splitting something up as far as you can, you will eventually
get to something that you can no longer split. These ultimate particles are supposed to be hard, rigid, compact, indivisible (the
literal meaning of "atom"), impenetrable (or else they would not
completely fill the space they occupy), uncreated, and indestruc-
tible. Each one is unique, individual, and identifiable; it could
be given a name, so to speak. They are constant in mass, volume,
and shape; and they persist through time. They interact with
each other only by direct impact—there is no "action at a distance." (That is why Galileo found it hard to accept the gravitational pull of the moon on the tides.) They move by changing

their location in an independent space. Newton treated them as dimensionless mathematical points, "vanishingly small." Any other property of matter (for example, elasticity) thus is a property, not of these ultimate particles, but of some composite or aggregate of them.

But the elementary particles which physics speaks of today, such as the electron, proton, and neutrino, are radically different. They are not things, which can be localized with unlimited precision in time and space. It would not be correct to say that an electron has a position and a momentum as if these were its own properties; they are not separable in theory from a physicist's decision to measure them. The more precisely he determines the location of an elementary particle, the vaguer becomes its momentum, and vice versa. These are complementary properties, according to Heisenberg's principle of indeterminacy; and this is not a defect of our instruments or abilities, but is a basic part of quantum theory. The physicist's measuring devices interact with what he is measuring. On the subatomic level, one might loosely say, the photons of light which reveal the electron to the physicist simultaneously kick the electron. You might suppose that it makes sense to say that a given electron traveled from this point to that point; but there is no way to say that "it" is the same electron, nor that "it" followed a definite trajectory between those two points, nor even that "it" existed at all between those two points. The phenomena can be described equally well by saying that the "first" electron was annihilated, and the "second" was created. No two electrons can be distinguished from each other. No electron can be named, so to speak, because no electron is unique or identifiable.

We cannot speak clearly of the electron as if it were a particle diffused through space, or part of the raw material of the world, with independent properties such as a location and a velocity. The electron is rather to be dealt with as a hypothetical construct, or inferred entity. It is a concentration of energy, which is theoretically unobservable, but which can be correlated with whatever properties of matter can be observed. Unlike traditional material particles, which collide and rebound with a precise exchange of energy, the electron is now regarded as a kind of wave disturbance, without precise coordinates; it undulates throughout a medium, or, more accurately, it is the undulation of that medium. But that wave doesn't literally exist in physical space; it is not composed of anything; it is not like a wave in water or in air; it is not made up of matter or energy. It is a concept, or mathematical device, which permits the physicist to predict how many electrons (or other elementary particles) will appear, on the average, within a given time. Thus it has been called a "wave of probability." The laws stating how the wave acts have the same theoretical status as other laws of physics; however, what they predict is not isolated individual events (such as the emission of a single alpha particle), but rather the likelihood of a given number of particles being emitted in a unit of time. This prediction, however has the same accuracy as the prediction of an eclipse or any other physical phenomenon. For this reason, modern science has largely abandoned the metaphysics of mechanism, although it retains the postulate of determinism (cf. Chapter 1).

To call an electron a "wave of probability" is not to underline our ignorance of what it really is, or the limitations of our instruments; it is as truly a property of the electron as (in Margenau's phrase) the color blue is a property of the sky. Of course, all the concepts of science are human creations ("Physics really began with the invention of mass, force, and an inertial system. These concepts are all free inventions," say Einstein and Infeld). But this "wave of probability" (or psi function) presents unprecedented problems of interpretation and comprehension.

In short, our understanding of what the world is made of has radically changed. In classical physics, some laws are indeed statistical—the laws describing the complex motions of the collisions of large numbers of molecules of a gas—but these probabilities can in principle be analyzed. In quantum mechanics, however, the part of nature that corresponds to "electron" is intrinsically uncertain. No isolated atomic event can be uniquely described; the probabilities are a priori limits to knowledge, not to be resolved into more basic entities, or explained by as yet undiscovered factors, the so-called hidden parameters. All that there is to know about an electron is expressed in its wave function.

Identity of Indiscernibles

The Pauli exclusion principle is part of the basic theory of quantum mechanics; it states (roughly) that if two elementary particles of the same type are localized in the same region of space, they must differ in at least one observable property; that is, they must occupy different quantum states. Thus, Leibniz' famous doctrine of the *identity of indiscernibles* has been curiously supported. It is said that Leibniz, wandering through the gardens of Herrenhausen, found that no two of the vast number of fallen leaves were exactly alike. He then decreed that no two things in the world could ever be exactly alike, for, if they were identical, they would not be two things, but one. There must be some reason to count them as two, he said; there must be something you could say about one that would not apply to the other. *Eadem sunt quorum unum potest substitui alteri, salva veritate* ("Two things are identical if one may always be substituted for the other, retaining the truth"). Berkeley proposed this challenge: imagine a universe consisting only of two identical spherical stars, revolving opposite to each other in a circular orbit in the same plane and at the same distance from the center; there is no other point of reference: what could you possibly say about either which would not also describe the other? (If there were a *Statue of Liberty* in Boston absolutely identical to the one in New York, would there then be one *Statue of Liberty* in two places?)

Space and Time

The concepts of space and time have also been revolutionized. In classical physics, space is absolute, infinite, independent, immutable, three-dimensional, Euclidean, logically prior to any material content, a necessary condition for the reality of motion, continuous (there are no holes in space), infinitely divisible (there is no smallest bit of space), homogeneous (all the diversity in the world comes from the position and motion of matter), and causally inert (since homogeneous). Traditionally, time has analogous attributes: it is absolute, infinite, independent of any physical content, continuous (there are no holes in time), infinitely divisible (there is no smallest interval of time), homogeneous, flowing uniformly (whether or not anything changes or moves), an objective feature of the world. Change ("becoming") is not identical with time, but occurs *in* time, just as matter occupies space. There is no "first moment." Time, like space, is causally inert; living organisms all grow older, but the passage of time itself has no effect on things. (That is why Goodman's paradox of "grue," discussed in Chapter 16, bothers us: it suggests that the mere passage of time may have causal efficacy.)

In classical physics, any motion in the world can be described by stating the successive positions occupied at different times by material particles within the frame of the space-time arena. The motion is due to forces (e.g., gravitational attraction) that are independent of the material particles and can be fully described by laws that form a finite, complete, and well-determined system; if we knew them all, and the position and velocity of all the particles, we could predict the future certainly and completely. This model is the basis of Laplace's determinism (Chapter 1).

In the new physics, however, space and time are not receptacles, or containers, but rather relations between events. As Einstein once said, if you took away events, you would not be left with an empty space and time, as classical physics supposed; nothing at all would be left. Matter is no longer said to move absolutely in a static, independent, space-time arena. Rather, nature is a field within which matter is constituted by local curvature or singularity. A bit of matter thus is no longer a thing moving in or through space; it does not retain its identity while in motion, but is more like a vortex or swirl in a liquid. "There is nothing in the world except empty curved space. Matter, charge, electromagnetism, and other fields are only manifestations of the bending of space. Physics is geometry," declared an eminent physicist.

Mass and energy are now held to be equivalent and interchangeable. Mass increases with velocity. If a clock is in motion, the rate at which it tells time seems to decrease as its velocity increases. Events that appear simultaneous to an observer in one system or framework may not appear simultaneous to an observer in another system; neither observation can be said to be absolutely correct, since there is no absolute and independent framework of time. Light travels at a fixed velocity, and this is the maximum velocity which is possible in the universe. Some parts of the world are therefore theoretically and forever inaccessible to man. If two events are so far removed that, because of the finite speed of light, they cannot be related, then neither event can be called "earlier" or "later" than the other; this sets limitations on the applicability of causality. The value of an interval of time now depends on the physical reference frame in which the two events at the beginning and ending of the interval occur. <u>Time is neither independent nor inert: it interacts with events.</u> There is no such thing as an instantaneous or simultaneous cross-section of the world, because light takes time to travel. Therefore, <u>a given moment of time can be specified only at a given location in space</u>. There is no "now" except "here." Space and time are relative to moving systems of reference, and so interfused that the measurement of a distance becomes a relation between a "here-now" and a "there-then."

Irreversibility of Time

One can easily imagine isolated events as happening backward, such as water running uphill or ashes turning into cigarettes. There is no logical contradiction in such occurrences. It would be like running a movie camera backward. One can pretend that a grave might open, a skeleton emerge, put on flesh, gradually become "younger" and smaller, and finally plunge into his mother's womb. These bizarre events violate established scientific laws; they represent physical and biological processes hitherto unknown, but not logically impossible. Any small-scale individual event can be imagined as reversible.

But it would be a mistake to think of time as reversible, or as running backward. The theory of thermodynamics introduces the concept of entropy and the so-called heat death of the universe. Entropy is a mathematical measure of the degree of disorganization of a system. For the universe as a whole, it can go only in the direction of greater randomness, and that is why the directionality of time cannot be reversed. In the long run, the energy levels of the world go only from higher to lower.

Physicists sometimes make such utterly baffling remarks as, a positron can be dealt with as an electron traveling from the future to the past. But thermodynamics requires the overall direction of time to be toward increasing entropy; quantum mechanics makes every measurement irreversible; and the cosmological theory of the expanding universe likewise is unidirectional. The fantasy of "time travel" is merely a fantasy. It involves self-contradiction. An actual person is what he is by virtue of having been born at a particular time to particular parents; he could not be the same person at another point in time.

Choice of Geometries

In discussing the analyticity of mathematics (see Chapter 6) I indicated that the choice of how to describe the world is not absolutely dictated to us by the world. This is illustrated by the story of the non-Euclidean geometries. For some two thousand years after Euclid, no one seriously doubted that he was describing the space about us. One of his assumptions was that through any given point in a plane, there is one and only one line parallel to a given line. Two lines are defined as parallel if they never meet, no matter how far they are extended in either direction. This "parallel postulate" did not seem to have quite the intuitive certainty of Euclid's other assumptions (such as that the whole is greater than its part), yet it remained virtually unquestioned. In the nineteenth century, however, mathematicians realized that the parallel postulate could be replaced by either of two other assumptions: (1) the postulate that there are *no* parallels (in the "elliptic" geometry of Riemann); or (2) the postulate that there is *more than one* parallel (in the "hyperbolic" geometry of Bolyai and Lobachevsky). These replacements result in geometries which at first seem bizarre—in which, for example, the sum of the interior angles of a triangle becomes either more than, or less than, 180°; or in which the ratio of the circumference of a circle to its diameter becomes less than, or more than, pi. These elliptic and hyperbolic geometries were proven to be as consistent internally, and as complete, as Euclid's; that is, the parallel postulate was shown to be independent of the other postulates of geometry. Gauss (so the story is told) was the first mathematician to become aware of this, but, fearful of the impact this discovery would make (and it was indeed overwhelming), he concealed his researches. (He wrote in 1811 that all <u>mathematical concepts</u> <u>are our creations</u>. In definitions, he said, <u>we must not ask, what</u> <u>has to be assumed</u>? <u>but, what is it convenient to assume?</u>)

You may protest that surely either lines are parallel or they are not parallel! Surely only one of these geometries correctly describes the world! Unfortunately, this is impossible to determine. Gauss and Riemann tried to verify the actual sum of the interior angles of a large triangle; they took careful angular measurements from three mountain peaks in Germany. However, the slight discrepancies they found from the Euclidean 180° could be attributed to the inaccuracy of their instruments; the distances between the mountains were too small. Nowadays we can measure enormous interstellar distances, but the rays of light which travel from the stars to our eyes may be equally well described as "straight lines in Riemannian space" or as "curved lines in Euclidean space." This is because light, in relativity theory, is gravitationally attracted and therefore "curved" by such massive bodies as the sun (as Einstein established in a sensational prediction concerning the eclipse of 1919). Thus, as Poincaré concluded, <u>one geometry is not truer than another, but</u> <u>more convenient. Man is again the measu</u>re.

Note that the term "reality" does not appear in this chapter. What are space and time "really"? Is the "wave of probability" real? No illumination is forthcoming from this line of inquiry! (see Chapter 1).

13

Is There Purpose in Nature?
The Evidence of Evolution

THERE ARE THREE distinct themes in biological evolution:

1. Progression: the more complex forms of life appeared later than the simpler ones.
2. Transformation: later forms of life descended from earlier ones.
3. Variation and natural selection.

Darwinism

It is the theme of variation and natural selection which is Darwin's essential contribution to modern thought. Before him, Herder had argued for progression but not transformation, whereas Robert Hooke maintained there was transformation but not progression, that is, later forms descended from earlier forms that were not necessarily simpler. Linnaeus and Buffon in the eighteenth century believed that the species now alive have descended from ancestors equally complex and developed; simple organisms could not give rise to more complex ones; species are fixed, and any variation is within the species. The last paragraph of Darwin's *Origin of Species* states that all forms of life have been produced by the laws of

> Growth with Reproduction; Inheritance; . . . Variability from the indirect and direct action of the conditions of life, and from use and disuse; a Ratio of Increase so high as to lead to a Struggle for Life, and as a consequence to Natural Selection, entailing Divergence of Character and the Extinction of less-improved forms.

Darwin did not discover any of these factors (although he coined the term "natural selection" by analogy to the artificial selection practiced by agricultural stockbreeders). What he did was to see these well-known phenomena in a new way. Previously it had been supposed that when God created the world, He created "to the limit of His capacity"; that is, that the whole order of nature had emerged at the moment of creation. Would a perfect and omnipotent God create less than a complete world? Therefore, whatever kinds of being *can* exist, *do* exist. (This is the pervasive philosophical theme of plenitude, or the Great Chain of Being.) Moreover, no living species can ever disappear. Thomas Jefferson wrote, in 1782:

> Such is the economy of nature that no instance can be produced of her having permitted any one race of her animals to become extinct; of her having formed any link in her great work so weak as to be broken.

For a species not to survive would reflect poorly on God; and it would open up the possibility that even man might become extinct. But other views were very much in the air: Benjamin Franklin and Malthus, for example, were aware of the factors Darwin mentioned; and Tennyson's poem "In Memoriam" in 1850 (eight years before Darwin's *Origin of Species*) refers to the natural selection of species. What Darwin saw for the first time was an *open-ended natural selection,* without purpose or balance or plan, in which anything might happen.

Evolutionary theory has changed since Darwin. His "use and disuse" of parts of the body are now known to have no effect on evolution. Lamarck had supposed (erroneously) that you could transmit to your offspring characteristics which you acquired during your life; but nothing you do and nothing that happens to you (short of the damage or destruction of your genes) can make any change in the genotype you inherited from your parents and will pass on to your descendants. On the contrary, natural selection only speeds up or slows down a process which is *genetically* determined. Thomson and Geddes make this point:

> [Natural selection] furnishes the brake rather than the steam or the rails for the journey of life; . . . instead of guiding the ramifications of the tree of life, it would . . . do little more than apply the pruning knife to them.

There are no characteristics at all—not size, nor strength, nor speed, nor longevity—which by themselves make for fitness, or favor survival. G. G. Simpson explains, in *This View of Life*:

> What natural selection favors is simply the genetic characteristics of the parents who have more children. If genetically red-haired parents have . . . a larger proportion of children than blondes or brunettes, then evolution will be in the direction of red hair. . . . The characteristics themselves do not directly matter at all. All that matters is who leaves more descendants.

Be fruitful, then, and multiply! But the crucial aspect of this process is that the gene combinations that turn up, and their interaction with the environment, is opportunistic, blind, and purposeless. That is the cream of the cosmic jest.

Genetic Mutations

Darwin, unacquainted with genetics, was puzzled by the mechanism of natural selection. If the children of a tall father and a short mother are of medium height (that is, if inheritance blends the constitution of the two parents) then the species will eventually reach a uniform intermediate height: what then does natural selection work on? (Darwin did not inquire into why there should be variation at all; he took it as a brute fact; just so, Newton did not see any point in asking for the cause of gravitation, or of the solar system.) It is now established that mutations—random changes in the genes, "errors in the DNA coding," caused by unknown factors, perhaps cosmic rays—and not Darwin's postulated "insensible variations"—provide the raw material for natural selection. Most mutations are in fact unfavorable to the survival of the species; many are fatal. It is disturbing, perhaps, to face this "paradox of advance through mischance, of ascent through accident" (Hans Jonas) ; but that is not the only reason for doubting that this world was made for us.

Nature's Ingenuity

What nature may be said to do is to try, in every possible way, to solve the problems of survival. She shuffles the genes so thoroughly that in the course of time (and if the entropy laws permit) any combination that can occur, may occur (just as any combination of numbers may eventually turn up on a well-balanced roulette wheel) . The varieties of methods of reproduction, for example, include hermaphroditic species; species in which a pair of individuals fertilizes each other; species in which the individual self-fertilizes; a tapeworm species in which the individual changes from male to female as it grows older; species in which sperm and egg cells float off to live lives of their own, and species in which this process alternates with more familiar sexual intercourse; an Australian fish species (the wrasse) in which, when the dominant male dies, the chief female in his harem becomes a male and assumes the dominant role; and species that are nonsexual but are descended from sexually reproducing species! Again, in the behavior of a parent toward its progeny, one finds endless variations, from utter devotion to cannibalism; in "married life," every arrangement, from monogamy to reciprocal violence to the absence of any arrangement. But about this lavish and restless prodigality and inventiveness of nature we must make the sobering comment that over 99% of all the species that ever came into being have failed to survive! What a departure from the principle of plenitude and the cheerfulness of Jefferson!

When we examine the intricate and complex mechanism of the human eye, we marvel that it should have come about "by chance"; but nature has "experimented" with almost every possible type of photoreceptor, ranging from single-celled spots of pigment that are sensitive to light, up to wonderfully complex light-receiving structures. The ones which are now functioning are the very few successes. In fact, it is the scallop *Pecten* which probably has the most remarkable optical apparatus in the animal kingdom; it has some fifty to one hundred eyes, each with a double retina; each retina is served by a separate optic nerve. Since there is a finite number of ways in which to solve a biological problem (e.g., to devise a photoreceptor or, say, an organ to control the salt content of the blood) and since nature's failures are extinct, there seem to be "convergent lines" in evolution. All species that have survived are adapted to their environment. In David Berlinski's phrase: "The whole gigantic panorama of life in its various forms is a matter merely of a system that misfires randomly if regularly and then manages to trap its usable mistakes." The variety of living creatures is no more evidence of nature's purpose than are the survivors of modern warfare evidence of the merciful aspects of war: in both instances we must first look at the population of the graveyard.

Purposive Adaptation and Functional Explanation

Opponents of this position will point to many striking examples of apparently purposive adaptation: the dolphin is born tail first, since it is an air-breathing mammal, and would otherwise drown. The ostrich has callosities on its undercarriage where it touches the hot desert sand when it sits down. Lemmings can barely survive the rigors of an arctic winter; they therefore multiply with extraordinary rapidity—they can breed at the age of three weeks; their gestation period is twenty days; and there may be as many as thirteen young in a litter. Fireflies have a special rhythmic code whereby some forty different species of males and females can find each other; a certain male, for example, will flash exactly twelve pulses in a third of a second. Some moths have colored spots on their wings that look like eyes (*ocelli*); this pigmentation confuses predators. In the gypsy moth, the male antenna has some fifty thousand different odor sensors, each one sensitive to one type of molecule; moreover, he can spot his mate a mile away. Survival of a species often depends on remarkable perceptual adaptations: the butterfly selects his mate by responding to an unimaginably minute amount of a chemical; the bee senses ultraviolet rays; some hunting birds have astonishingly sharp sight. Forsythia is yellow; if it weren't, bees (which are allegedly red-green color-blind) would never find it. Human beings also have various intricate sensory devices: for depth perception; for filtering out stimuli; for perceiving a gestalt out of only a few clues. The human body has a delicate and fragile system of nerves to maintain a steady internal state despite extensive changes in the outside world. Compensatory activities demonstrate "the wisdom of the body": an over-heated animal drinks to provide sufficient fluid to sweat, and sweating is a means of cooling. Shivering generates heat in the muscles. Goose flesh is an attempt to keep warm by fluffing out what used to be hair.

These frequently hair-raising examples, however, have been adroitly selected, and are ambiguous. The wisdom of the body can be matched by its stupidity: the same compensatory activities also form scar tissue, which produces cirrhosis of the liver as well as asphyxia; the appendix is apparently useless; cancer is the body's supreme folly. *Homo sapiens* is one of the few species unable to synthesize within his own body vitamin C (ascorbic acid); it is essential to life. Only man and the other primates are plagued by kidney stones; all other species produce the enzyme uricase, which oxidizes uric acid into a compound that can be dissolved and excreted. The human sinus drains poorly (and gives us trouble) because our four-footed ancestors held their heads down, not up. Child birth is painful and hazardous. Senility is degrading. No intelligent designer of a human body would ever do so poor a job! And, let us place that flashing firefly in appropriate perspective: there is a predatory cannibalistic female firefly that has learned to imitate the mating signals of other species; thereby she lures the unsuspecting amorous male to his death!

More significant than the examples offered on both sides of the debate about selection is how they are employed. The paradigm way for science to explain is to subsume the fact in question under a general law (Chapter 10). But it is sometimes claimed that this method may not suffice to explain the activities of living creatures; unlike rocks, they act purposefully. Thus, it is important to realize that any reference to *purpose* (we shiver "in order to get warm") may be replaced by a general law about *function* (shivering generates heat; if we don't shiver, then we don't get warm). The question "Why do human beings have kidneys?" need not be answered: "for the *purpose* of regulating the blood's salt content." Rather, it can be answered: "Kidneys contribute to life by regulating the blood's salt content; if that *function* were not accomplished, the species would suffer." This answer does not just shift emphasis (not like "your relatives will all die before you" versus "you will outlive all your relatives"). The purposive, or teleological, explanation introduces anthropomorphic (or theistic) elements which distort the situation, as it would if you were to say that a chain hangs in a catenary in order to reach its lowest center of gravity, or that the sun moves southward in the winter for the purpose of escaping the cold. If it were not for certain expedients, a species would become extinct: if dolphins were born head first, they would drown; fireflies without a built-in metronome would leave no offspring; moths lacking ocelli would be eaten; red forsythia would not catch the bee's eye. But the overwhelming majority of species has in fact vanished. Nature is the great destroyer.

If a living system maintains a specific property (e.g., internal temperature or blood salinity) despite changes in the outside environment; or if it has compensatory mechanisms or "governors" for negative feedback; or if it acts with apparent purposefulness for an end contained within the system, then it may be called *teleonomic*. (Note that this is not Aristotle's teleology, or final cause, which disappeared from the natural world with Darwin.) A teleonomic system is the result of natural selection, as much as a disposition to learn, or the ability of the hand to grasp, of the eye to see, of the spider to spin a web, of the bird to build a nest, or of the salmon to smell its way upstream. To explain why birds migrate southward in the autumn, one might suggest four teleonomic frameworks:

1. Ecological. Since birds eat insects, they would starve in the northern winter.

2. Genetic. Birds are "programmed" to do so by their genetic constitution, acquired during their evolutionary past.

3. Intrinsic physiological. Birds respond to the decrease in the hours of daylight—photoperiodism.

4. Extrinsic physiological. Birds respond to cold air, winds, etc.

None of these teleonomic descriptions requires any deviation from the paradigm of scientific explanation.

Nature's Successes

Let me illustrate adaptation in another way. One of nature's successes is the fluke-worm, *Redia*. Charles Sherrington, in *Man on His Nature*, describes its life cycle:

> It starts from the ripe egg as a little thing with two eye-spots and between them a tiny tongue-shaped bud. It travels about the meadow-pool . . . it bores into the lung of the water-snail. There it turns into a bag and grows at the expense of the snail's blood . . . they wander about the body of the snail. They live on the body of the snail, on its less vital parts, for so it lasts the longer. . . . They breed and produce young. The young wander within the sick snail. After a time they bore their way out of the dying snail and make their way to the wet grass . . . they encyst themselves and wait. A browsing sheep or ox comes. . . . The cyst is eaten. The stomach of the sheep dissolves the cyst and sets free the fluke-worms within it. The worm is now within the body of its second prey. It swims from the stomach to the liver. There it sucks blood and grows, causing the disease called "sheep-rot." . . . The worms inside the sheep's liver mature in three months and produce eggs. These travel down the sheep's liver-duct and escape to the wet pasture. Thence as free larvae they reach the meadow-pond to look for another water-snail. So the implacable cycle rebegins.

It remains to add that sheep-rot caused the death of half the sheep in Ireland in 1862, and over a million sheep in Argentina in 1882, and that the related human disease Bilharziasis ("snail-fever" or "blood-flukes") today affects more than a hundred million persons annually—it is (after malaria) the second most common human disease. It seems to me a reasonable bet that the tiny worm called *Redia* will be happily proliferating long after *Homo sapiens* is extinct.

(In discussing the concept of disease in Chapter 17, I stress the importance of the point of view from which biologists and physicians structure and classify diseases. Malaria is not a disease from the viewpoint of the anopheles mosquito; if the preceding paragraph had been written by an intelligent worm, there would have been no irony about "nature's successes". It is for anthropocentric reasons that we favor sheep over worms. There are no diseases in nature; nature is as indifferent to "disease" as to "dirt." It is we who eat potatoes and corn who refer to a "blight" when they are infested by parasites: why don't we call it "the foddering of the parasite"?)

Can Evolution Be Predicted?

We have seen that one of the criteria for a good scientific hypothesis is that it be falsifiable (Chapter 9). If nothing whatever can possibly disprove it, then it is not very useful as an explanation. Can the theory of evolution make predictions, so that it could be verified or falsified? It asserts that genes, which are subject to mutation, are shuffled at random, so that an enormous number of gene combinations, or genotypes, are possible. (10^{963} is one estimate for human beings, who have at least 100,000 genes.) Relatively few of these possibilities are ever realized. Whatever combination does result is subjected to the pressures of whatever environment it happens to find: climatic changes? new predators? food shortages? geologic upheavals? Any one genotype may produce a range of different mature individuals, or phenotypes, depending upon interaction with the environment. Even identical twins are not exactly alike at birth. Conversely, different genotypes may be represented in similar phenotypes. Moreover, organisms can adapt to the same environment in different ways. In the Arizona desert, plants and animals have managed to surmount the lack of water by means of quite different expedients. It is the phenotype that is exposed to natural selection. The environment of any one organism includes other organisms, which it may or may not eat, and which may or may not eat it. Any change in an organism alters the environment of all other organisms with which it interacts. "An evolving population," says the biologist C. H. Waddington, "is, as it were, playing a game in which it has some choice as to which card it puts down for any given trick. It hasn't much choice as to which card it is dealt." The initial conditions that must be considered in making a prediction of evolution are of an order of magnitude and complexity which overwhelms our finite resources. Yet no scientific theory can ever be used to make a prediction unless the initial conditions are specified; and all theories require the elimination of irrelevant factors (*ceteris paribus,* "other things being equal"); this constraint presents enormous practical difficulties to the biologist. The astronomer would find it quite impossible to predict eclipses if comets the size of the sun came tearing through our solar system every minute or two, randomly and from all directions.

In any event, both evolution and genetics are concerned not with individual living creatures, but with classes, in particular, species. (Similarly, the temperature and pressure of a gas are properties of a class of molecules; the physicist finds it meaningless to refer to the temperature of a single gas molecule.) The *species* is now defined as a "gene pool" that has become reproductively isolated; a species is a group of living creatures that does not interbreed with other groups. This is a more dependable approach to defining species than grouping according to physical properties, or appearances, since no property which can be used to distinguish one species from others is in fact possessed by all the members of the species. A species can maintain its genetic integrity in many ways: by an elaborate ritualized courtship; by high specificity in the time or place of reproduction; by a narrow range of responses to different sounds, smells, or colors. All of these peculiarities act as barriers to unproductive mating. Some biologists believe species tend to branch only when there occurs a geographical or ecological barrier that prevents genetic exchange. And gradualism or continuity seems to be the rule: at no single point, for example, does a tissue become a kidney or one species branch and become another. Since evolution considers not the single organism, but only the species, the difficulties in prediction are practically insurmountable.

Problems in Evolutionary Theory

There are problems with the explanatory adequacy of contemporary evolutionary theory. If survival value alone is to account for the attributes of living creatures, why is it that so many of these attributes do not seem to be relevant to survival? What is the value of the tuft on the breast of the wild turkey? Why are there so many different shapes of antelope horn? Why does the cow have a multiple stomach, whereas the horse, which is about the same size and is also a vegetarian, does well with a simple stomach? Why are there different human blood groups—why hasn't the fittest blood group been naturally selected by now? On the other hand, why should a species ever lose organs once useful, the eyes of the mole, for example, or the toes in the flipper of the whale? Perhaps these apparent exceptions to the criterion of survival value can be explained by the interrelation of genetic characteristics, so that features that are neutral vis-à-vis survival are genetically linked with others that have survival value.

Another sort of issue is posed by parallel evolution: why is the skull of the Siberian wolf so very similar to that of the Tasmanian wolf? These species have been subjected to different environmental pressures for all the millions of years, ever since Australia became separated from the Eurasian continent—a sufficiently long time for the evolution of the Australian kangaroo. Is it because there is only a limited number of ways in which an organism can "make a living"? or must one postulate some other factor? perhaps some sort of "archetypal grooves" or constraints? (The biologist O. H. Schindewolf holds that a *taxon*—a classified group of organisms—comes into actual existence when its first species appears; and also that taxa exist objectively. Thus, according to Schindewolf, the class of birds originated in one step with *Archaeopteryx*, the first animal to fly by means of feathers.)

Does Evolution Have Any Direction?

Can any overall trend or direction be discerned in the open-ended evolutionary process? Nothing is clearly established. To say that it moves toward better adaptation is analytic, since whatever species *do survive* at any given time *are adapted* to survive at that time. Is the size of the organism a factor? But the bacterium is tiny. Is individuality a factor? But blades of grass, like bacteria, are as much the results of evolution as are human beings. Everything alive today is the culmination of a long chain of mutations and adaptations. Have animals evolved toward greater complexity? But the hoof of today's horse is surely less complex than the four toes of *Eohippus,* its remote ancestor. In what direction do birds evolve, if the ostrich has lost the ability to fly, but can run faster than other birds? Why should the evolutionary process ever have gone further than, say, the rabbit? or the ant? Why have plants not evolved toward greater complexity or higher organization?

The list of questions is virtually endless. The rate at which evolutionary changes occur seems to vary enormously. Some species have not changed at all within vast time spans: the coelacanth is apparently identical to its most ancient ancestors; algae found in rocks over three billion years old closely resemble their descendants today. Could a time possibly arrive when both the environment and the genetic code would become perfectly stable, and evolution cease? Can we be sure that evolution is going on now? Is the increased human life span a mutation? or resistance to TB? Could evolution ever reverse or repeat itself? The ancestors of the whale left the sea and then returned. Could dinosaurs reappear? Any species alive today is what it is because of a particular history or sequence of events that spans billions of years. The residual influence of the past is never entirely lost. There is a connectedness to all life: you yourself would be different now if some reptile in the Paleozoic era had wandered north instead of south. Is evolution a universal law of nature (like gravitation, for example) which would apply wherever living creatures appear, or does it hold on this planet only? Nothing, as I said, is clearly established.

Two distinguished biologists disagree flatly on the course of evolution. Julian Huxley believes that "the biological process culminating for the evolutionary moment in the dominance of Homo Sapiens . . . could apparently have pursued no other general course than that which it has historically followed." But G. G. Simpson asserts that "the assumption . . . that once life gets started anywhere, humanoids will eventually and inevitably appear is plainly false." Human beings have greater power over their environment than other animals have, and they are more independent of their surroundings; but still man is, for Haldane, "a worse animal than the monkey."

(A parenthesis on *sex* and *death*: primitive animals [e.g., Paramecium] reproduce by fission; that is, the mature creature divides into two, each half becoming a new young adult. If there are no mutations, the genetic material remains the same. The new animal thus does not have the advantage of the diversity provided by the sexual mingling of parental genes and might not therefore have the variety of reserves which opportunistic evolution favors. On the other hand, unlike the creature born of parents, which grows old and dies, the animal which reproduces by fission can keep on dividing and live on as long as its food supply holds out. In a sense, then, sex and death [Eros and Thanatos!] may be said to have come into the world together. And, in another, odd sense, they may go out of the world together: as the human life span increases indefinitely and the planet gets more and more crowded, there is likely to be pressure to reduce—perhaps eliminate—not sex, of course, but births.)

What Is Life?

Modern biochemistry has established that all genes of all living creatures are made up of the same substances (DNA, RNA, and proteins). A man's genes differ from a dog's, say, only in the way they are arranged. The same contractile protein produces the streaming motion of the amoeba and the moving finger muscles of the pianist. Heredity operates in the same way in plants, bacteria, and human beings. This chemical unity of all life makes it conceivable that life originated only once. Darwin tried to avoid the problem of the origin of life, but he was pressured into adding, in the second edition of *The Origin of Species* (published six weeks after the first), this passing reference: "Life having been originally breathed (by the Creator) into a few forms or into one. . . ." There is nothing chemically unique about the structure or functioning of living materials; many have by now been synthesized in test tubes.

Biologists now define a living organism as

> an entity that can utilize chemicals and energy from the environment to reproduce itself, can undergo a permanent change (mutation) which is transmitted to succeeding generations, and . . . can evolve into a distinctly new species.

The emphasis in this definition is on self-duplication and mutation; many time-honored "characteristics of life" are not included: organic unity, self-regulation, regeneration of parts, ability to react to stimuli, spontaneity, goal-directed or purposive behavior, and memory or learning. (And what a far cry from Henry James' definition of life as "that predicament which precedes death!") There are, inevitably, borderline entities such as the virus, which have features of both living and nonliving matter—how to classify them seems to be a matter of convention.

Can the living cell itself be synthesized in the test tube? The task is enormously complex; and the probabilities—presently, at least—are against it; but there is no logical or theoretical reason why it cannot be done. Similarly, no reason is known why there should not be living creatures elsewhere in the universe—the incredible complexity of the living cell may be matched by the incredible vastness of space. There are over a million galaxies within reach of our telescopes; our own Milky Way galaxy contains a hundred billion stars similar to our sun; if each of these "suns" had one planet physically similar to our earth, there would be a hundred thousand trillion planets on which some sort of life might be possible. These numbers stagger the imagination; but speculation should be tempered by the sober fact that no slightest bit of evidence exists. Furthermore, we must remember the intimate functional relation between life as we understand it and the physical attributes of our earth. When the solar system was formed, if the earth had been about 10% closer to the sun, some four-fifths of our planet would have been too hot to support life. If the earth had accumulated more than its present mass, birds might never have evolved, since the ability to fly requires a delicate balance of gravity, air density, and the amount of bone needed for support. And if the earth's axis had not been inclined to the plane of its orbit around the sun, we would have had no seasons.

Our Moral Responsibility

The moral for philosophy is clear: if there is any purpose in nature, we have put it there; it is no longer a figure of speech that man can make himself. The biologist now asks: what are your standards for admission to membership in the human race? The unborn fetus may now be diagnosed by amniocentesis; a decision may be made (based on its strength? brain size? freedom from disease?) as to whether this potential person should become an actual person (Plato's selective breeding!). We may in the foreseeable future become parents by ordering from genetic engineers just the baby we want, and adopting it prenatally. We are about to direct and transform the human species *irreversibly*. We shrink from this terrifying responsibility.

14

"Human Nature" and Scientific Method in Anthropology, Psychology, and Psychoanalysis

Is THERE A GROUP of character traits which will identify human beings at all times? Philosophers have differed widely in their answers to this question.

Is There a Constant Human Nature?

David Hume wrote:

> Would you know the sentiments, inclinations, and course of life of the Greeks and Romans? Study well the temper and actions of the French and English. . . . Mankind are so much the same in all times and places, that history informs us of nothing new or strange in this particular. Its chief use is only to discover the constant and universal principles of human nature . . . the regular springs of human action and behavior.

Adam Smith spoke of the economic propensity which "comes

with us from the womb and never leaves us till we go into the grave." Russell regarded the desire for power as the psychological invariant. Rousseau thought that the "noble savage," man in a "state of nature," is perfectly good; Calvin maintained that man in his natural state is utterly depraved. In ancient China, Mencius said that people are innately good; but according to Hsün Tzu, they are innately evil.

On the other hand, Sartre believes that human beings have no essential nature at all. Dewey argued that, although there may be a core of basic human needs and emotions, they may be expressed in various ways; the social importance of education lies in its ability to shape these malleable needs. Thus, James demanded that we find a "moral equivalent" for whatever it is that drives us to make wars.

Mill thought it pointless to try to develop a science of "sociology" because, he said, "Human beings in society have no properties but those which are derived from, and may be resolved into, the laws of the nature of the individual man." Dilthey, on the other hand, declared, "What man is, only his history tells." Perhaps he was echoing Marx, who said, "The whole of history is nothing but a continual transformation of human nature."

Many explanatory typologies of human nature have been devised. Perhaps the oldest is the Chinese Yang (male, active) versus Yin (female, passive) principles. The Greek physician Galen (c. A.D. 200) used the hot-cold and wet-dry principles, which in early Greek science determine the four "elements," to sort out the four "humors" (choleric, phlegmatic, sanguine, and melancholic); these determine human temperament, bodily type, susceptibility to disease, and so on.[1] More recent typologies include James' tough-minded and tender-minded; Nietzsche's Dionysian and Apollonian; Freud's oral, anal, and genital;

---

[1] This is the rationale involved:

Principle	Element	Humor	Temperament
hot + dry =	fire	choler	choleric
cold + wet =	water	phlegm	phlegmatic
hot + wet =	air	blood	sanguine
cold + dry =	earth	black gall	melancholic

Jung's extraverts and introverts; D. H. Lawrence's redskins and palefaces; Sheldon's endomorph, mesomorph, and ectomorph; and Riesman's tradition-directed, inner-directed, and other-directed.

Theoretical views about human nature are not without practical effect. Assumptions about a fixed nature of man can have such grotesque ramifications as Aristotle's approval of slavery and Thomas Aquinas' justification of mutilation as a punishment for crime. One can point also to the rearing of children in early Calvinist households; for example, since whatever the infant wants is by definition a manifestation of original sin, children were forbidden to eat whatever foods they liked and forced to eat foods they disliked. How different from the current belief that whatever a child "naturally" wants must be good for him!

Man Is Found Only in Societies

All attempts to isolate human nature assume that there must be some entity there to be isolated. But the fact is that the man not shaped by a particular culture, as anthropology reveals, has never existed. Human behavior is everywhere channeled by society. *Homo sapiens* has never responded to a stimulus except through the "intervening variable" of a culture. "My culture tells me when to have an appetite for what," writes the anthropologist Dorothy Lee. There are people who enjoy eating red ants and beetles, and who look at milk as if it were a mucous discharge. People have been known to starve rather than eat a taboo food. Only such limiting human environments as the life raft or the concentration camp eliminate the cultural, and reduce man to the biological: he then becomes an animal whose sole and all-absorbing need is survival.

Are there then no cultural invariants which would be evidence of a constant human nature? (An ancient Egyptian papyrus—possibly the oldest letter in the world—begins, "Dear Mother, will you stop worrying about me?") Kluckhohn, for example, argues that "some patterns turn up in all culture . . . marriage always appears; murder is always differentiated from justifiable homicide; every culture prohibits some of the varieties of incest." But these terms are often too vague to be of any use. "Marriage," for example, appears in such varying forms that the only common element is sex. Lévi-Strauss claims that nature becomes culture when the prohibition against incest emerges, but this definition is far too broad: there are exceptions to any generalization about incest.

It seems more reasonable to regard the relation between human nature and culture as a complex interaction. *Homo sapiens* is not an animal who acquires culture; rather, he is a species in process, who is now and has always been *making himself*. This view has been advanced by the anthropologist Clifford Geertz, in *New Views of the Nature of Man:*

> Culture, rather than being added on to a virtually finished animal, was a central ingredient in the production of that animal itself. The slow growth of culture through the Ice Age altered the balance of selection so as to play a major directive role in his evolution. The perfection of tools, the adoption of organized hunting and gathering practices, the beginnings of true family organization, the discovery of fire, and, most critically, the increasing reliance upon systems of significant symbols (language, art, myth, ritual) for orientation, communication, and self-control all created a new environment. . . . By submitting himself to governance by symbolically mediated programs, . . . man determined, if unwittingly, his own biological destiny. He literally created himself.

Thus, to try to separate human nature from culture is like trying to separate the physical subatomic particle from the field. Whatever the innate capacities (if any) of *Homo sapiens,* they can be observed only as manifested in actual societies.

[In discussing the person and his body (Chapter 17), I stress the extent to which illness and disease are socially conditioned; of course, mental illness, a fortiori, varies widely. The well-adjusted American extravert is not always the ideal of mental health! Ruth Benedict shows how the pattern of a culture, its pervasive ethos and values, act to shape the individual personality; thus, the Zuni Indians are "Apollonian" and the Kwakiutl are "Dionysian":

> It does not matter what kind of "abnormality" we choose for illustration, those which indicate extreme instability, or those which are more in the nature of character traits like sadism, or delusions of grandeur or of persecution, there are well-described cultures in which these individuals function at ease and with honor. . . .
>
> The most notorious of these is trance and catalepsy. Even a very mild mystic is aberrant in our culture. But most peoples have regarded extreme psychic manifestations not only as normal and desirable, but even as characteristic of highly valued and gifted individuals.

Remember the influence of mental states, conventions, and so forth on perception of the facts (Chapter 4). It is not only in the Soviet Union that political dissidents and deviants are declared to be insane!]

Functionalism

Aristotle, in his *Politics,* assigned the city, or *polis,*

> to the class of things that exist by nature, and man is by nature an animal intended to live in a *polis.* . . . The *polis* is prior in the order of nature to the family and the individual. The reason for this is that the whole is necessarily prior to the part.

In other words, man's activities may be explained by the way he functions in a city. Functionalism in the anthropology of Bronislaw Malinowski stresses the interdependence of institutions in their social context and as related to human needs. Thus, burial customs may be explained as promoting a feeling of social solidarity; and kinship practices as aiding survival. These terms, however, are seldom clear enough to show the covariance of two properties, or to make specific predictions. (How can one measure social solidarity?) The biologist will indeed speak of the functional utility of a process or structure to an organism or to a species (e.g., if the human being lacked kidneys, the salinity of the blood would not be regulated); but such biological terms as life span and reproduction are conceptually clear, and their relationships to specific structures and processes may be verified (thus the virgin female fruit fly, *Drosophila,* outlives the inseminated ones). In anthropology, however, functionalism does not produce empirical laws; it is therefore not so much an explanation as a useful guide to one's inquiries.[2]

Psychological Models of Man

We began this chapter by inquiring whether there are universal and constant characteristics of human nature; and we decided that if there are any traits common to all people, they are so embedded in diverse cultures that we cannot say anything significant about them. However, psychology, as the empirical study of human behavior, asks another kind of question: are there regularities to be found in the way people learn things, for example? or in their verbal skills? or in their emotions? or in what may loosely be called their mental life? To answer these questions, the psychologist, like the observer in other branches of science, needs a hypothesis by which to select and organize facts (see Chapter 9). What model of man does he tacitly assume for this purpose? Is man an organism which reacts to environmental stimuli in order to reduce tensions? or is he an active transcender of biological drives? Is he the animal that fears death? Is he "essentially a battlefield . . . a dark cellar in which a maiden aunt and a sex-crazed monkey are locked in mortal combat, the affair being refereed by a rather nervous bank clerk"? Is he a "ping-pong ball with a memory"? a pigeon in a box? a problem solver? a stimulation maximizer? an energy converter? an equilibrium achiever? a symbol creator? a game player? a status seeker? a reward seeker? a digital computer? a servo-mechanism? a telephone exchange?

[2] *Structuralism* has been recently championed by Lévi-Strauss and others; but his thesis of the binary oppositions and reciprocal relations between cultural elements is so vague that it is more a metaphor than a scientific model.

Which of these models is the true one? (Each one has been advanced, more or less seriously.) The criterion of an acceptable model of man is not truth or falsity, but utility in sorting out the facts and organizing our knowledge of human behavior. To say that man is "nothing but" one of these, however, would be to commit the reductive fallacy. And if a model cannot be correlated with observable human acts, and if it is not falsifiable, then it will be of little scientific value; that is why Jung's archetypes, the "structure of the collective unconscious," cannot be regarded as scientific.

Behaviorism

Two schools of psychology—behaviorism and psychoanalysis—are worth examining for their contributions to the scientific study of human activities. Behaviorism often provokes an antagonistic emotional reaction—which may support its own theory of conditioning. In its early, unsophisticated versions, it was no doubt guilty of the reductive fallacy. John B. Watson reduced experience to nothing but stimuli and responses. Thus he ignored the social and interactive dimensions of experience; he abstracted the individual's segment of the act from the other persons and objects involved in the complete act. He did not realize that nothing in the world is all by itself a stimulus or a response; these are constructs that require a context and a hypothesis. Behaviorism today is not just a theory of stimulus and response: it is the assumption that behavior is a function of previous natural events, and that laws describing and correlating these events can be discovered. Behaviorists do not now question the existence of such "states of consciousness" as images, hopes, and expectations; but they claim that it is not necessary to appeal to those states (nor to any extranatural phenomena) in order to predict behavior. There is no doubt that psychological terms have mental referents which are useful. However, if we find it convenient to explain Bert's provoking manners by his "grandiose self-image" or his "vanity," we are denoting not some obscure mental entity, but rather his disposition to strike an attitude, preen himself, and admire his own work extravagantly. And, if his vanity is to be inferred solely from these activities, there is no point in saying he does them *because* he is vain. B. F. Skinner writes:

> The term *drive* is simply a convenient way of referring to the effects of deprivation and satiation and of other operations which alter the probability of behavior . . . it enables us to deal with many cases at once. There are many ways of changing the probability that an organism will eat; at the same time, a single kind of deprivation strengthens many kinds of behavior. The concept of hunger as a drive brings these various relations together in a single term.

We explain nothing when we say that an animal eats because he is hungry. An individual reacts differently to the same stimulus at different times (if indeed there is such a thing as the same stimulus at different times). "Stimulus" is a complex scientific construct, not a simple sense datum. Before the observer responds to a stimulus, his "state of the organism" intervenes—his memory, belief, habits, background, expectations, and so on. But there is nothing mysterious about the organism's disposition or preparation or competence. Human beings (like other organisms) have certain capacities but not others: a man can learn to swim but not to fly. But these capacities are manifest only in accomplishment (as language competence is manifest only in performance; see Chapter 19). A capacity never issuing in action is a pretty dubious sort of entity.

An *intervening variable* is a construct that modifies and shapes the response to a stimulus. It is inferred for its explanatory value, but it is not itself to be observed. Thus, the state of the organism is the variable intervening between stimulus and response; and the pattern of culture is the variable intervening between the biological need and the way in which it is satisfied. It would be a mistake to regard these intervening variables as entities. When we see that trees are swaying, and people leaning as they walk, we refer to "the wind"; but all we can measure is the velocity, pressure, and temperature of molecules of air. We observe people buying and selling, and we infer that they have a "profit motive."

We hear that some people are setting fires and overturning automobiles, and we say, "the mob was in an ugly mood." Winds, motives, moods, and dispositions are, like the state of the organism and the pattern of culture, unseen variables that intervene between independent causes and observed dependent effects; they are posited because of their convenience in explanation.

Two Directions in Psychology

Psychology as a science has been propelled in two contrary directions: toward finding the elementary units of human behavior, and toward discovering the structure of the whole person. In the same way, in early physics Thales and the Greek atomists sought to find out what stuff things are made of, whereas Pythagoras emphasized the overall organization of the things in the world. Do the events that psychology studies consist of ultimate atomic constituents? Wilhelm Wundt believed that states of consciousness would eventually be analyzed into such elementary units as sensations, images, and feelings. Spearman and other early proponents of "factor analysis" argued reasonably that a finite number of traits or parameters could explain parsimoniously the individual differences among people—perhaps "intelligence" can be constructed out of numerical ability, verbal skill, memory, perceptual speed, reasoning ability, and spatial perception (on this last factor, some illiterates do better than some Ph.D.'s). This psychological atomism is opposed by the Pythagorean emphasis on structure proposed in Gestalt psychology by Von Ehrenfels, Wertheimer, Köhler, Koffka, and Lewin. They stress the interdependent unity of all organic responses and the need for such general organizing concepts as personality and adolescence. Skinner's (elementaristic or stimulus-response) studies on the control of behavior by the environment and Piaget's (structural or cognitive) emphasis on the intellectual capacities of the mind are, however, not contradictory but supplementary. Just as physics has discovered that the ultimate particle and the field are inextricable, and anthropology has been unable to separate human nature from culture, so psychology realizes that the part-whole distinction is spurious.[3]

Psychoanalysis

Freudian psychoanalysis presents a unique situation. It has never been completely systematized; Freud himself (naturally enough) kept changing his views during his life. Psychoanalysis originated in the clinic rather than in the university; its ambiance continues to be outside the academy. Its statements are replete with metaphors ("the libido is dammed up") which may be misleading. Its method of investigation rests on free association and the interpretation of dreams; even its leading proponents do not agree on therapeutic techniques. One psychotherapist called it "an unidentifiable technique applied to unspecific problems with unpredictable outcomes. For this technique we recommend rigorous training." Does it actually cure? If so, how? The evidence is scanty. H. J. Eysenck discovered that "spontaneous remission" of neurosis (i.e., disappearance of all the symptoms, with no therapy at all) occurs within two years to 65% of all patients, and within three years to 90%. General medical practitioners with no Freudian training also manage to treat neurotics with some success. How important are the trappings of psychoanalysis —the couch, the foreign accent, the beard, the suggestibility, the glamour of being analyzed?

[3] We may show schematically how these two kinds of theories emphasize different aspects of the learning process.

Stimulus-response theories	*Cognitive theories*
Gradual learning through trial and error	Sudden learning through the solving of problems
Emphasis on discrete stimuli and perceptual elements	Emphasis on relation patterns and the gestalt
Reinforcement from outside	Inner exploratory drive
Emphasis on conditioning	Emphasis on insight
Acquiring habits and skills one at a time	Eliciting latent "cognitive structures"
Continuity between the lower animals and *Homo sapiens*	Levels or stages in a hierarchy

The significance of Freudian psychoanalysis is not merely that it often works—fad diets work; and witch doctors cure people—but that it provides a formidable theoretical apparatus by which to explain behavior. The elements of consciousness are analyzed into the id, the ego, and the superego; all conflict and stress are taken as inductive evidence of this hypothesis. There is said to be continuous development of the person from earliest infancy; persistent residues from remote childhood continue to affect adult behavior. Free will is an illusion; the psychical life is completely determined. Sexuality is the chief (perhaps the only) source of psychic energy. The Freudian theoretical apparatus also includes such doctrines as the pleasure principle; the reality principle; the death wish; the Oedipus complex; repression; sublimation; projection; transfer; and identification.

Is It a Science?

How shall we evaluate the Freudian schema? It is not clear whether concepts such as the id are inferred entities, hypothetical constructs, or intervening variables; unlike unobservables in physics, the electron, for example, they are not uniquely correlated with what can be observed. Freud seemed to think they would someday be reduced to biochemical variables. Are they metaphors? or myths?

Unlike other scientific hypotheses, Freudianism cannot be verified by prediction. Ernest Jones writes, in his preface to Freud's *Collected Papers*:

> Few episodes in the history of scientific research provide a more dramatic test of true genius than the occasion on which Professor Freud made the devastating discovery that many of the traumas to which he had been obliged to attach aetiological significance had never occurred outside the imagination of the patients.

Thus, it doesn't matter what really happens to you, or what you actually dream, but rather what you remember to have happened, or what you now think you dreamed. Freud claimed that the Oedipus complex is universal: *all* boys want to kill their father and marry their mother. Any contradictory evidence can always be denied by Freudians. As Stekel writes, on the symbolism of dreams: "All dreams have a bi-sexual tendency. Where the bi-sexuality cannot be perceived, it is hidden in the latent dream content."

Thus Freudianism is clearly no more falsifiable than fatalism or than divine providence. Freudians do offer some piecemeal empirical verification; for example, that three different character traits (parsimony, orderliness, and obstinacy) tend to occur together, as a result of a certain kind of early training; but specific consequences can seldom be deduced and predicted. Any kind of act whatever could be interpreted either as hostility, for example, or as repressed hostility. (Heads I win, tails you lose.) The Freudian system of concepts, in short, is not tied down by operational rules or coordinating definitions to what can be observed.

Perhaps the most serious defect of Freudian psychoanalysis as a science, however, is the peculiar way in which the data are "manufactured by the analyst." The psychoanalyst Judd Marmor writes that patients

> seem to bring up precisely the kinds of phenomenological data which confirm the theories and interpretations of their analysts! Thus each theory tends to be self-validating. Freudians elicit material about the Oedipus complex and castration anxiety, Jungians about archetypes, Rankians about separation anxiety, Adlerians about masculine strivings and feelings of inferiority, Horneyites about idealised images, Sullivanians about disturbed inter-personal relationships, etc. . . . What the analyst shows interest in, the kinds of questions he asks, the kind of data he chooses to react to or ignore, and the interpretations he makes, all exert a subtle but significant suggestive impact to bring forth certain kinds of data in preference to others.

Thus patient and analyst interact with each other; the outcome of the analysis must be something they both agree upon. If the patient rejects the analyst's interpretation, it is beside the point to ask whether this is the error of the analyst or the obdurate resistance of the patient. Erikson warns that the analyst must be aware of himself as he "makes himself part of the client's life-history"; there is "a core of *disciplined subjectivity* in clinical work which it is neither desirable nor possible to replace with seemingly more objective methods." And Martin Buber suggests that the analyst is himself in the process of being cured! The data of psychoanalysis are spoken words (no one is ever psycho-analyzed by mail!) and speech (as we see in Chapter 19) is a directed and reversible activity. Any interpretation whatsoever of the patient's condition upon which the analyst and the patient can agree thus verifies itself.

15

The Study of History:
What Is the Past?

WHY SHOULD PHILOSOPHERS be concerned with the study of history? Isn't the past irrevocably fixed? History would indeed be of limited philosophical interest were it not that men, unlike animals, *are* what they have *come to be*. Animals may have individual biographies, but they have no meaningful history: cats and cows today are as they were in ancient times; Odysseus might be a stranger to us, but his faithful dog is not. The growth of human culture (that is, of man) is continuous and cumulative. To study our past is to understand better how we came to be as we now are.

"The Past"

Stories about the dead are inspired by the curiosity of the living. That is why history is being rewritten constantly—not simply because new facts are discovered, but because it is "always written wrong." The past is in a steady process of imaginative reinterpretation and reconstruction; we want it to be meaningful to us in the present.

But isn't the historian bound by the facts? Can he alter what has actually occurred? As in the sciences (Chapter 9), the problem lies in the determination of the facts. No historian can examine or record all that occurs, even within a short time period. Even the chronicler or annalist whose concern is "just the facts" must winnow them ruthlessly. No event per se is history. No newspaper can publish all the news; some one must decide whether or not it's "fit to print." The historian must pick and choose and organize in accordance with his insight as to what is significant. This process is influenced by a number of factors:

1. Our interests change: we probably care less now about the love affairs of the French kings than about how the French peasantry lived. (Our histories of ancient Rome tell as much about us as they tell about the ancient Romans; this is again the problem of cultural relativity, Chapter 11.)

2. Our conceptual apparatus changes: we now have available to us, for example, the Marxist hypothesis that the American Civil War was a class conflict, and the Freudian insight into why Bakunin loved violence and why Martin Luther was rebellious.

3. Our view of the basic historical segment changes: thus, Toynbee holds the most intelligible unit to be not the nation but the "society" (he cites five since A.D. 775—Western Christianity, Orthodox Christianity, Islam, Hinduism, and the Far East). Braudel chooses "The Mediterranean" as his unit.

4. The "personal equation" (interests and idiosyncrasies) of the historian changes.

5. The audience for whom he writes changes; this may have an effect on his selection and organization.

Sometimes the historian's standard of significance verges on the ludicrous. Here is one historian's complete biography of King George V:[1]

[1] A. J. P. Taylor, in *English History, 1914–1945,* quoted by David Fischer, with appropriately raised eyebrows, in his *Historians' Fallacies.*

George V (1865–1936), second son of Edward VII: married Princess Mary of Teck, 1893; king, 1910–1936; changed name of royal family from Saxe-Coburg to Windsor, 1917; his trousers were creased at the sides, not front and back.

For all of these reasons, and probably others, nothing could be more naive than the "Baconian fallacy" that all the historian has to do is to collect the facts, or than Mach's view that "the bare data confront us." Namier said:

> The function of the historian is akin to that of the painter and not of the photographic camera; to discover and set forth, to single out and stress that which is the nature of the thing and not to reproduce indiscriminately all that meets the eye.

But even the photographer must select, focus, arrange, emphasize, organize, evaluate, compose, define, and omit; he, too, searches for "the nature of the thing." As Carl Becker put it, echoing Voltaire, history "must play on the dead whatever tricks it finds necessary for its own peace of mind." The garment we wear called "the past" is remodeled for us to conform to the new styles.

It seems awkward or even perverse to conclude that "the past" is not absolutely fixed and is amenable to prudent manipulation. But remember that "the past" does not literally exist at all; only the present exists. The past is not a datum given to us: it is *inferred* from present evidence. Just as the geologist infers the "pastness" or age of the rock he is examining now, so the historian critically inspects memoirs, letters, diaries, newspapers, artifacts, etc., and infers a past history. History differs from geology in that the historian attributes meaning to his data (as we can similarly distinguish a human action from an event; see Chapter 20). He looks at three standing stones and says, this was a Druid temple. He records the earthquake in Lisbon in 1755, but not other quakes, because this is the one that inspired Voltaire's *Candide*.

Patterns and Selectivity

The patterns said to be found in past events are selected by the historian; like the hypotheses of the scientist, they may be suggested, but are neither imposed nor dictated, by "the facts." At a particular time the facts may have been that in Belgium many men were running around, shouting, fighting, and dying; the historian later designates this the decisive Battle of Waterloo. Is there always a structure to what happens? Is there only one structure? Is the structure evident at the time? Was the Industrial Revolution, or the Gothic Age, or the Hundred Years War evident to those who participated in it? We refer offhandedly to the sexual revolution; and to the revolution in the Catholic Church: will future historians so elect to describe what is going on now? (I like a whimsical idea of Jorge Luis Borges about literary predecessors: we would say, for example, that the predecessors of Kafka are Zeno, Kierkegaard, and Robert Browning; but what if Kafka had never lived? Each writer thus creates his own predecessors: no one ever is, all on his own, a predecessor. It is not merely that predecessors cannot be identified until later, but that no such thing even exists until later!) What exists are individual persons doing things one at a time, "a wilderness of single instances." Historical terms are, as Santayana puts it, "merely rhetorical unities" that "break up on inspection into a cataract of miscellaneous natural processes and minute particular causes."

The metaphysics of absolute idealism (Chapter 1) regards all events, present and past, as concatenated into a seamless web that cannot—without distortion—be analyzed into discrete events. Mark Van Doren's poem "Past is Past" expresses this view:

> To wish a word unsaid,
> To wish a deed undone—
> Be careful, for the whole
> World that was is one.
>
> Pull the least piece away,
> And bigger ones may fall;
> Then granite; then great timbers,
> And the end of all.

But historical pluralism, as defined by Maurice Mandelbaum, seems much more plausible:

The grand sweep of events which we call the historical process is made up of an indefinitely large number of components which do

not form a completely inter-related set. . . . [Historical pluralism]
denies that every event is related to every other event.

Is there, then, no limit to the historian's selectivity? Is there
no hard core or bed-rock of indisputable facts that the historian
must recognize? Can a totalitarian government rewrite the past
as a matter of political expedience? I am told that one edition
of the *Great Soviet Encyclopedia* devotes an excessive number of
columns to the Bering Sea because just prior to publication the
entry for Beria had to be deleted. Is he the only unperson? Was
there ever a man named Trotsky? Under our eyes today, the
achievements of Stalin and Khrushchev are being re-written. But
let us not disregard the beam in our own eye. Winston Churchill
claims in his *History* that the Monroe Doctrine could not have
succeeded had it not been supported by "the friendly vigilance of
the British Navy." Is that a fact? Columbus' landing place has recently been reidentified and it has been suggested that he discovered America in 1467, not 1492. A Finnish historian finds that the
Russian winter of 1812, which is supposed to have destroyed
Napoleon's army, was a mild one. The Catholic Church has recently "decanonized" St. Christopher—it seems there never was
such a person. In brief, the hard core of indisputable facts is
not so very hard. Ranke demands that history tell us *"wie es
eigentlich gewesen"*; but there is no such thing as "the way it
really happened." The past in Dewey's phrase, is always "the past-
of-the-present."

But these considerations do not make history incurably slanted,
partial, relativistic, nonobjective, or mythical. The historian
never indeed knows all there is to be known about an event, but
neither does the physicist. The historian "goes beyond the evidence," but so does the physicist. The historian selects his facts
and decides how to describe them; so does the physicist. There
may be more than one "true" account of the past; but neither is
our physics the only conceivable description of the world. Just
as science is self-correcting, so different historical accounts may be
confronted, compared, and contrasted; emphasis and bias may
be made manifest; evidence may be scrutinized; arguments may be
evaluated. The alternative to absolutism does not have to be
nihilism; just because we don't have certainty about the past, it
does not follow that anything goes.

Frameworks of Historiography

Let us examine some of the frameworks or hypotheses that historians have used as implicit bases for selecting facts and exhibiting their interconnections (that is, their philosophies of history).

I. We may begin with Ecclesiastes:

> The thing that hath been, it is that which shall be; and that which is done is that which shall be done; and there is no new thing under the sun.

It is an ancient idea that history is *cyclical*; the Persians, Babylonians, and Hindus believed that it repeats itself endlessly. Is this view naive? Alexander Goldenweiser argues that there is only a limited number of possible solutions to most practical problems of human life. (How many kinds of pot can you cook in? In how many ways can you paddle a canoe?) Repetition is therefore likely. Pitirim Sorokin says, more emphatically, "the basic forms of almost all socio-cultural phenomena are limited in their number; hence they inevitably recur in time, in rhythmic fashion."

II. A second group of philosophies of history may be called *functional* because of the way in which they isolate and stress certain causative factors:

1. Buckle, for example, believes that the history of civilization depends on climate, soil, and geography. Of course such factors are important: personality is affected by diet; maturity is in part a function of climate. Ancient Greece and Rome, situated near swamps, were almost wiped out by malaria. Simkhovitch attributes the fall of Rome to the exhaustion of the soil. Taine shows that in Egypt the devil is personified as the typhoon; in Scandinavia as the Frost Giant. But physicalistic and telluric factors, although necessary conditions for civilization, are not sufficient. Inland peoples will probably not invent canoes, but coastal peoples—the ancient Peruvians, for example—likewise may not. The Hopis and Navahos, in almost identical geographical circumstances, have vastly different cultures. Although the Fiji Islands are cold and stormy, the natives wear no clothing; in torrid Uganda the people are fully clad. Thus, a functional theory of history has both strengths and weaknesses.

Other functional theories of history may be indicated schematically. In each case, the historian has selected a particular causative factor to which he attributes major significance in the interrelations of past events:

2. Race is stressed by historians as ancient as Tacitus (who contrasted the virtues of the unspoiled Germans with the vices of the decadent Romans) and as modern as the Frenchman Gobineau and the Anglo-German H. S. Chamberlain. Both were anti-Semitic advocates of Nordic supremacy; they believed that racial endowment is the determinative factor in history.

3. Hereditary ability is paramount in historical interpretations that focus on the influence of such families as the Medici, the Adamses, the Bachs, the Kennedys, and the Soongs. Francis Galton, the founder of eugenics and himself a member of a distinguished family which included Charles Darwin, was a proponent of this theory.

4. Psychological factors are identified by Freud and many post-Freudians as the moving force in history. In this view, civilization results from the sublimation of deep impulses and unconscious basic drives. Eros (the libido, or sex drive) and Thanatos (the death wish) are personified as the causative factors in history.

5. The *Communist Manifesto* begins, "The history of all hitherto existing society is the history of class struggles." Marxism is not the only theory of economic determinism; Charles Beard's interpretation of how the American Constitution was adopted is another example. The modes of economic life and the relations of production are deemed to explain the legal, political, intellectual, religious, and other "ideological" aspects of a society and its history.

6. Carlyle said, "The History of the World is but the Biography of Great Men." Emerson and James also found the motive power of history to be the appearance of superior individuals.

What happens when two functional theories conflict? Sidney Hook offers the amusing example of Trotsky's account of the role of Lenin in the Russian Revolution. As a Marxist, Trotsky was committed to the inevitable success of the proletarian revolution; but Lenin's "Theses of April 4," which set the course of the revolution, Trotsky wrote, were published in his own name and his only. The central institutions of the party met them with a hostility softened only by bewilderment. Nobody—not one organization, group, or individual —affixed his signature to them.

How, then, could the revolution have succeeded without Lenin? How can Marxist economic determinism be reconciled with Lenin's apparent indispensability? Lenin would somehow have been produced, according to Trotsky, because he

> was not an accidental element in the historic development, but a product of the whole past of Russian history. . . . Lenin did not oppose the party from outside, but was himself its most complete expression. . . .

This analysis is not unlike Kautsky's claim that, had Napoleon died in 1785, another soldier would have risen from the ranks to perform Napoleon's historic task!

III. The idea of *progress* as a philosophy of history is relatively new. Prior to Voltaire and the French Revolution, the "Golden Age" was usually placed in the remote past. (Progress must be distinguished from historical evolution and from change. *Change* is pervasive and objective; it is any difference in position, size, or quality. If the change is gradual and has a direction, it is *evolution*; this may or may not be pervasive, but it, too, is objective. However, *progress* is change in the direction of human interests; it is neither pervasive nor objective.) Giambattista Vico first suggested in the early eighteenth century that men control their history, so that it could be directed progressively. In different ways, Saint-Simon, Comte, Kant, Hegel, Fichte, Bergson, Spencer, and Whitehead would agree that history shows progress.

IV. History is a great drama of sin and redemption, according to the *Christian* view. In the year 4004 B.C., God created beings who were imperfect copies of Himself. But Adam and Eve succumbed to the temptation of the Devil, so they and their sinful descendants were condemned to suffer. God then tried to redeem mankind by the incarnation of His Son. According to St. Augustine, history is the conflict between the "City of God" and the "City of Satan" until the final day of reckoning. (The Christian view might be regarded as a special example of the progressive theory.)

V. *Organismic* theories consider society to be a kind of living organism. Spengler believes that all civilizations grow, from infancy, through youth, maturity, and senility, to death. All cultural phenomena are thus said to be "organically" interrelated. In ancient Greece, for example, the unit of government (the city-state), the development of Euclidean geometry, a religion of finite deities, the characteristic orders of architecture, and belief in a closed universe were all declared to be interconnected as if they were parts of a living whole. "Everything that is Classical," Spengler summarized, "is comprehensible in *one* glance." Nor was it accidental, he insisted, that double-entry bookkeeping was invented in 1494 by Fra Luca Pacioli; Spengler ranked him with his contemporaries Copernicus and Columbus. The analogy between a society and an organism is also made, but more loosely, by Sorokin and Toynbee.

Closely related to the organismic theories are those that postulate a *Zeitgeist,* or spirit of the age, to account for cultural phenomena. These theories explain Gothic cathedrals, for example, as a manifestation of the "Gothic spirit," which is said to infuse all the products of that era. However, we can more accurately understand Gothic cathedrals as a solution to certain problems in engineering and economics. Stone was then widely used for building because of the fear of fire in wooden buildings; ceilings were necessarily heavy, and supporting walls had to be very thick, with little space for windows. But the invention of the flying buttress and the ribbed vault distributed the weight of the structure and made possible thinner walls and larger openings. Arches were pointed so that openings of different sizes could reach the same highest point. The art of staining glass was also then being mastered. Thus, the soaring buoyancy of the Gothic cathedrals is attributable less to a mysterious *Zeitgeist* than to the solution of specific practical problems. To speak of "Gothic man" is to use a metaphor; to seek for the collective consciousness which produced "Gothic art"—cathedrals, music, and poetry—is to pursue a will o' the wisp. There is no single dominant outlook, or *Weltanschauung,* that influences all the arts. The pointed arch is also to be found in Islamic architecture. Nothing in English painting corresponds to the poetry and drama produced in the Elizabethan era. The skyscraper has nothing in common with atonality in music. It is convenient to use such general concepts as the "spirit of an epoch," but they have no explanatory or predictive value; it is fallacious to assume that whatever events are produced in a given chronological period must have a common essence.

The Myth of Historical Inevitability

In *War and Peace* Tolstoy vividly portrays the bewilderment of the millions of people caught up in the crises and upheavals of the Napoleonic Wars. "On the 12th of June [1812]," he writes, "the war began, that is, an event took place opposed to human reason and all human nature." And he wonders:

> What led to this extraordinary event? What were its causes? Historians, with simple-hearted conviction, tell us that the causes of this event were the insult offered to the Duke of Oldenburg, the failure to maintain the continental system, the ambition of Napoleon, the firmness of Alexander, the mistakes of the diplomatists, and so on. . . .

> The causes of this war seem innumerable in their multiplicity. The more deeply we search out the causes the more of them we discover; and every cause, and even a whole class of causes taken separately, strikes us as being equally true in itself, and equally deceptive through its insignificance in comparison with the immensity of the result, and its inability to produce (without all the other causes that concurred with it) the effect that followed. . . .

> And consequently nothing was exclusively the cause of the war, and the war was bound to happen, simply because it was bound to happen. Millions of men, repudiating their common sense and their human feelings, were bound to move from west to east, and to slaughter their fellows, just as some centuries before hordes of men had moved from east to west to slaughter their fellows. . . .

> Although in that year, 1812, Napoleon believed more than ever that to shed or not to shed the blood of his peoples depended entirely on his will (as Alexander said in his last letter to him), yet then, and more than at any time, he was in bondage to those laws which forced him, while to himself he seemed to be acting freely, to do what was bound to be his share in the common edifice of humanity, in history.

One enduring myth is that human history has an overall plot, and that if we could only figure out what it is, we would have a clue to what the future holds. But there is no evidence at all to support so romantic a view.

Appraisal of Histories

How are we to evaluate these philosophies of history? As may be expected, none of them is entirely true, none is entirely false. They are frameworks for collecting and organizing data; like metaphysical theories or like the psychologist's models, they succeed if they fructify our self-understanding. Thus, they may not be equally satisfactory even when they are equally accurate. No crucial experiment can test the validity of a theory of history, any more than it can the truth of a metaphysical theory. Edmund Wilson declares that the Russian Revolution was "the moment when for the first time in the human exploit the key of a philosophy of history was to fit an historical lock." But locks often have more than one key. Did the success of Lenin's revolution "prove" Marxism? And if he had failed, would Marxism thereby have been disproved? Were the French ultimately ousted from Algeria because of concessions made to the rising nationalism, or in spite of it? Raymond Aron observes that

> When an Empire begins to break up, the blame is ascribed indifferently to those who for too long refused to reform it, and those who, by permitting reform, accelerated the course of events. The facts never decide the issue between the opposed theories.

There is no Archimedean point of view; and neither the bird's eye view nor the worm's eye view is infallible.

History is far from being exclusively scientific or factual; it is also in large part creative. Macaulay regards history as a branch of literature. The historian, like the novelist, tells a story: this is how things happened. This may be considered to be a *genetic* explanation. As Ernest Nagel shows, it is also the way in which the scientist answers such questions as, why does the ocean contain about 3% salt? or why does English have so many words of

Latin origin? Historical geology and Darwinian evolution also explain by demonstrating how things came to be as they are. Thus, the explanatory aspect of history would differ from that of the social sciences. Although both disciplines face the problem of the plurality of causes, and the necessity to select and impute causes, the social sciences (ideally) explain by embedding the fact to be explained within a general law. However, there seems to be no compelling reason to insist that such a "covering law" or "deductive-nomological" model be the only legitimate one for historical explanation; nor that the cyclical, functional, progressive, organismic, and other frameworks used by the historian to structure his data be metamorphosed into scientific hypotheses or general laws to be verified or falsified. That would be to miss the point of how the study of history operates in fulfilling the commandment "Know thyself."[2]

---

[2] Here are two enlightening examples of the construction of a meaningful past: the Crusades, which loom so large in European history, are now described by Islamic historians as Christian fanaticism, or as European exploitation of the Arabs, or as imperialism, or even as a precursor of Zionism; but Islamic writers at that time spoke of the Crusaders only as Franks or as infidels, not distinguished from other invaders or marauders—there was not even an Arabic word for Crusades! And the heroic and suicidal defense at Masada in A.D. 66, in the Jewish revolt against the Romans, now considered one of the outstanding events in Jewish history, is not even mentioned by the Rabbinic and other chroniclers of that time—their interest was rather in such religious scholars as Johanan ben Zakkai; our only information about Masada comes from Josephus, who was a renegade Jew.

16

Probability, Rationality, and Induction

I MAINTAINED in Chapters 3 and 4 that our knowledge about the world is never certain; only analytic propositions are known to be true a priori. Synthetic propositions (propositions with factual content) are made true by a process of verification. This process depends ultimately upon the evidence of our senses, and is always subject to revision. The truth of synthetic propositions is therefore a matter of probability.

But what exactly does probability mean? Various usages of this term may be distinguished:

1. *Opinion.* "Bourbon probably tastes better than Scotch."
2. *Prudence.* "Always carry an umbrella because there is a probability of rain."
3. *Measure of ignorance.* "We may never get beyond probabilities in finding out why President Kennedy was assassinated."
4. *Inductive generalization.* "All ravens are probably black." "All politicians are probably dishonest."
5. *The weight of the evidence.* "Caesar probably invaded Britain." "Darwinian evolution is more probable than the biblical account of creation."

6. *Symmetry in the world.* "A normal coin will probably come up heads half of the time." "Any one hand at bridge is as probable as any other."

7. *Relative frequency.* "Of the next thousand babies born in New York City, there will probably be more boys than girls." "The probability that a man aged thirty will survive to his next birthday is .945."

Diverse Meanings of Probability

We can identify four different concepts that relate to the meanings of probability just illustrated.

Most apparent is the connection between probability and the psychological element of *belief*: the greater the probability is declared to be, the more strongly you believe it. This is the simplest view of probability, and the most pervasive. It is the oldest view, and, in a sense, also the newest. In spite of the obvious hazards in relying on a state of mind as a criterion of probability, a recent widespread personalistic, or subjectivistic, interpretation developed by De Finetti, Ramsey, Savage, and others sees probability as a special measure of self-disciplined belief or opinion.

Probability sometimes refers to the *weight of the evidence* or the degree of confirmation or corroboration of a hypothesis. This usually cannot be stated as a frequency—see example 5.

Probability is stated mathematically in example 6, by dividing the favorable instances into the total number of possibilities. It is deduced analytically and a priori. A coin has only two sides; there is no reason why heads should be favored over tails; therefore, without tossing any coins, you can say these outcomes are equally probable. This is the so-called principle of indifference or of insufficient reason. But how do you know that this is really true for coins? Until recently, the birth of boys and of girls was considered equally probable for the same reason. Now it is known that actually more boys are born than girls (their death rate in infancy is also higher). But suppose you tossed, say, a million normal coins and got 600,000 heads and 400,000 tails. Would you abandon the view that the odds of getting heads are 50–50? This is the Achilles' heel: when a probability is regarded as deductive or *analytic,* no empirical evidence can contradict it; it is compatible with any results; it does not restrict the frame of possibilities. But in that case, why on earth should the probability apply to coins, for example, but not to babies? When in fact are actual events equally possible, or "indifferent"? (Nothing so like as eggs, said Hume!) There is, alas, no logical relation between the two ways in which a coin or a baby *can* turn up and the frequency with which the alternatives actually *occur.*

The fourth concept of probability avoids the deductive or analytic view; rather, it relies on experience, that is, on the statistical sense of *relative frequency.* In example 7 we count the actual number of men who die between their thirtieth and thirty-first birthdays and divide this figure by the total number of men in the city or other area examined. In the example, 1,000 men were studied; during the course of the year 55 men who were between thirty and thirty-one died, so that 945 men survived. The frequency with which men aged thirty survive a year is stated relative to the total. It is this numerical value which cannot be assigned in example 5 to the "weight of the evidence." It is stated as a fraction or decimal in a continuous range, with the limits of 0 (impossibility) and 1 (certainty). This relative frequency concept of probability is independent of the other three concepts; it is empirical, self-corrective, and pragmatically successful; it is therefore widely favored. It is not, however, free of theoretical difficulties. Since this probability can be assigned only to a class or series of events (it is the "gambler's fallacy" to forget this rule) it does not explain any one particular case (such as whether Bert, now aged thirty, will survive or not). Moreover, Bert (like every individual) is a member of more than one class: he is a lawyer, a vegetarian, and a cigarette smoker; the life expectancy of each of these classes is, say, 72, 81, and 63. Which is Bert's? (The numbers of course cannot be averaged.) Every event likewise may be described in more than one way and may therefore be included in more than one class of events; this is a particular problem in discussing human actions (Chapter 20). Thus all of the evidence available may not suffice to determine any given situation. (That there are limits to the classes of events is one view of the postulate of induction.) Furthermore, there are questions of probability that cannot possibly be understood in terms of the frequency of actual occurrences, such as events that have never occurred before (e.g., a Pope being bitten by a piranha) or such as that the probability that any two integers taken at random will be relatively prime (i.e., have no common factor) is $6/\pi^2$. (Of course it is an error to assume that the most probable distribution of events will occur in any given instance. In the Dreyfus trial, the prosecution argued that Dreyfus' correspondence must have been in code, because the frequency of the letters in it was "abnormal." Poincaré testified that the most probable distribution was, in any single case, highly improbable. Poincaré had identified himself on the witness stand as the greatest living expert on probability, a tactical error he later justified by pointing out that he had been testifying under oath.)

Importance of Probability

It is important to clarify the meaning of probability because it is such a widely used concept in contemporary scientific explanation. Genetics, for example, is entirely probabilistic in describing the combinations of dominant and recessive genes. Geneticists predict that within a given family over a long period of time the probabilities are that three-fourths of the children will be brown-eyed and one-fourth will be blue-eyed; no prediction can be made about any specific child, any more than about the next single toss of a coin. In the theory of evolution, as we have seen (Chapter 13), the difficulties of prediction are due to the enormous number of variables that affect the probability of a particular gene pool's encountering a particular environment.

In physics, the jerky, irregular Brownian motion of small particles suspended in a liquid is explained by the probabilities of the random impact of other particles. The theory of heat is probabilistic and statistical, rather than mechanical (which is a reason for the inadequacy of the metaphysics of mechanism; see Chapter 1). The second law of thermodynamics may be stated thus: all real processes tend to go toward a condition of greater probability—this is what is meant by the irreversibility of "time's arrow." Heat always tends to flow from the hotter of two adjacent bodies to the cooler one, although the reverse is logically possible. The long-range direction of events is toward randomness and greater entropy. In quantum mechanics (Chapter 12) probability is of the essence: physicists do not speak of the individual electron, but only of the probabilities inherent in it. The evidence for so-called gravity waves, or for extrasensory perception, or for the causal connection between cigarette smoking and lung cancer is statistical inference. Thus, it is important to determine exactly what is meant by a coin's propensity-to-fall-heads-half-the-time, and whether this probability is as objective a property of a coin as its melting point.

Rationality

Some subjectivists define probability as the degree of belief shown by a rational gambler, but rationality itself is a problematic concept. Philosophers have long tried to come to grips with it. They have called it the grasp of necessary connections; or, thinking in terms of grounds and consequences; or, awareness of organizing principles; or, the relational element in intelligence (only connect!). (The medieval belief in the rationality of God may be at the root of the scientific world view.) In the eighteenth century, the rational man was defined as one not dominated by his instincts. Kant regarded rationality as behavior guided by rules: "Everything in Nature works in accordance with laws. Only a rational being has the power to act in accordance with his idea of laws . . . reason is required to derive actions from laws." For Max Weber, rational action is the deliberate choice of means to attain explicit goals, in the light of all existing knowledge; the essence of capitalism is the rational organization of all facilities in the constant pursuit of gain, undeterred by, for example, the barriers of institutional religion. In the words of Ludwig von Mises, "action based on reason . . . knows only one end, the greatest pleasure of the acting individual."

These disparate views nevertheless fail to account for a residual area of nonrational choice. Suppose there are two covered urns, each containing an unknown quantity of similar metal balls. One urn, you are told, contains gold balls (worth $100 each) and silver balls ($10 each); the other urn contains platinum balls ($1,000 each) and lead balls ($1 each). You are allowed to select only one ball: into which urn do you put your hand? You may of course have personal or private considerations that affect your decision. You may be so poor and hungry that the difference between $1 and $10 is crucial—or you may be so wealthy that even $100 won't mean much to you, so that you might as well aim for $1,000. Barring such special personal circumstances, however, the choice is more a matter of temperament than of rationality. The adventurer will gamble on a platinum ball; the conservative may want to maximize the minimum utility, that is, try to get the best possible of the worst possible outcomes (the "maximin" rule). As Hempel put it, "man is a rational being indeed: he can give a reason for *anything* he does!"

Psychoanalysis and anthropology have recently shown that the concept of rationality in action may be even more tenuous. That well-known neurotic who refuses to shake hands because he is afraid of germs has a reason for his conduct. His fear of germs may be excessive or unwarranted, but is his action therefore irrational? If I touch every lamppost as I walk down the street, in order to keep ghosts away, don't I have a reason? Does the falsity of my belief in ghosts and their connection with lampposts make my behavior irrational? Suppose my car battery has died. Does my ignorance of this fact when I turn the ignition key make my behavior irrational? Was it irrational ten years ago to spray DDT on crops? or to keep babies in swaddling clothes? Is the aborigine irrational when he would rather have a pretty feather than a ten-dollar bill? Is it rational always to buy at the lowest price? or to prefer intangible status to material possessions? Was Freud rational in choosing to have constant pain in his cancerous jaw rather than the dullness which a sedative would induce? Was Marc Antony irrational when he dallied with Cleopatra and did count the world well lost? Are the Israelis and the Arabs rational?

There seems no rational way to put in order such incompatible human ends as selfishness and altruism, justice and mercy, freedom and security, our own interests and those of later generations. Life in the twentieth century, when extreme conditions seem to have become almost commonplace—concentration camps, terrorism, torture, assassination, mass murder—brings into question all of our comfortable preconceptions about what rational men can and will do. Moreover, decisions are often actually made out of habit, or boredom, or in ignorance (both of our own changing values and of possible alternatives). Thus, there is no single definition of, or simple standard for, rationality. But it would be a more serious mistake to conclude that there is any alternative to reliance on reason or that there is no objective basis for making decisions. The new studies called Decision Theory and the Theory of Games try to work out a definition of rationality in terms of a consistent ordering of your preferences so as to maximize your utilities, under conditions of uncertainty and risk. The Theory of Games also takes account of the special case when your decisions must be based on decisions made by other persons with competing interests. From this point of view, social policy may be defined as a rational endeavor to maximize the utilities of society as a whole.

Induction

One of the usages of probability at the beginning of this chapter was "inductive generalization." We say that all ravens are probably black, because we have seen a large number of ravens, and all of them have been black. We generalize from our past experience and feel justified in predicting that the ravens we have not yet seen, or may never see, are also black. This type of inference is called induction, and there is this problem about it: how can we be sure we are right? We have been wrong about the births of boys and girls: why not also about the color of ravens? Is a sample ever large enough? One of the criticisms leveled at Aristotle's logic (Chapter 6) is that his use of the form "all x is y" cloaked such different kinds of assertion as the inductive generalization ("All politicians are liars") and the complete enumeration of a class ("All cabinet members are Republicans"). In the latter instance, the induction is complete: we can talk to each of the cabinet members, and we do not have to generalize to unexamined members of the class. When we say that 945 of *any* 1,000 thirty-year-old men will survive a year, we are extending our inference from an observed relative frequency to an unobserved one. In short, the concepts of probability and induction are closely connected. Furthermore, in scientific explanation (Chapters 9 and 10), the facts seldom unambiguously determine the selection of a hypothesis: various criteria must be applied and weighed. And no hypothesis is ever completely verified (Chapter 8), so reasons must be given for a decision. Thus, rationality is also intimately associated with the concepts of probability and induction.

Why do we believe that sugar will continue to taste sweet tomorrow, just because it tastes sweet today? How do we know that there are limits to the classes of events in the world? Or that the world is not (or will not become) completely and chaotically random? Sometimes these questions are answered by the postulate that the future will resemble the past; but why must it? If you reply, because it always has, you merely repeat the problem. That was the past future; what about the future future? The philosophical turkey reasoned that since she had been fed by the farmer every morning of her life she always would be; but she discovered the problem of induction on Thanksgiving Day. If you point to the "uniformity of nature," the question still is unanswered: why should nature be uniform in the future just because it has been so in the past? The answer is, it is not nature which is uniform, but human procedure: it is our decision to act as if the future will resemble the past.

"Nature is uniform" is an analytic proposition. It does not restrict factual possibilities. If a stone should fall up, we would say there must be some natural reason for this phenomenon. Thus, the justification of induction is pragmatic. If the world were utterly chaotic, and stones fell up or sideways as often as down, it would be pointless to rely on experience; but even such a world would be uniform in its randomness. If human success is possible in any way at all, that way must incorporate the continued application of inductive inference. Anyone who becomes aware that there is a problem in induction has in a sense already solved this problem. Induction may be defined as the marshaling and evaluation of evidence; what could rational behavior be, other than reliance on evidence?

Two New Riddles

Two recently proposed problems will serve as arguments for the appropriateness of this pragmatic approach. One is Goodman's "new riddle of induction." He shows that all the existing evidence supports equally the hypotheses "all emeralds are green" and "all emeralds are grue" (*grue* is defined as green now and blue after 1984). We prefer the predicate *green* to the predicate *grue*, he says, only because it is "better entrenched." Inductive generalization may thus be accused of a certain arbitrary conservatism. The second problem is Hempel's paradox of confirmation. He points out that a proposition is logically equivalent to any of the forms into which it may be validly converted. Thus, "all ravens are black" is logically equivalent to its contrapositive "all non-black things are non-ravens." Whatever evidence confirms either of these propositions will therefore also confirm the other. "This white handkerchief is a non-raven" confirms the contrapositive, "all non-black things are non-ravens," and therefore also confirms "all ravens are black." We shrink intuitively from these conclusions.

Both problems arise, however, from a disregard of the pragmatic function of logic in inquiry. What purpose is served by introducing "grue"? or by the conversions of a proposition? The situation reminds me of my grandfather's ingenious convertible spring-controlled kitchen stool and stepladder combination. It had so sensitive a mechanism that a footstep on the ladder might set off the springs and convert it suddenly into the stool. Once as a boy I sneezed while sitting on the stool; it leaped up and turned into the ladder; I broke my ankle. My grandfather therefore banished the device to the attic. I remember being awakened at night by its apparently spontaneous conversions (caused, I suppose, by the vibrations of passing streetcars). Nowadays I am awakened at night by the apparently spontaneous conversion of a proposition into its contrapositive.

It is man who is the measure. These difficulties are beside the point; they fall into place when we keep firmly in mind the purpose of probability, logic, and science: to organize human experience.

17

The Person

"KNOW THYSELF": the primal philosophic injunction! But what does it mean? "To thine own self be true," says Shakespeare. Kierkegaard tells us that to avoid despair one must "will to be that self which one truly is." According to the psychologist Carl Rogers, under therapy "the individual explores what is behind the masks he presents to the world, and even behind the masks with which he has been deceiving himself . . . to an increasing degree he becomes himself . . . a person."

The Self: I and My Body

The concept of the *self*, or the *person,* or the "real me" is frequently taken for granted as a metaphysical ultimate, that is, as a primitive term or entity which cannot be reduced to, or analyzed into, anything simpler, and is somehow there to be found. The *body* of course is neither ultimate nor simple: it is composed of familiar chemical elements, into which it will disintegrate. But am *I* the same as my body? or is it I who have a body? Note that

185

the question is not, *who* am I? but *what* am I? There is clearly
a strong sense in which I am not identical with my body. This
insight has been expressed in a multitude of ways. "The spirit
is willing but the flesh is weak"; "Our bodies are our gardens, to
the which our wills are gardeners" (Othello); "You bury only
my body, not me" (Socrates); "This body of mine is Gautama's
body, and it will be dissolved in due time . . . but Buddha will
not die" (Buddha); the Orphic pun on *soma sema* ("the body
is a tomb"); and not least by the old Jewish patient who complained to Erik Erikson, "Doctor, my bowels are sluggish, my
feet hurt, my heart jumps, and, you know, Doctor, I don't feel
so good myself."

The issue may be put thus: is my body an object of my experience, or is it the source of my experience? Do "I" discover
"my body?" When I first touch my foot, is that a different kind
of experience from my first touching a table? "I" can cause
changes in "my body"—does this mean that "I" am separable
from "my body"? Are my eyes transparent windows through
which I look, so that conceivably "I" could look through other
eyes? Could "I" possibly be in another body? smile with another
mouth? feel sad in another heart? My eyes are the only eyes I
cannot see. My body is the only body I can control directly; it is
the only avenue through which I can influence the world outside. As a baby, I had to learn the difference between my thumb
and my mother's nipple: if all events occurred as and when I
wished, would I ever find out where my body ended? Is it logically
possible, asks Schlick, that I might say, I have a pain in the
candlestick? (Note that these issues are philosophical rather than
scientific; they are concerned with the meaning of concepts, not
with the facts; the criterion for settling such questions is not
empirical possibility but freedom from logical contradiction.)

Continuity of the Person

What is it that makes for the *continuity*, or sameness, of the
person? Would you be the same person if you changed your

clothing style radically? or your hairdo? or if your features were altered by plastic surgery? Would you be the same person in a wheelchair? or if your skin color were different? or your sex? What if these changes had occurred ten years ago? or right after you were born?

Perhaps the continuing identity of the person is not bodily. (Emphasis on the mind—the *"Ego cogito"*— dates from Descartes.) What if you had another nationality? spoke a different language? had a different religion? (religious conversion is often described as a rebirth). Is there an essential core, a true self, an inner you, an identity of the person, which would be the same if you had been brought up from birth by foster parents, say, in China? Sartre and the existentialists deny this; they say that you are what you are as the result of a series of "accidents," fortuitous circumstances (such as race, sex, and nationality) which might have been other than they are. You delude yourself if you think you can find a real inner, personal essence.

The problem is to find a criterion of *individuation:* what is it that identifies a person as a distinct entity? Rosencrantz and Guildenstern in *Hamlet* are always on stage together. At their first appearance, this is said:

> *King.* Thanks, Rosencrantz and gentle Guildenstern.
> *Queen.* Thanks, Guildenstern and gentle Rosencrantz.

Is it possible that the king and queen are confused? or even that Shakespeare did not distinguish between Rosencrantz and Guildenstern as persons? Tom Stoppard raised the interesting possibility, in his play *Rosencrantz and Guildenstern Are Dead,* that they themselves may have had doubts as to who was who. (One of them introduces himself as the other, and has to be corrected!) Mark Twain described an interview in which he explained to his interviewer that he was one of identical twins; one twin had drowned in his bath when two weeks old, "but we didn't know which . . . one of us had a peculiar mark, a large mole . . . that was *me.* That child was the one that was drowned!"

Is existence at a certain place and time part of the person? Consider the relation between spatial location and sameness: I hold in my hand the "same pen" I had in China; but, if we could somehow move the Hudson River to China, it would not be the "same river." Being in a certain place is part of being the same river, but not of being the same pen. What about being the same person? Consider temporal location. If you see a photograph of yourself at the age of three, you ask, was that angelic child really me? If you are told you will someday be a toothless doddering imbecile, you say, Oh no! that won't be me! Thus we may intuitively reject identification with ourselves at points far distant in time (cf. the self-contradiction in "time travel" in Chapter 12).

Is ancestry part of the person? The genes you inherit from your parents, and which were fixed at the moment of your conception, will normally be transmitted unchanged to your descendants. This sum of genetic determinants, or *genotype*, lives on, not because it is immortal, but because it replicates itself. How you grow as a person after the moment of your conception depends upon the continuous interaction between your unchanging genotype and your changing environment. Because environments differ so widely, a vast number of different mature phenotypes is possible from a single genotype. For this reason it is practically impossible to isolate innate from acquired behavior patterns. Also for this reason, the Darwinian theory of evolution, based on natural selection among phenotypes, finds it difficult to predict the future course of evolution (Chapter 13).

The effect of environmental changes may clearly be seen in Japanese teenagers today—they tend to be a head taller than their parents—and in the children born in Israeli kibbutzim, who are so different from their European-bred parents. René Dubos writes,

Genes do not determine traits, genes only govern the responses of the person to environmental stimuli . . . man's body and brain have not changed significantly during the past hundred thousand years. The same set of genes that governed man's life when he was a Paleolithic hunter . . . still govern his anatomical development, physiological needs, and emotional drives. . . . Human nature . . . is the historical expression of the adaptive responses made by man during his evolutionary past and his individual life. Genetic and experiential factors operate in an interrelated manner in all biological and behavioral manifestations. . . . The child is pro-

grammed by the conditions of intra-uterine and early post-natal
life. . . . He can never change his past.

As long as you are alive, your body grows and decays. The cells
that make up your body are constantly being discarded and replaced. Where do the replacements come from? From some fish
now swimming in the Pacific Ocean, some plant now growing
in Idaho. Metabolism is the process of remaking one's body by
absorption and ingestion. If the body's cells are almost entirely
replaced every seven to ten years, what makes one's body the
same body? Only its relatively constant form. An analogy would
be an army regiment marching: every minute some soldiers may
drop out and be replaced by others; after a while perhaps not
one man who started is still marching, but it is the same regiment.
A club is a similar case: all of its founders may be deceased, the
original building sold, but it may continue to be "the same
club" because the new members follow the same traditions.

How important is bodily form? In *The Brothers Karamazov,*
Grigory has fathered a six-fingered child: "don't christen it," he
declares, "it's a confusion of Nature!" (Real monstrous births are
more frequent than you might suppose; there is an unsettling collection in the museum at Salzburg.) The local priest must decide
whether to baptize the "confusion"; that is, he must determine
whether or not it is human. What latitude does he have?

If your cat (Tobermory!) began to talk and read and study
philosophy, would you ever call it human? When Actaeon was
turned into a stag and Narcissus into a flower, did they continue
to be the same persons? In Kafka's "Metamorphosis," a man
awakens to find that he has the body of a large cockroach: is he
still the same person?

In the new biological technique called "cloning," a cell can be
removed from a living animal and nurtured into full independent growth. The new animal is genetically identical to its single
"parent." This technique has apparently been somewhat successful with a frog. Suppose it were performed on a human being.
Would the cloned person be a continuation of the cell donor? If
human beings could reproduce by fission, as the amoeba does,
each half would have not only the same genes but the same memories. Would there be one person or two?

Discontinuity in time also raises questions about personal identity. Rip van Winkle was presumably the same person after his twenty-year slumber; but in the new science of cryogenics, the body can be frozen and "kept alive" almost indefinitely—after hundreds of years is the person the same?

When Does Life Begin and End?

The relation between the person and his body has other aspects. When does life begin? that is, when does a blob of tissue become a person? The Catholic Church for centuries permitted abortion prior to the "quickening" of the fetus (during the first eighty days of pregnancy). When does life end? Today the heart can be artificially kept beating for long periods. "With enough tubes in a person and surrounded by oxygen there is hardly any way a patient can die," a doctor has said. President Eisenhower was kept alive by electrical stimulation of the heart, forced feeding, and artificial respiration long after he could not possibly perform these functions by himself. A wealthy Midwestern matriarch with encephalitis was kept alive in a coma for five years; tended seven days a week by three shifts of nurses, she never said a word, never made a voluntary movement; her brain was dead. Physicians now propose three criteria for the irreversible loss of consciousness which would be defined as death: lack of response to stimuli, even those normally very painful; no movement or spontaneous breathing; and no reflexes. The "flat" encephalogram would be deemed corroborative evidence of death. Under these circumstances, may a surgeon extract a still-beating heart, or another organ, to transplant it? Is there an ethical distinction between putting a person to death and withdrawing the means whereby he is kept alive? Recently in a Brooklyn hospital two infants were born, a few hours apart; one had a deformed heart valve that would have caused the child's death within weeks, the other had a brain defect likewise incompatible with survival. Physicians transplanted the heart from the brain-damaged infant to the one with heart disease: "we were trying to make one whole individual out of two who had no chance of survival."

Memory

Let us consider memory as a possible criterion for the continuity of the person. Rip van Winkle remembered his past; what if a person in a cryogenic experiment, on being rewarmed to life, remembers nothing? With sophisticated brainwashing, your memories now can be edited, or elided, and replaced with others: do you then become a different person? Are you the same person after hypnosis? or after psychoanalysis? Are Dr. Jekyll and Mr. Hyde the same person? If two persons are brainwashed, and their memories switched, along with their habits, tastes, and plans, do they exchange identities?

(A parenthesis on illness and disease: these are quite different concepts. It is the person who is ill, but the body which is diseased —remember Erikson's oldster. The physician may cure a disease; but this cure may or may not heal an illness. A disease is caused either by a germ [e.g., cholera] or by the injury or malfunction of a bodily organ, system, or tissue [e.g., heart failure]. But normal healthy persons usually carry around within them many disease-causing microbes; some additional factor, therefore, must be required to cause the disease. In some instances a germ-caused disease has been "cured" by a placebo. A person may be ill without having any bodily disease at all; on the other hand, one may have a disease but at certain stages show no signs of illness, for example, diabetes, venereal disease, and arteriosclerosis. A person may have any of these diseases and feel perfectly well. There is both a personal and a psychological component to illness, whereas disease is presumably a bio-physical reality. But it would be a mistake to consider a disease as an objective entity, somehow waiting "out there" to be discovered and labeled. The human body at any given moment varies from the "normal" in many ways; but it is the medical profession that identifies symptoms, classifies syndromes, and establishes the categories of disease. "Disease occurs as a natural process," according to Dr. Fábrega, ". . . but any disease—smallpox, leprosy, syphilis, hypertension, cardiovascular disorders, cancer, etc.—is in part a cultural construct." In the nineteenth century, for example, consumption was considered as the characteristic attribute of heightened or artistic sensitivity [remember *Camille*]. Goiters [the compensatory hypertrophy of the thyroid gland] were once admired: Rubens' 1625 portrait [now in the Prado] of the famous beauty Maria de' Medici highlights her sizable goiter. Goiter was so prevalent in certain areas that Napoleon complained that his Alpine troops could not wear the standard uniform because of their swollen necks. Today almost everybody gets pyorrhea after a while: is it a disease? Is senility a disease? Is death?)

The Rights to Your Body: Self and Society

Homer tells the story of the beautiful tall Queen of the Amazons, who is slain in battle. As she lies dead on the field, a Greek named Thersites plunges his spear into her unseeing eye. Achilles, enraged beyond measure, kills Thersites on the spot. We all share Achilles' sense of outrage, I think. But have you a right to the integrity of your body after death? Should your beliefs against autopsy, for example, or against cremation, be given priority over the right of your survivors to knowledge or to protection against disease? Does the person have any rights after death?

Do you have an absolute right to your body even during your life? A court in New York has stated, "Every human being of adult years and sound mind has the right to determine what shall be done with his own body." But there are laws as well as strong feeling against self-mutilation. Kant condemned masturbation on the ground that you ought not violate the humanity which subsists within your person by treating your body as a mere device for your own gratification. Cotton Mather was an early advocate of innoculation against smallpox—an outraged citizen threw a bomb into his study. It took that great genius Christopher Wren to perform the first blood transfusion in England, in 1657. A law in Belgium prohibits any operation on the human body, except to save life or cure disease; three doctors are currently being sued for a sex-change operation. Do you have the right to change your sex? Do you have the right to be sterilized? How do you feel about van Gogh's cutting off his ear to send to a friend? In short, the notion that you are not the owner, but only the trustee, of your body has a long history.

On the other hand, what right does society have over your body? Does it have the right to order sterilization of mentally defective individuals, vaccinate masses of people during epidemics, spray insecticides on crops, fluoridate drinking water? Does it have the right to order drug "therapy" to tranquilize schoolchildren who are hyperactive "behavior problems"? what about violent prisoners, or people in old age homes that lack sufficient nursing personnel? Should Jehovah's Witnesses be compelled to submit to blood transfusions to save their lives?

Should experimentation on the living human body be prohibited? Such a ban would impede the growth of medical knowledge since experimenting on animals does not yield adequate information. The premature marketing of the drug thalidomide had horrible results. Yet, to this day no one knows how aspirin works: should it therefore be taken off the market? *Not* trying out a new drug also constitutes an experiment.

It seems unquestionable that society should obtain the consent of the subject or patient, and inform him fully of the risks involved in experiments or medical procedures. What if he is mentally deficient? or an infant? or senile? or a prisoner who is being cajoled and subtly coerced? We must never forget the Nazis, with their human guinea pigs, people in cages, and mass graves.

Bodily transplants raise additional issues. Recently a twenty-eight-year-old man named Tommy Strunk was dying of kidney disease. Only a kidney transplant could save him, and the best donor was his twenty-seven-year-old brother Jerry. But Jerry was in a mental hospital, not competent to authorize surgery on himself, although he loved Tommy. A Kentucky court approved the surgery, on the ground that Jerry depended on Tommy's friendship and understanding; Jerry's well-being "would be jeopardized more severely by the loss of his brother than by the removal of a kidney."

In a study published by Skeels in 1966, carried out for some thirty years, a group of mentally retarded one-year-old children were in the course of time brought into the normal range of intelligence by increasing their developmental stimulation and the intensity of their relation with mother surrogates. A control group, initially higher in intelligence, was left in a nonstimulating environment; all but one of these individuals became mentally retarded and were institutionalized. Does this experiment violate your sense of the rights of the person? On the other hand, another study, recently reported, examined the effects of the long-term use of anticoagulant drugs by persons who had suffered strokes. A large number of patients was divided into two groups, only one of which received the treatment. The ethics of withholding a beneficial treatment from the control group was questioned—but the results of the study indicated that the treatment was not only not beneficial, but probably harmful.

Two other situations concern the issue of the social control of the person's body. Kidney disease victims can be helped, their lives perhaps saved, by renal dialysis. But dialysis machines are scarce. In Seattle, a committee was organized to allocate the machines. Its job was to determine "the worth to the community" of each of the sufferers: among the criteria was whether or not the sufferer was a churchgoer. The second situation involves American soldiers in North Africa during World War II. Penicillin was scarce: should it be given to soldiers wounded in battle or to men with venereal disease? The army decided in favor of the latter: they could be restored to combat fitness more quickly; and battle wounds are not contagious.

The dialectical opposition between the person and society extends beyond the body: there is a right to privacy. Is this right invaded by pollsters? by sex researchers? by educational experiments in the ghettoes? by inquisitive anthropologists? by experimental psychologists? Are the rights of the person infringed by economic and psychological incentives to limit family size? or (not so long ago) to increase it? Mussolini offered a bonus to large families; our income tax structure continues to reflect a similar partiality.

The tensions between the right to bodily integrity and the needs of society, and between the right to privacy and the right to knowledge, should never be relaxed. There is no simple solution or clear boundary between them; this is part of the problem of what it is to be human. If you join a mountain climbing expedition, and rope yourself to the other climbers, you expect to be saved by them if you should slip; and you assume the risk of being killed yourself by their mishaps or incompetence. But this is the best way to climb a mountain.

Creation of the Person

A good part of this chapter has consisted of unanswered (unanswerable?) questions. The person must be seen as an ongoing integral process, which resists analysis into any simpler constituents. It is a metaphysical ultimate for which traditional categories are conceptually inadequate. To ask whether the body is the object of experience or the source of experience is to forget that the process of becoming a person rests on both modes. The body is both the self and the world. I am not the same as my changing body, yet I am not different from it. I am not separable from my body, yet I am not identical with it. My memory is part of what constitutes me; yet I am reluctant to say that I would be a different person if I had another memory. I would not be who I am if I had had a different parentage; but the constraints placed upon me as a person by my genetic endowment are minimal. I am not independent of society; yet I am not entirely the creature of society. There is, in short, incessant interaction between the growing person and the natural and social environments which both make his growth possible and yet resist his efforts (just as the artist's medium resists the artist). While alive, the process is never complete; the potentialities are never exhausted. The person is no more certain of his outcome than any other artist is. For it is the person who learns, who makes choices, who doubts, who acts and strives, who grows, who is guided by morality, who has an inner standpoint, who is creative. When Socrates said, Know thyself, he did not mean Discover thyself, but Create thyself.

18

Mind and Body

THE METAPHYSICAL PROBLEM of what there is in the world—especially the conflict between materialism and idealism (Chapter 1)—ultimately focuses on the problem of mind and body. Let me clarify why this problem exists.

States of Consciousness

I sit and stare at the fireplace, thinking of Paris. My "image of Paris" has two distinctive characteristics:

1. It cannot be observed by anyone else; it is *private* rather than public; I have "privileged access" to it; what I say about it cannot be corrected by anyone else. "The psychic is what is given only to one," says Munsterberg.

2. My "image of Paris" has no particular location or size. In a vague way, I suppose, it is inside my head. But where? in front or back or center? If I now imagine the Eiffel Tower, is my image of the Eiffel Tower smaller than my image of Paris? An image is *nonspatial*; it does not occupy space at all.

196

It is convenient to refer to phenomena such as mental images as *states of consciousness*. Characterized by their privacy and nonspatiality, they include thoughts, beliefs, ideas, purposes, hopes, intentions, attitudes, wishes, and memories. States of consciousness also include such processes as attention, deliberation, expectation, anticipation, problem-solving, awareness, perception, and preparation to respond.

If we define such states by the characteristics of privacy and nonspatiality, then it is debatable whether *emotions* qualify for inclusion. Thus James asks, in his *Psychology,*

> What kind of an emotion of fear would be left if the feeling neither of quickened heart-beats nor of shallow breathing, neither of trembling lips nor of weakened limbs, neither of goose-flesh nor of visceral stirrings, were present, it is quite impossible for me to think. Can one fancy the state of rage and picture no ebullition in the chest, no flushing of the face, no dilation of the nostrils, no clenching of the teeth, no impulse to vigorous action, but in their stead limp muscles, calm breathing, and a placid face? The present writer, for one, certainly cannot.

Whether the emotions are states of consciousness in the accepted sense, rather than bodily states, is therefore an open question.

More interesting is the state of consciousness called *pain*. It is the darling of the philosophers because of its psychological and physiological peculiarities:

1. Prizefighters and football players can be soundly battered, yet feel no pain. Bullet wounds are usually not painful; soldiers frequently do not even know they have been shot.

2. Some people are "pain-blind." They may bite through their tongues or be burned by cigarettes, but feel nothing. (Thus pain often serves as a warning to us; it has biological survival value.)

3. Captain Ahab would, long afterward, feel pain in the leg bitten off by Moby Dick. This "phantom limb" phenomenon is common among amputees.

4. We sometimes locate our pain in the wrong place. This is "referred pain" and can complicate medical diagnosis.

5. A placebo is about half as effective as morphine in stopping pain, according to statistical evidence.

6. There is wide individual variation in pain sensitivity; the threshold can often be raised or lowered by suggestion, distraction, self-hypnosis, or "cognitive dissonance." If a sudden disturbance makes you forget your toothache, did the pain temporarily stop? or did the pain continue without your being aware of it?

7. Autistic children seldom cry: do they therefore feel no pain?

8. Patients with incurable painful diseases, after being given a prefrontal lobotomy, sometimes report that "they still have the pain, but it doesn't bother them."

9. Does the masochist enjoy his pain? Animals can be conditioned to "enjoy" pain: a dog can be trained by reinforcement to give himself an electric shock; he will wag his tail while being shocked.

10. There are important social and cultural determinants of pain. Patients from large families tend to be more aware of pain: is this because they have had more people to complain to? Is childbirth painful? Euripides' Medea, deriding male heroism, asserts that she would rather fight a hundred battles than bear a single child. According to some women, labor would be unendurable were contractions not intermittent; yet other women knowledgeable in the techniques of prepared childbirth assert that labor need not be painful at all. In primitive societies that practice the "couvade," the woman gets up immediately after childbirth and fools the wicked spirits by going to work in the fields, while the father lies down and moans loudly. Margaret Mead claims that in Manus (New Guinea) married women are said to derive only pain from sexual intercourse until after they have borne a child.

11. The feats of the shamans—they walk barefoot on flaming coals, swim in icy rivers—are mysterious; so is acupuncture; but so is aspirin.

All in all, the perception of pain seems to involve the background, upbringing, memory, expectations, attitudes, anxieties, and social milieu of the person. We can agree both with Descartes, who said pain is spiritual, and with Thomas Aquinas, who said it must be material since angels surely feel no pain.

The Mind-Body Problem

A mind-body problem exists because states of consciousness interact with states of the body. The mind clearly acts on the body: we "drive" our bodies; we control our appetites; the thought of food makes our saliva flow; a ghost story produces gooseflesh; if a nursing mother becomes overanxious, her milk may be affected; a cardiovascular patient who "gives up" is likely not to recover; thoughts about sex have physical results (St. Augustine complained, my body doesn't obey me!); hysterical paralysis or blindness is caused by fear or neurosis; and such "involuntary" activities of your body as the expansion and contraction of your blood vessels, the beating of your heart, and the formation of your urine, can all be affected by your mental efforts.

There is strong evidence, too, that the body acts on the mind. Our mental processes are affected, for instance, by alcohol, coffee, air pressure, bodily posture (Yoga Asana), breath control (Pranayama), and fasting; mystical visions usually occur on mountain tops (where the air is thin) or after prolonged asceticism. Most striking is the variety of drugs that can be categorized by their distinctive mental results: sedatives, hypnotics, anesthetics, analgesics (painkillers, e.g., morphine, aspirin), convulsants (e.g., strychnine), anticonvulsants (e.g., dilantin), psychedelics (which alter perception, e.g., LSD), ataractics (tranquilizers), euphoriants (e.g., amphetamine), and antidepressants.

How do we account for the interaction between what is nonspatial and what is spatial; between what is nonmaterial and what is material? The Tower of Babel failed to reach from earth to heaven, not because technology was primitive, but because concepts were confused. Are our concepts of mind and body equally confused? Can we, perhaps, account fully for states of consciousness, which are unquestionably part of our experience, in the language of physical science? States of consciousness may clearly be *caused* by physical stimuli, as color perception is caused by light of a certain wavelength, or as hallucinations are caused by drugs; or they may be invariably *correlated* with physical conditions, as dreams seem to be with rapid eye movement, or (as we might well discover) alertness might be with some tightening of the scalp. Are states of consciousness therefore *identical* to certain physical states (as some philosophers maintain about the emotions)? Traditional materialism answers affirmatively. Just as a blazing red fire seems real enough, but is in fact actually the way in which a large number of molecules appears to us when they combine with oxygen, so mind has been said to consist of a combination of material particles (Lucretius), or the way in which such particles move (Hobbes), or a property they have (Diderot), or the way in which they are organized (La Mettrie), or in something they secrete (Cabanis). Is the relation between the mental and the physical merely empirical (so that to deny it would be like saying that an iron bar could float on water or that a stone could fall upward) or is it logical (so that to deny it would be like saying that a circle could be square)? Both you and I can see my pen, read my book, hear my voice; is it empirically impossible, or is it, rather, logically self-contradictory, that you should feel my pain? have my dream? see my image? Are these propositions synthetic or analytic?

Dualism

Dualism is the plausible metaphysical proposal that no problem exists because mind and matter are equally fundamental, entirely independent, and mutually irreducible. Physical science can explain how one body can impart motion to another body, but only mind can influence mind. The state of consciousness cannot be in contact with, or be reduced to, matter. How, then, does the act of my will move my limb? How does swallowing a drug influence my mind? Descartes, who argued for dualism, identified the tiny pineal, or cone-shaped, gland in the brain, whose function was unknown, as the point at which the mental decision is transmitted from the *res cogitans* (thinking substance) to the *res extensa* (spatial or physical substance). But this is one of the great philosophical howlers. If the division between the mental and the physical is radical, exclusive, and exhaustive, if these are the only two kinds of thing in the world, of what could a link between them possibly consist?

We showed in Chapter 17 that the person is not separable from his body. Dualism opens the door to such unpalatable possibilities as a mind existing without a body; or a mind occupying two or more bodies (metempsychosis? reincarnation?) or the body of an animal; or two minds occupying one body; or satanic possession; or dybbuks. Whatever phenomena these statements purport to refer to can be adequately described without such dubious phraseology.

Other dualists (e.g., Leibniz) argue that when God created the world he preestablished a harmony between the parallel closed circuits of mental and physical events, so that my mental decision to raise my arm and the physical event, the movement of my limb, although ontologically independent, are constantly conjoined. Geulincx suggested the analogy of two separate clocks, wound up so as to continue to tell the same time. Malebranche saw no difficulty in having omnipotent God solve the problem via constant miracles: whenever you decide to raise your arm, God on that occasion miraculously makes your arm rise. Spinoza, not a dualist, dissolved Descartes' riddle by declaring that the act of the will and the movement of the body are one and the same event seen under different aspects; there is only one reality, but it has two attributes, namely, thought and extension. Epiphenomenalism is the view that causal interaction goes in only one direction: mental states are the by-products of bodily states, but they are inert and "less real," like shadows, or like the whistle caused by water boiling in a kettle (which has no effect on the water), or like the gleam remaining on the television after it is turned off. (The Christian Scientist is a reverse epiphenomenalist: for him it is the body which is "less real.")

Modern Views of Mind

Modern philosophy, like the burnt child who dreads the fire, is reluctant to refer to mind as an entity. It prefers, rather, to speak of mental states, or states of consciousness, which it understands functionally, that is, as ways of acting, or dispositions to behave. If you say you remember how to do something, that means that you are now able to do it; your memory is not an entity over and above your manifested ability. If you say that Bert has a knack for fixing radio sets, that means that if you show him a broken radio, he will do things to make it work; you would not ask to see his knack. If Bert has a sharp wit, that is a way of characterizing the manner in which he says things; he is not thereby equipped with an entity of any sort. Caesar's ambition was not something other than his overt political maneuvers; it consisted of them. Intelligence (or modesty, or vanity) is not a thing, but (like solubility or brittleness) a disposition or tendency to react to stimuli in certain ways. Although we may have occasion to say that the dog believes his master is outside the door, we would never say that the dog believes his master is far away; not because we think that a dog has a limited capacity to believe, but because we see that a dog acts in a certain way at some times and not at others.

Suppose a visitor to New York City asked you to show him Columbia University. You would take him to Broadway and 116th Street, point out the Library, the lecture halls, the laboratories, the dormitories, the Faculty Club, etc. If he said, no, what I want to see is the university, he would be committing a category mistake. The university is not the same kind of entity as buildings, books, and test tubes. Neither is mind something which can be seen or touched. To think of it as inhabiting the body is what Ryle calls the dogma of "the ghost in the machine."

Contributions of Science

Modern science has made enormous strides in correlating the physical with the mental. There is a bewildering array of more or less reliable evidence that schizophrenia may be caused by the lack of a certain regulator chemical in the brain; that manic depressive psychosis may be alleviated by lithium carbonate treatment (just let your imagination play with the idea of eliminating mental illness in the world by dropping a chemical in the water supply!); that learned patterns of behavior (e.g., avoidance of the dark) can be transferred from trained rats to untrained rats by injecting into the latter material extracted from the brains of the former; that changes in the size of the pupil of the eye can indicate how hard a person is thinking, and whether he likes or dislikes what he sees; that biocybernetic techniques can identify a brain signal associated with "expectancy," another one correlated with the color at which a subject is looking, and a whole group that indicate "relaxed awareness"; that there are specific, identifiable areas of the brain that can be stimulated mechanically to produce (or suppress) hunger, sexual desire, and curiosity; and that, as Dr. José Delgado maintains, "functions traditionally related to the psyche, such as friendliness, pleasure, or verbal expression, can be induced, modified, and inhibited by direct electrical stimulation of the brain."

Recently a defendant in a murder case in New York pleaded not guilty by reason of insanity resulting from his chromosomal imbalance. There are normally twenty-three pairs of chromosomes, including one pair which determines sex characteristics and is designated as XX in women and XY in men; but the defendant had a chromosomal configuration, XYY, which some researchers claim is sixty times more prevalent among men convicted of violent crimes than among the general male population.

> No puppet master pulls the strings on high,
> Portioning our parts, the tinsel and the paint;
> A twisted nerve, a ganglion gone awry,
> Predestinates the sinner and the saint.
>
> Each, held more firmly than by hempen band,
> Slave of his entrails, struts across the scene:
> The malnutrition of some obscure gland
> Makes him a Ripper or the Nazarene.
>
> —George Sylvester Viereck, "Slaves"

Science has indeed made great strides; but note that the philosophical problem persists: my image of Paris may indeed be found some day to be *caused by* physical stimuli, or *correlated with* physical conditions, but will it therefore be *identical with* those physical states?

One Language or Two?

The doctrine of *physicalism* asserts that any sentence referring to a (nonmaterial, nonspatial) state of consciousness can be correlated with, or translated into, a language containing only terms that denote material spatiotemporal objects and properties, with no residue. This physicalist language would suffice for all of science (remember Carnap's remarks to Einstein, Chapter 2). Physicalism is not a metaphysical doctrine (such as materialism or dualism or mechanism), but rather a methodological or linguistic program. The sentence "Bert has a toothache," for example, would be translated into sentences that describe what Bert says and does, his cries and gestures, and the observable data of physiological, neurological, dental, and X-ray examination.

But another current in modern philosophy, the *double language* theory, denies the adequacy of the physicalist program. It insists that having a toothache is *not* equivalent to cries and gestures, nor to saying or doing anything, nor to being disposed to behave in a certain way; nor is "having a toothache" exhausted by any statements of physics, biology, or neurophysiology. The toothache is essentially neutral. It may be described by the physicalist "language of body" and it may be denoted by the psychological or phenomenal "language of mind." The distinction between these two languages corresponds loosely to the distinction between knowledge by description and knowledge by acquaintance (Chapter 2). In some European cities there are two telephone directories: one lists the subscribers alphabetically by name, the other lists the same subscribers geographically by street and number. Just so, the toothache may be classified under the captions "physical" and "mental." As in James' view of the emotions, the same "fear" can be described in two languages. Neither language has philosophical priority; neither must be reduced to the other. This is not an issue of metaphysics, although it is reminiscent of Spinoza's metaphysics of one reality with the two attributes of extension and thought. (Suppose you are told that an old, dusty, faded painting in your attic, which you have glanced at countless times, is in fact a famous missing Rembrandt; now you see the same entity under quite a different caption, but only your language has changed.)

Difficulties in Self-Knowledge

I began this chapter by characterizing my image of Paris as private. And in discussing the basis of knowledge in Chapter 2 I used the example "I know that I have a headache, because I feel it." My claim to have direct knowledge of my private states of consciousness, however, raises some problems. It is naive to suppose that I can look into my mind, as if it were an internal television screen, and report what I see there, just as I report on what I see outside myself. Exactly how do we observe, or attend to, our own states of consciousness? How do we take notice of a state of attention? or of an act of volition? Kant thought that any self-examination, or attention to a mental state, would disturb or distort it. (How could Kant possibly know, except by introspection, that introspection alters the state being introspected?) Wilhelm Wundt argued that the observer in psychology could, like the observer in physics at that time, ignore the fact that he is an observer. It is tempting to accept one's own mental states as "self-presenting" and exactly what they appear to be, but this view is not warranted. James put it, "if to *have* feelings or thoughts in their immediacy were enough, babies in the cradle would be psychologists, and infallible ones."

There are at least six difficulties involved in the understanding of oneself:

1. There is a *linguistic* parameter. Introspection or knowledge of one's mental states, like knowledge of anything else, requires adequate terms or concepts. "We have no power of thinking without signs," says Peirce; Wittgenstein states, abrasively, "You learned the *concept* 'pain' when you learned language." You may have felt pain, that is, or been in pain, or had pain; but you didn't have the *knowledge* without the necessary terminology. Not every experience becomes knowledge. The psychoanalyst Moses Burg, reporting on the rising incidence

of schizophrenia in Japan, has noted the relevance thereto of language:

> In the Japanese language there are many different ways of saying "I." Each of these "I's" has distinctive nuances [and is] used in different psychological circumstances. However, there is no single word for "I" which expresses a unitary, underlying self. . . .
>
> In English, . . . it is possible for one person to communicate to another person statements of action, states of being, etc., in words which do not embody in their linguistic structure nuances of assumption by the self and assignment to the other of various degrees and varieties of such interpersonal relations as superiority-inferiority and intimacy-distance. . . . This omission of interpersonal reference is just as impossible in Japanese as it is to speak a sentence in English in which the verb has no tense.
>
> Thoughts, feelings, perceptions, attitudes, and modes of consciousness are expressed as if the person involved had blurred or non-existent ego-boundaries. . . .

2. The self-presenting states of consciousness are often confused or inchoate. If you were to ask me, is that really Paris you are imagining? or, are you sure you have a headache? I might begin to wonder. The mere fact that you question me might suffice to alter my self-awareness and make those "self-presenting" states uncertain.

3. The process of self-awareness takes time. What I am really doing is retrospecting what my mental state was a little while ago. How can I understand myself *right now*?

4. The whole idea of privileged access to one's own mind is confused. If you had accused Caesar of being ambitious, he would have denied it indignantly. The angry man is often less aware of his own anger than are those who observe him. (Brother Juniper was comparing himself with two of the other monks in his monastic order. "It is true," he said, "that I cannot rival Brother Anselm in piety, nor can I compete with Brother Benedict in austerity, but when it comes to humility, by God, I'm the tops!") It did not require Freud to show us that we are not always the best judges of our own states of consciousness. We fear self-knowledge because it is so often bad news!

5. The claim of privileged access also breaks down in another way. If you tell me that you remember how to get from the

road to the lake, but in fact you get lost whenever you try to get there, I begin to doubt your claim. But what do I mean when I say that *I* remember? Regardless of how certain my memory may seem to me, or how vivid my recollection is, I will have to admit that I really don't remember, if I try but never get there. My "memory" is worthless. Thus, such states of my mind as remembering, knowing, etc., must (like belief in Chapter 8) be justified by appropriate action. The criterion for the existence of my internal mental capacity is its appropriate external exercise.

6. There is a logical problem: the man who says, I am a fool! is no longer as foolish as he may have been. We do indeed find out about ourselves as we find out about others; but to ascribe folly or evil or ambition or wit to ourselves is not the same as to ascribe it to others. I might or might not be mistaken when I say that I am ambitious; but it will differ from the way in which you will be mistaken if *you* say that *I* am ambitious. There is a *conceptual asymmetry* here. The risk of self-deception may be built into the procedure itself; it might be impossible to analyze one's own hopes and fears correctly. Self-commentary, in the words of Ryle, is "logically condemned to eternal penultimacy."

I ended the last chapter by saying, "When Socrates said Know thyself he did not mean Discover thyself, but Create thyself." Do you suppose Socrates knew all along how difficult both activities are?

19

Minds, Machines, Meanings, and Language

IN APPRAISING the grounds of knowledge in Chapter 2, I expressed my doubts about intuition as a basis of knowledge. It is quite remarkable how the reliability of intuition has been discredited. Poets, mystics, and transcendentalists have always had powerful intuitive convictions of certainty; and from Descartes to Husserl there has been a strong philosophical tradition that "clear and distinct ideas" directly intuited by the mind can be trusted. Nevertheless, no one has yet provided a clear and distinct idea of what these clear and distinct ideas are. Bergson was a great advocate of intuition as a direct, immediate, total apprehension of reality; he depreciated verbal or symbolic knowledge because it mediates, and analyzes, and gives a "motionless view of a moving Reality." He argued that biological evolution has favored the insect, who relies on instinct, at least as much as it has favored the human being, who (misguidedly) relies on reason. But this romantic craving for insight confuses experience with knowledge. An ineffable intuition cannot be expressed or communicated or discussed or verified or made coherent. As

Russell remarked, with his frequently acidulous felicity, instincts have been granted to the birds, to the bees, and to Bergson.

Decline of Intuition

We can identify twelve elements in the erosion of confidence in our ability to acquire knowledge directly by intuition:

1. Many recent developments in mathematics have cast doubt on intuition. In a field in which intuition seemed to enjoy unusually respectable status, the non-Euclidean geometries (Chapter 12) were only the first shock. Standards of what is intuitively obvious, or needs no proof, have been continually corrected and refined. How naive is Schopenhauer's remark that Euclid's obsession with substituting reason for intuition is as if a man should cut off both his legs in order to walk on crutches! The nineteenth century saw such "counter-intuitive" discoveries as: (a) there are as many even numbers as even and odd numbers combined (because there is a one-to-one correspondence between the two infinite sets); (b) there is an equal number of points in lines of different lengths, and as many points in a line as in a square (Cantor) —the number of points is infinite in all these cases; (c) a curve (which has no width) can cover the entire surface of a sphere (Peano); (d) a tangent cannot always be drawn to a continuous curve: there are continuous curves that cannot be differentiated anywhere (Weierstrass).

2. Logic is now understood as an explication of how symbols are used, and not a reasoning process, or chain of mental occurrences, running from premises to a conclusion. Russell's Theory of Types, Brouwer's dispensing with the law of the excluded middle, and Gödel's Theorem all appear counter-intuitive (Chapter 6); so does Hempel's paradox of confirmation (Chapter 16).

3. Darwinian evolution and genetics establish the continuity of all living things, and weaken the claim that human mental activities are qualitatively unique. Karl Jaspers adroitly asks,

who was the first ape to notice that he wasn't an ape? Human genes are composed of the very substances (DNA, RNA, and proteins) that make up the genes of all living creatures. The argument that human "essence" is discontinuous with the rest of nature cannot withstand the contrary evidence of anatomy, paleontology, and embryology, for example.

4. The progress of science in correlating or reducing mental states to physical states has weakened our confidence in an entity called mind (Chapter 18).

5. The decline of supernatural religions acts to deflate any supernatural claims for intuitive knowledge.

6. Analysis of mental activities shows that introspection is not always reliable. Intelligence, volition, ambition, belief, and so on, are now better understood, not as mental entities, but as dispositions to behave in certain ways. Their significance is as much public and social as private (Chapter 18).

7. In Freud's view of the unconscious, we are seldom aware of all our own basic drives, impulses, and motives; only the tip of the iceberg of our consciousness is visible. We rationalize. This tends to reduce the stature and trustworthiness of intuition.

8. Marx, opposing Hegel, argued that consciousness is not autonomous, but depends on class; there is therefore no intuition of the truth as such, but only of a bourgeois, or feudal, or proletarian view of truth. Philosophy is, like literature and art, an ideology or class product; there is no justification for claiming its universal validity.

9. In the sociology of knowledge (Chapter 11) it is also denied that mind can grasp the truth directly and absolutely, on the ground that the validity of ideas is never independent of how and where they originated. The sociologist Vilfredo Pareto argued that people "tend to paint a varnish of logic over their conduct" by providing various plausible explanatory "derivations" which conceal their underlying modes of conduct or "residues."

10. Rationality (as discussed in Chapter 16) becomes, upon analysis, rather hazy as a distinctive attribute of mind.

11. It used to be thought that such things as "the golden moun-

tain" must have some kind of "intentional" existence, because you and I can both think of it and assert true propositions about it. But the substantial clarification of descriptive phrases (Chapter 7) relieves us of concern about how the mind can by self-examination or intuition produce any "intentional" entities. Descriptive phrases are not names.

12. One of the lesser known travels of Gulliver was to the island of Lagado, where a professor at the Grand Academy showed him a computer machine, and explained:

> Everyone knew how laborious the usual Method is of attaining to Arts and Sciences; whereas by [this] Contrivance, the most ignorant Person, at a reasonable Charge, and with a little bodily Labour, may write books in Philosophy, Poetry, Politicks, Law, Mathematics, and Theology, without the least assistance from Genius or Study.

This is still a little far-fetched! A century ago, Engels rhetorically asked: "Man will some day reproduce the brain in a machine, but will the essence of thought thereby be captured?" But if the essence of thought is to operate with signs, or to follow rules, or to pursue a goal, or to solve problems, or to weigh alternatives, or to make decisions based on evidence, then the essence of thought is already captured; the brain, however, with its enormous number of nerve cells, is probably much too complex to reproduce in a machine! Developments in cybernetics have removed some of the mystical aura surrounding mental processes.

Minds and Machines

"Intuition is bankrupt!" says Quine. The twelve factors that have contributed to the erosion—or perhaps collapse—of our confidence in intuition have had profound results. The great insight of Descartes, *cogito ergo sum*—the self or person is a being that *thinks*—is intact. How could our unique mental abilities be duplicated by a machine? If we no longer can rely on a direct mental apprehension of the truth, what has happened to man's place in the world? The parallel between minds and machines is disturbing. But to ask whether a machine can think is to foreclose any fruitful analysis.

There are some mental activities (such as playing chess) that can certainly be performed by the computer. If the machine makes the proper move, should we inquire whether it "thinks"? or "weighs the possibilities"? or "remembers previous moves"? or "wants to win"? or "has an image in mind"? When you add a column of figures, do you "think"? If you get on a train in China, ignorant of the language, but with a slip of paper which has the ideogram of a station, and you watch for it and get off properly, then you have acted intelligently, whether the ideogram in fact means "Celestial Tranquility" or "Down with the Running Dogs of Imperialism." Many "mental processes" requiring "intelligence" or "deliberation" or "the essence of thought" are now being performed successfully by machines. Computers have also written poems and composed music. We inquire in Chapter 22 into the creativity, spontaneity, novelty, and infinite variety of mind. Does it indeed have greater variety than a machine?

The computing machine is a complex interrelation of electric switches. Each switch at any moment is either on or off (current either does or does not travel through it) ; and it is never both on and off. The switch thus corresponds to the proposition in logic, which is either true or false (excluded middle) and never both true and false (contradiction; see Chapter 6). Thus, there is a formal analogy between a machine and a set of propositions. A machine may be regarded as the concrete embodiment, or instantiation, of an axiomatic system; it is, so to speak, the word made flesh. Therefore, the limits established by Gödel on the consistency and completeness of axiomatic systems apply to machines. Since no one can say whether these limits clearly apply to the mind, do we now have a theoretical differentiation between the powers of minds and machines? This is an open question. So far as I can tell, there are at this moment two sorts of task which the machine cannot perform (i.e., for which no adequate program has yet been written) : the recognition of pattern; and the translation of languages. (There is some reason to suspect that these may be aspects of a single problem.) It is human linguistic activity which we must explore in this chapter.

Language and Mind

That there is a close interrelation between language and mind is of course not a new discovery. ("Ontology recapitulates philology," says J. G. Miller, in a witty parody of the biological aphorism, "ontogeny recapitulates phylogeny.") I have quoted Wittgenstein, "if we spoke a different language, we would perceive a somewhat different world." Let me add a remark by G. E. Moore: "It seems to me very curious that language . . . should have grown up as if it were expressly designed to mislead philosophers"; and by Heidegger: "Existence is itself essentially linguistic." Indeed, before our century, Nietzsche wrote, "By the grammatical structure of one group of languages, everything runs smoothly for one kind of philosophical system, whereas the way is, as it were, barred for certain other possibilities." And, going back, Mill said, "The . . . rules of grammar are the means by which the forms of language are made to correspond with the universal forms of thought." Chauncey Wright observed, "[the] languages employed by philosophers are themselves lessons in ontology." Lichtenberg pointed out that verbs of personal existence are irregular in all languages and remarked that "all our philosophy is an improving of linguistic usage." Much earlier, Bacon said, "words plainly force and overrule the understanding." (He called this the "Idol of the Market Place.") Aristotle called spoken words "the symbols of mental experience"; and Heraclitus said, "the Logos is revealed in speech." No doubt one can go back even further.

How did language originate? There is no human community anywhere, no matter how primitive, without language; and human language is radically different from animal communication. How did human language start? Like the sounds made by animals (the "bow-wow theory")? as exclamatory interjection (the "pooh-pooh theory")? as imitation of sounds (the "ding-dong theory")? Was the earliest utterance, in Hamann's words, "neither a noun nor a verb but at least a whole period"? Was it poetry?—as Vico maintained. There is just no evidence whatsoever on the origin of language.

In Chapter 7 I discussed how language bites on to the world. Let me add here some empirical considerations relevant to the intimate relation between language and mind.

Natural Languages

Natural languages (this category excludes artificial languages such as Esperanto, formal languages such as logic and mathematics, and such "languages" as art, or music, or flowers, or drafting, or the genetic code) have six identifiable characteristics:

1. The foundation of language is *speech*: writing, signs, or gestures are not of the essence.
2. Speech acts are *social* and *directed*: speaking, like fighting or like making love, is an act done to someone else. And speaking is *reversible;* that is, the speaker can also be a listener. (Talking only to one's self is like masturbating.)
3. Language is an institution of a *community*: it is governed by the *rules* of those who speak it; it is not innate, but must be learned. Infants (in fact or in fiction) who are reared by animals (Kaspar Hauser, or the wild child of Aveyron) must all be later taught how to speak. (Wittgenstein refers to a "language-game" as a "form of life.")
4. Units of sound (phonemes) may be combined in various ways, according to the syntax or morphology of the language,[1] into a *system, "ou tout se tient"* (Antoine Meillet) : the whole thing holds together. The vocabulary of individual sounds is not as important as the relationships between them. (This is the thrust of linguistic structuralism.) Human beings can therefore use language creatively; they can speak and understand sentences never uttered before. Max Black calls this the "productive aspect" of language.

[1] Different languages of course use different combinations of the twenty to forty phonemes which we can pronounce. Greek and Latin, for example, had to translate the Hebrew phoneme *sh* into *s* (as in Moses, Solomon, Jesus, Isaiah) . Russian had to borrow the Hebrew *sh* letter.

5. Language is *meaningful*: it expresses thoughts and wishes; it evokes responses; it connects with the world; it helps determine "the facts" (Chapter 9) and our self-knowledge (Chapter 18).

6. Languages are in a process of constant *change*. New words are being coined all the time. T. H. Huxley coined *agnosticism;* Whewell coined *physicist* and *scientist* in 1840; Thomas Gray introduced *picturesque* in 1740; the first appearance of *capitalism* is in 1854; *civilization* does not appear in Samuel Johnson's *Dictionary* (1775); *gas* was coined by Van Helmont; *altruism* by Comte. If we still shudder at *camp* or *funky,* we should remember that Herbert Spencer denounced *educational,* and Mill called *sociology* (the coinage of Comte) a "convenient barbarism." Shakespeare coined (or at least is the first recorded user of) *assassination, bump, critic, disgraceful, dwindle, fitful, gloomy, impartial, lonely, sportive, bare-faced,* and *countless.* And words disappear: *swive* and *insisture,* for example.

Meanings of words frequently change. *Villain* once meant "serf" or "peasant"; *nice* meant "precise"; *naughty* meant "needy"; in Chaucer, *lust* means "innocent delight." When is a change of meaning legitimized? Dictionary editors face this question constantly. The lexicographer Philip Gove has posed a number of questions on legitimate usage. Can a road have a *blemish?* Does a camera *reveal?* Can charity be *relentless?* Can you *encounter* a dearth of material? Is a fact ever *elusive?* Can silence be *incessant?* Can one *sense* heresy? He quotes F. Scott Fitzgerald, "My uncle finally said, 'Why ye—es,' with a grave, hesitant face." (Can a face be *hesitant?*) And Agnes Repplier, "The child's quick temper subsided into listlessness." (Can temper become listlessness?) W. O. Douglas, "The question . . . was a seesaw contest of opposed ideas." (Can ideas be in a *seesaw* contest?)

Expansion of meaning, of course, is frequently deliberate: a metaphor is, literally, a carrying beyond. When Henry James refers to "blotting-paper voices," or Chandler to "stainless-steel voices," or Faulkner to "the viciousness of stamped tin," the tension between the primary meaning of these words and their new usage fuses disparate elements to create imaginative new effects. Sometimes an established sense of a word is actually a "dead metaphor" (e.g., a fork in the road, an eyelid, an electric bulb). When do we applaud a metaphor (an "iron will") and when do we condemn it as a catachresis, or misuse ("to take arms against a sea of troubles")?

Can a native speaker ever "misuse" his language? James Michener's editor objected to his using *transpire* for "occur." Michener insisted, however, and it was this very usage by him which was cited as the authority in the subsequent *Random House Dictionary*. I once got on a very crowded bus in New York, and asked the driver, "How are you doing?" "I'm doing a land-house business," he replied. Should I have corrected him? A German learning English once complained to me that, when he tried to study, his mind often went cotton picking (he meant wool gathering). Was he wrong? He also once said, "in 1933 the Communist party in Germany was in shatters" (shreds and tatters, no doubt!).

The judicial process is another area in which meanings grow and change. Law courts are called upon to decide whether tomatoes are "fruit" and whether airplanes are "ships." Does an ordinance which prohibits "vehicles" in the park exclude —or should I say include— bicycles? ambulances? baby carriages? Does the Constitutional requirement that "Congress shall make no law . . . abridging the freedom of speech, or of the press" forbid libel and slander actions? or restrictions on pornography? Is a corporation a person? It has been defined as "invisible, incorporeal, intangible, immortal, existing only in contemplation of Law, a mystical body not found in the world of sense, an impalpable creation of human thought, a figure of speech, an abstraction, a fiction, a mere name." But the corporation is held to be, as the person is, the subject of legal rights and obligations; it cannot be deprived of life, liberty, property, or the equal protection of the laws.

One aspect of how a word functions is in its pure sensory stimulus, as of course poets realize. It is not merely the *mot juste* which cannot be replaced; every word carries a unique atmosphere. The eighteenth-century actor David Garrick said that "that blessed word *Mesopotamia*" spoken by the famous preacher George Whitefield could make people laugh or cry. James wrote: "an excellent old German lady . . . used to describe to me her *Sehnsucht* that she might yet visit 'Philadelphia,' whose wondrous name had always haunted her." One step in Hatha Yoga withdrawal is "to repeat 12,000 times, with a quiet mind, the Syllable of Obeisance AUM." Would any other syllable get the same result? When Max Beerbohm was told that *gondola* was the most beautiful word in English, he retorted that *scrofula* sounded the same to him. Santayana believed that "languages express national character." Would Israel be a different nation today if Yiddish rather than Hebrew had been adopted? What if North Americans spoke Spanish? Why do we use roman numerals on monuments? Language functions expressively as well as cognitively.

The evocative overtones of a word raise the problem of synonymy (which in turn complicates the issue of deciding whether a proposition such as "a bachelor is an unmarried man" is analytic or not; see Chapter 5) . The dictionary offers us, for example, the following synonyms for *help*: aid, assist, strengthen, support, succor, sustain, benefit, improve, relieve, alleviate, further. Are these interchangeable with *help* in every context? Are there not significant shades of difference among them? Consider the nuances in the variations within a single word: *design, designer, designing, designate*. Consider the overtones of alleged synonyms: animals sweat; men perspire; ladies glow. I am firm; you are obstinate; he is pig-headed. Russell suggested: I have reconsidered; you have changed your mind; he has gone back on his word. It has been asserted that the only pair of genuine synonyms in English is *gorse* and *furze*.

Linguistic Variety

I have mentioned the influence of language on philosophy. It is therefore important to take into account the fact that there is great variation between linguistic structures. Thus, the relation between the subject and the predicate, and the sharp distinction between nouns and verbs, which seem so basic to us, are far from universal. In some languages, people do not say "the sky is blue," but "the sky blues"; they would therefore not be likely to regard colors as the properties of substances. (Note that we say, "the moon shines.") In some languages of the Caucasus, they do not say, "I see him," but "he is seen by me." Do the active and the passive "have the same meaning"? Linguists disagree. Is "coming into the world" the same as "being born"? Japanese has three "passive" voices: a "true" passive ("it is bought"); a potential ("it can fly"); and suffering the result of an act (e.g., someone's death). A passive may also be used to soften a request ("will it be done?" rather than "will you do it?"). Hopi verbs have no tense; Hopis do not understand "tomorrow is another day" because they regard the day as returning, rather than new. Navaho verbs, on the other hand, indicate whether the action referred to is in progress, or is about to happen, or occurs from time to time. (How much subtler than our "present" and "future"!) The Dravidian Kota language has no adjectives; thus, "he is a strength-man."

Note some peculiarities of language. In English we eat bread, but we do not eat apple. We pluralize *house* and *foot,* but not *deer* or *snow.* Does it make a difference whether the woman caught two fish or two fishes? (Some philosophers think that these linguistic idiosyncrasies reflect profound ontological substructures.) In Japanese there is no separate word for numbers, such as *five;* there are different ways of saying five men, five birds, five trees, etc. In French, *le poêle* (m.) means stove; *la poêle* (f.) means frying pan. Some linguists find significance in whether a noun is masculine, feminine, or neuter. Latin has no definite article *the;* perhaps that is why the ancients had no problems about "intentional existence" and definite descriptions (that is, *mons aureus* means either *the* golden mountain or *a* golden mountain). Chinese has no verb *to be;* Hebrew has no word for *is.* Hungarian has one word for *he, she,* and *it*—and we wonder how they manage until we realize that English has one plural *they.* Russian has one word for "foot and lower leg." Why doesn't English? Chinese has a word *pa* meaning "a short man standing as tall as he can"; another word, *hoo,* means "to find bail for the lighter offenses of females." The Arabs have some six thousand words for *camel,* including about fifty for pregnant camels. If you find this multiplicity startling, look at *Webster's New International*: it lists about a thousand words for *grass.* In Russian there is no single, simple word for *to go* or *to come;* rather, the verbs that express these concepts simultaneously reveal, for example, how often the act is done, how long it lasts, and so on.

John Searle has remarked how extraordinary it is that sentences in one language can be translated into another.

Word Origins

If there is a close connection between language and mind, then, of course, etymology would be another source of interest. Philosophers as diverse as Dewey and Heidegger have been unduly influenced by word origins. Austin says, "a word never—well, hardly ever—shakes off its etymology." He points out that in an *accident,* something befalls you; when you make a *mistake,* you take the wrong one; in an *error,* you stray; when you *deliberate,* you weigh up. Some philosophers think it significant that (etymologically) to *refer* is to carry back, that to *tell* is to count, and that *thing* once meant a public assembly.

Some common verbs, for example, *fix,* have an astonishing variety of meanings: repair, arrange, do, make, order, mix, procure, finish, lend, give, use, get, bespeak. And there are some elemental words that have in fact antithetical senses. (Freud was much impressed by a book written on this subject by Karl Abel.) Thus, *loose* means the same as *unloose; valuable* as *invaluable; cleave* means both to "cling closely" and to "divide by force"; *with* has a sense opposite to its usual one (of association) in *withdraw, withstand, withhold,* or *withershins* (contrariwise). In old Saxon, *bat* meant "good." In Latin, *altus* means both "high" and "deep"; *sacer,* both "sacred" and "accursed"; *clamare* means "to cry out," but *clam* means "silently." In German, *Boden* means both "attic" and "ground floor." Compare German *Loch* and English *lock.* Phonetic alterations sometimes distinguish opposed senses: Latin *siccus* (dry) and *succus* (juice); German *stumm* (dumb) and *Stimme* (voice). In certain German-English pairs, the consonant order has been reversed, but the meaning has been preserved: *Topf, pot; Balken, club; kreischen, shriek; täuwen, wait.* In Egyptian, there are such single words as "oldyoung" (meaning "young"); "farnear" (meaning "near"); and "outsideinside" (meaning "inside"). Karl Abel concludes "Man has not been able to acquire even his oldest and simplest conceptions otherwise than in contrast with their opposites; he only gradually learnt to separate the two sides of the antithesis." Freud uses this linguistic material as evidence for his own views that children like to reverse the sound of words, that slips of the tongue often use contraries, and that dreams frequently employ opposites.

Vagueness, Ambiguity, and Context

Much has been written on the vagueness of natural language. Such words as *rich, rational, sane, happy, living* seem incurably indeterminate, their edges irremediably blurred. Waismann speaks of their "open texture"; Quine of "the marginal hangers-on" of their extension. This vagueness might, theoretically, be eliminated; we might decide, for example, that a hill becomes a mountain at 400 feet or that *rich* means "having $1,000,000"; but at what a price! Language would be utterly impoverished.

If vagueness is like the blurred focus of a camera lens, then ambiguity is like a double image: it projects more than one meaning. Many simple words are thus afflicted with "polysemia"— multiplicity of meaning: *bank, ball,* and *jade,* for example. Consider a *hard* rock, a *hard* question, and *hard* liquor: are these different words, or one word used metaphorically? Another aspect of ambiguity is "amphiboly": Peirce quotes, "A lawyer told a colleague that he thought a client of his more critical of himself than of his rivals." There is also the ambiguity of scope: is a beautiful young girl the same as a young beautiful girl? And ambiguity of word order: compare "he stepped on the rock deliberately" and "he stepped deliberately on the rock."

Structural linguistic ambiguity plagues the programers of translating machines; examples are endless: "He made an observation" (did he say something or did he see something?) ; "he pressed his suit" (a tailor or a lawyer?); "our mothers bore us"; and the triply ambiguous "Helen made the robot fast while she ate." One gem is the translation by a machine of "the spirit is willing but the flesh is weak" into "whisky is good but meat is rotten." How would you program a machine to translate "business is business" or "boys will be boys" or "that's that"?

Here we see that context influences meaning. (F. C. S. Schiller argued this position before the time was ripe.) Whenever words are spoken, there is a background or situation, a tone of voice, an accompanying shrug or gesture, a raising of the eyebrows. That is why many jokes which you laugh at when you hear them aren't funny in print. When the philosopher Jeremy Bentham wanted someone to read aloud to him, he was careful to employ only persons who had monotonous voices. If you were to remind me that I had made you a certain promise, I might reply nastily, "O.K., O.K., so I promised!" If you continue to disagree with me, I might hint, "The door isn't locked, you know." When Frederick the Great showed some of his poetry to Voltaire, Voltaire commented, "Sire, you are a great king!" Suppose you hear me say, "Bert is sober today." To understand language we must always examine the context, read between the lines, see how the locution is put to use, note what effect it has. The same words may be spoken with irony, or sarcasm, or innuendo; they may be a request or an invitation. What reply is being made here:

> *Macbeth.* If we should fail?
> *Lady Mac.*   We fail!

A "speech act" encompasses not only the spoken words but also *illocution* (what was accomplished in the utterance, in view of the relevant conventions) and *perlocution* (the actual effect on the hearer). These are, along with *sense* and *reference* (Chapter 7), important aspects of meaning. (J. L. Austin stressed this.)

A Perfect Language?

Can a language be corrected or improved so as to become perfect? Every natural language is limited by its vocabulary; that is why English has had to import *ersatz, hubris, élan, chutzpah, taboo, simpático,* and *shibui.* Could we eventually remedy all the inadequacies of English (or of any other single language)? Suppose we borrowed whatever expressions we had to; and suppose we clarified *love* into *eros* and *agape;* and *know* into *savoir* and *connaître;* and supplied Aristotle with the word he wanted when he wrote, in the *Nicomachean Ethics,* "the man who exceeds in his desires is called ambitious, the man who falls short unambitious, while the intermediate person has no name." Could we then arrive at a logically perfect language (as was hoped for by Descartes, Leibniz, Cassirer, Frege, Husserl, and the early Wittgenstein)? Could we ever attain the perfection of formal languages such as *Principia Mathematica*?

This question reveals a profound misunderstanding. As Wittgenstein later put it:

> Our language can be seen as an ancient city; a maze of little streets and squares, of old and new houses, and of houses with additions from various periods; and this surrounded by a multitude of new boroughs with straight regular streets and uniform houses.

Language is not logic. There are no invariants in language; grammar has no essence; syntax and morphology differ from language to language. Nothing in language "corresponds with the world" or reflects "the grain of reality." Languages can be translated only roughly. None is ideal. There is no clear standard for perfection or adequacy, as there is for a chess set with a pawn missing, or a dictionary with a page torn out.

It is amusing to note how chauvinism enters into the evaluation of languages. Bentham said, "of all known languages, English is . . . that in which . . . the most important of the properties desirable in every language are to be found." Diderot insisted that French had the greatest "naturalness" in its word order. The sixteenth-century Spaniard Huarte said that "the rational soul meeting with the temperament necessary to invent a very eloquent language" must hit on Latin. Fichte said German was the best language. Cornford declared that "when once we go beyond the names of objects like tables or trees and of simple actions such as running and eating, no Greek word has an exact equivalent in English, no important abstract conception covers the same area."

Language and Meanings

The "original sin of metaphysics," says John Searle, is to "read the features of language into the world." One of the most fruitful achievements of philosophical analysis is the disclosure of how language and grammar often mislead us. Moore, Russell, Ayer, and Ryle have warned against "systematically misleading expressions." We must not suppose that an "insane murderer" and an "alleged murderer" are two kinds of murderer, merely because the two phrases are grammatically similar; an "alleged murderer" may not be a murderer at all. If we say that "the Queen of England is pretty" and that "the Queen of France is imaginary," we must not be deceived into thinking that there exists in the world some entity called "the Queen of France" about which we can make true statements. Descriptive phrases such as these do not denote, as Russell showed in his Theory of Descriptions (Chapter 7). If we say, "this road goes to London" and "this line goes to infinity," we must not think that infinity is a place like London and that we will get to it at the end of the road; rather, it means that the line will never end. If we say, "I am hunting a lion" and "I am imagining a unicorn," we are misled if we infer that the unicorn must have some sort of objective existence since it is the object of a transitive verb.

Nevertheless, traditional philosophy has been strewn with blunders no less egregious. The ontological argument for the existence of God rests on the assumption that the phrase "something than which nothing greater can be conceived" denotes a being that exists in reality. Words or phrases used as if they were names may actually have no reference at all (Chapter 7). "The average American loves baseball" denotes no one; neither does "procrastination is the thief of time." Philosophers concerned with "the ontological commitment of discourse" are fascinated by such insidious linguistic parallels as "there is a possibility that Bert may come" and "there is an apple that Bert may eat"; "there is a meaning which can be given to Bert's cries" and "there is a book which can be given to Bert's wife"; "Bert's enterprise lacks tenacity" and "Bert's book lacks a cover." In these examples, we must not be recklessly induced to hypostatize verbal twists into metaphysical entities; possibilities, meanings, and tenacity are not in any way like apples, books, and covers. Opponents of abortion caution us that we may abort a "possible Darwin." What kind of a Darwin is that? We have noted, as one of the grounds for dissatisfaction with traditional logic (Chapter 6), the fact that the form "all x is y" cloaks sharply different kinds of assertions.

Students of structural linguistics have also stressed the difficulty in making any formal distinctions between such superficially similar, but radically different, usages as "Bert is eager to please" and "Bert is easy to please"; or between "Bert expected her to come" and "Bert persuaded her to come."

Thus, any connection between this living, changing, vague, ambiguous, faltering, irregular, diverse, makeshift, haphazard, piecemeal, misleading, and imperfect human enterprise called language, and some realm of eternal Meanings, should be regarded skeptically. We must staunchly resist the temptation to suppose that meanings subsist timelessly in some celestial warehouse, waiting to be thought of, as if they were minerals in a museum awaiting a suitable verbal label. Communication in language stands (or wobbles!) on its own two feet; it is continuous with gesture; it is not a process of coding and decoding independent meanings. When a child first learns to speak, we are wrong if we assume that he is acquiring a technique by which to express some nonlinguistic thoughts or by which to understand the thoughts of others. When the poet asserts that he needs (for example) a word somewhere between *stimulate* and *encourage,* we must not be deluded into supposing that he has "some meaning in mind" for which an appropriate word must be found: there may not *be* any such word, *or meaning!* Not every experience becomes knowledge (Chapter 2). Although I sometimes think that a word I am looking for "is on the tip of my tongue," it does not always turn up: I may be mistaken. If I am unhappy right now with the way I am expressing myself, that does not imply that "I have something in mind" more accurate or satisfactory. "How can I tell what I mean," asks C. Day Lewis, "until I see what I say?"

But the error is widespread. Thus Chuang-tze (a fourth-century B.C. follower of Lao-tze) said,

> The fish trap exists because of the fish: once you've gotten the fish, you can forget the trap. The rabbit snare exists because of the rabbit: once you've gotten the rabbit, you can forget the snare. Words exist because of meanings: once you've gotten the meanings, you can forget the words.

And Michael Drayton (a contemporary of Shakespeare) wrote that, beneath the surface of the mind, there is

> . . . something more
> That thought holds under lock
> And hath no key of words to open it.

> 'Tis but the smallest pieces of the mind
> That pass the narrow organ of the voice
> The great remain behind in the vast orb
> Of the apprehension!

And, in the words of the Russian psychologist Vigotsky, "Thought is born through words . . . a thought unembodied in words remains a shadow."

All of these metaphors are seriously misleading. *"Meanings" do not exist apart from words* even though *meanings are not identical to words*. Meanings are related to words much as propositions are related to sentences (see Chapter 7). Meanings are not supernatural entities somehow attached to words, or infused into words, as souls are to bodies. If two words "have the same meaning," they can be *used* interchangeably; but there is not some one thing possessed by the two words in common, as if it were a car owned jointly by Bert and Fred. A word when used may be more or less adequate to its purpose: that is, a word fits a meaning or purpose as a shirt fits a body, more or less well; but, although there are naked bodies, there are no naked meanings. "One always in speaking says more than one intends to," says Sartre; but, alas! there is no other or better way to say what one intends. (Remember Cratylus, who gave up speaking altogether.) Croce also seems to me to err in saying that expression is to the mind what bookkeeping is to a business; this suggests (mistakenly) that a mind could carry on without language as easily as a business could without records. The relationship is complex. Mead oversimplifies when he claims that mind is reducible without residue to language; so does Husserl in saying that "we can make our speech conform in a pure measure to what is intuited in its full clarity." These formulations minimize and distort the problem of how language is actually used. The human linguistic predicament is unique and inescapable; we are immersed in it; we can never see it from the outside. "We feel," says Wittgenstein, "as if we had to repair a torn spider's web with our fingers. . . . Philosophy is a battle against the bewitchment of our intelligence by means of language."

The Functions of Language

Of course language functions in many different ways. Its most familiar function, with which we have been concerned in this chapter, is *cognitive*: language transmits information. But it also operates noncognitively, or *expressively,* when we attend to the words themselves and to their atmosphere. Poetry often combines the cognitive and the expressive:

> The fair breeze blew, the white foam flew
> The furrow followed free
> We were the first that ever burst
> Into that silent sea.
>
> —Samuel Taylor Coleridge, "Rime of
> the Ancient Mariner"

> When Ajax strives some rock's vast weight to throw,
> The line, too, labors, and the words move slow;
> Not so when swift Camilla scours the plain,
> Flies o'er th' unbending corn, and skims along the main.
>
> —Alexander Pope, "Essay on Criticism"

> I sprang to the stirrup, and Joris and he;
> I galloped, Dirck galloped, we galloped all three.
>
> —Robert Browning, "How They Brought the
> Good News from Ghent to Aix"

In these verses the rhythm and sound of the words are expressive in themselves. Language is also used expressively in prayer; and when a man whispers "sweet nothings" into his wife's ear, or tells her she looks "scrumptious"; and in such sounds as "wow!" and "scram!"; and when a politician or preacher or salesman uses words to evoke emotional responses.

A third area of language is the ceremonial. Here the words are not necessarily either cognitive or expressive, but *performatory*: they are themselves the sole instrument of the action. Examples are the railroad conductor's "all aboard!" and the croupier's *"les jeux sont faits."* Also performatory are "I thank you, apologize, warn, greet, guarantee, promise, welcome," etc. These words are complete speech acts. They do not describe the acts of thanking, apologizing, warning, etc., but constitute those acts. They are not propositions which can be true or false. If a man says, "I bid you good morning," that does it (even though he may hate you!). The use of language solely to establish social relations is called "phatic communion" by Malinowski; in our culture, "hya doin'?" exemplifies this. In all of these performatory utterances, as in oaths, incantations, passwords, and rituals, there must be no change in the exact words. If you are asked whether you take this woman to be your lawful wedded wife, and you answer "yes" instead of "I do," you may turn out not to be married. The difference between "my arm goes up" and "I raise my arm" may well be performatory; that is, the latter sentence does not isolate an obscure volition over and above the rising of my arm, but serves to make me responsible for the action (see Chapter 20). In its performatory function, language is continuous with gestures and symbols: the handshake, the military salute, the lawyer's LS on a document, the gestures of the auctioneer and baseball umpire. (Gestures of course also function expressively.) Austin estimates that there are over a thousand performatory verbs in English.

Language also functions to tell a story, to declaim, to hypnotize, to play a part, to imagine, to soothe, to ask, to deceive, to demonstrate one's feelings, and in endless other ways.

Ostension and Established Meanings

Dewey quotes an anecdote from Ogden and Richards' *Meaning of Meaning* which perfectly illustrates the problem of *ostensive definitions*. How do people actually learn what words mean? How does language get off the ground in the first place?

> A visitor in a savage tribe wanted on one occasion "the word for *table*. There were five or six boys standing around, and, tapping the table with my forefinger I asked 'What is this?' One boy said it was *dodela,* another that it was an *etanda,* a third stated that it was *bokali,* a fourth that it was *elamba,* and the fifth said it was *meza*." After congratulating himself on the richness of the vocabu-

> lary of the language the visitor found later "that one boy had thought he wanted the word for tapping; another for . . . the material of which the table was made; another . . . the word for hardness; another . . . the name for that which covered the table; and the last . . . gave us the word *meza*, table."

I remember as a boy reading, in a story about whaling, "the boats hit the water with a simultaneous splash." The accompanying illustration showed two small boats being released from the davits of a sailing vessel and sending up clouds of spray on reaching the water. I thought, naturally, that *simultaneous* meant "full of wet spray." Could it be that I have made other errors which I have not yet discovered? There is no alternative to learning what words mean other than being shown the objects they denote, but the method is not infallible. Quine calls this problem the "inscrutability of reference." Try pointing to the shape of a cloud, to its size, to its color. Ostension presupposes a contrast: can you point to air? Ostension, like language, is embedded in social convention; it, too, is a "form of life."

It is merely a historical or empirical fact that words are used as they are; but once a word has been given a use, it is awkward to ignore it. There is little point in "correcting" people who "misuse" such words as *decimate* and *livid;* remember Michener and *transpire.* Wittgenstein asks, "Make this experiment: *say* 'It's cold here' and *mean* 'It's hot here.' Can you do it?" Words are mere breaths of air, or scribbled pencil marks, but as used in a "language game" by a speech community they are not arbitrary. No concentration or mental effort on your part can accomplish the lofty aim of Humpty Dumpty:

> "When I use a word," Humpty Dumpty said, in a rather scornful tone, "it means just what I choose it to mean—neither more nor less."
>
> "The question is," said Alice, "whether you can make words mean so many different things."
>
> "The question is," said Humpty Dumpty, "which is to be master —that's all."

If the Emperor declares, "I am a divinity, all men must bow before me in adoration," there is mighty little satisfaction to be gotten if you say to yourself, as your forehead scrapes the floor, that you are only doing it for the exercise.

Animal Language

I mentioned earlier the unsolved problem of the origin of language and the fact that human language differs radically from animal communication. An animal utters a fixed number of signals, each of which is associated with a specific behavior or situation. No bee ever repeats another bee's dance unless it has had the same experience which prompted the first bee's dance. Animal communication is automatic, invariant, monotonous, and more or less congenital. Thus, the vervet, an African monkey, sounds a special "snake chutter" when it spots an Egyptian cobra or puff adder, and a different warning sound when an eagle or a cheetah is near; it also emits a specialized "lost cry" when a baby is separated from its mother. Each of these sounds is produced only and always in response to the proper stimulus. When a mode of animal communication has a dimension (e.g., the pitch of a bird song), that dimension is generally related directly to the degree of the animal's fear, for example, or hunger (that is, the shriller the pitch, the more frightened or hungry the bird). Some bird songs are entirely innate, or "precoded" (doves have no ability to change their vocalizations); others are entirely learned (some birds adopt the vocal patterns of their foster parents). Finally, there are bird "dialects."

Human language is always learned, however; it is not mechanically controlled by specific external stimuli or internal states; it is not restricted to the communication of information; it is innovative and creative. People can accommodate to new situations; they can behave diversely; they can pronounce and understand an infinite number of new sentences. Animals, although intelligent enough to solve problems and follow complicated instructions, do not have this ability. Human language is sui generis, and as much an attribute ("species-specific") of *Homo sapiens* as building dams is of beavers.

Explanation of Linguistic Ability

Human language sets us apart and therefore requires an explanation. There are few sharp boundaries between men and animals. Babies and kittens, for example, play in the same way and perform identical biological functions. Chimpanzees have almost the same physiological equipment for speech that human beings have, but no chimpanzee has ever learned to say a word. (However, in a research project begun by Allan and Beatrice Gardner, chimpanzees are being taught to use and combine "linguistically" a number of visual signs. Chimps also seem to learn the sign language of the deaf. And there is some evidence that there is an area in the left hemisphere of the human brain specifically associated with interpreting segmental phonemes.) The organs that human beings use for speech have not evolved uniquely for that activity; speech is an "overlaid" function, accomplished by organs which have other jobs to do. That is why we cannot ordinarily speak when we are under heavy physical exertion, or when eating unmasticated food. Our control over our speech organs is tenuous. Yet all children, regardless of intelligence, easily learn to speak the language of their community, correctly and accentlessly.

The language-learning capacity of children has been the crux of a dispute between Noam Chomsky and B. F. Skinner. Chomsky maintains that a special ability must be posited to account for language learning, but Skinner asserts that language is learned, just as everything else is, by "operant conditioning" (stimulus, response, and reward or punishment). This is a twentieth-century version of the seventeenth-century dispute between Locke and Leibniz: is the mind at birth a blank tablet (*tabula rasa*) on which experience writes? or are there veins in the marble which influence what we learn? Chomsky writes,

> The general features of grammatical structure are common to all languages and reflect certain fundamental properties of the mind ... certain language universals that set limits to the variety of human language . . . are not learned; rather they provide the organizing principles that make language learning possible. . . . By attribut-

ing such principles to mind, as an innate property, it becomes possible to account for the quite obvious fact that the speaker of a language knows a great deal that he has not learned.

In arguing for a tacit linguistic *competence* which underlies actual *performance,* Chomsky maintains the distinctions drawn earlier by Saussure between *langue* and *parole* and by Hjelmslev between *schema* and *usage.*

I believe that it is not warranted to postulate a specific human attribute called linguistic competence. For all the reasons mentioned in this chapter, there are no universals in linguistics, no invariants among all languages. There is indeed much that remains mysterious about language; for example, whether all the rules may be stated explicitly (recall the example cited in Chapter 2 of ordering adjectives and of substituting *highly* for *very*); but knowing how to use language is no more mysterious than other instances of knowing how. It is also curious that an adult cannot learn a second language in the easy way he learned his first; but neither can an adult learn to swim as easily as a child can. Would an infant learn to speak if, although isolated from adults, he were constantly within earshot of a radio? No one can say. (Macaulay as a child did not speak until once when a lady expressed concern after accidentally spilling hot tea in his lap; his first words then were, "Thank you, madam; the agony has somewhat abated.")

Continuity of Language with Other Human Activities

Descartes, in his *Discourse on Method,* asserted that it would be possible to make a machine so similar to an ape that we would be unable to tell them apart, but that no machine could ever duplicate the variety and innovativeness of human speech. But language is not in fact unique in the spectrum of human capacities. It is a part of an enormous range of social intercourse that embraces religious rituals; etiquette at a formal banquet; behavior in a crowded subway; in a museum; toward strangers on the street; when to smile; conventions of facial expression, posture, and stance. When you sit at a person's desk, and he answers the telephone, you studiously gaze into the middle distance and pretend not to hear what he is saying. One of the many difficulties which American troops faced in Vietnam was that our image of the self-reliant honest man, the man who stands up straight and looks you right in the eye, is the Indo-Chinese image of the gangster or barbarian. If you should drop in at the cocktail hour at any international gathering, you would observe the phenomenon of the migratory conversational unit: as some people in a group move closer to the others, others draw back, because some nationalities tend to stand closer together while talking than others do; a small group might in an hour circumnavigate quite a large room. Although the rules for driving a car may be learned quickly, they suffice to guide us through a potentially infinite number of different situations, often unpredictable and novel, seldom if ever reencountered. We all learn these codes of stance, mannerism, gesture, tactility, interpersonal behavior, and so on, in the same way that we learn the rules of language; yet we are equally unable to state them fully. People who violate them are looked at askance. I once saw a man lying on the floor of Grand Central Terminal in New York in order to examine the ceiling conveniently. That is indeed a notable piece of architecture, and best examined when on one's back; but the glances cast in his direction by the solid citizens who had to step over him would have petrified a lesser man. An amusing interchange of letters appeared in the *London Times*:

> Can anyone tell me the present rules for hand-shaking? I mean socially. Either I stick my hand out and they look at it as if it's the first one they've ever seen, or I decide not to, and they're reaching up my sleeve for it. What about hosts and guests? Shake on arrival but not on departure? Does sex come into it? Class?

The answer appeared a few days later:

> Shake hands with a Frenchman whenever you have not spoken to him for more than five minutes. Shake hands with an American almost as often as you would with a Frenchman. Shake hands with an Englishman as seldom as possible, and when forced to do so do it as quickly as possible. Wear your watch on the right wrist, so that in the event of being too quick on the draw you can quickly pretend you only wanted to know the time.

The *New Yorker* cartoon on p. 233 is also appropriate.

"*Lucille, do we kiss the Friedlanders?*"

Drawing by Saxon; © 1974
The New Yorker Magazine, Inc.

It seems to me ill advised to isolate language from the vast range of human social behavior. Our unreflective awareness of appropriate social conduct is similar to our intuitive sense of grammatical usage. The human species has evolved certain physiological capacities (e.g., to swim, but not to fly) and certain neurological dispositions to learn; no one can now say how specific these learning mechanisms are, but there seems to me no compelling need to postulate a special linguistic ability.

20

Intention, Action, and Free Will

THINK OF ALL the different terms by which we describe a single action, say, the killing of a person: murder, manslaughter, war, self-defense, capital punishment, lynching, euthanasia, infanticide, geronticide, religious sacrifice. In each case, someone is put to death, but the acts of putting to death are differentiated by the intention of the author of the act. *Intention* is an answer to the question, why did you do it? It is an explanation for human actions. This is a commonplace in the criminal law, which has long recognized *mens rea* (wicked or guilty intention) as a sine qua non for crime. Only intention distinguishes stealing from borrowing. And the law courts, free of philosophical qualms, have declared that "the state of a man's mind is as much a matter of fact as the state of his digestion." Theology has also thought intention a clear-cut concept. Abélard wrote:

> Actions which are right and actions which are far from right are done by good men and bad men alike. . . . God considers not the action but the spirit of the action. It is the intention, not the deed.

235

Difficulties with Intention as an Explanation

However, it becomes quite difficult to clarify exactly what intention is, and how it explains human actions. The following situations point up this difficulty:

1. Your enemy is traveling on an airplane; you insure his life and place a bomb on the plane, timed to explode in flight. Do you also intend to kill the other passengers? When you intend an action, do you intend the *consequences* of that action?

2. If you say you did not know there would be other passengers, are you thereby exonerated? Do you intend what you *ought* to know? In that case, did all Germans intend to torture their victims in the concentration camps? Did Einstein intend the destruction of Hiroshima?

3. Your enemy comes to lunch; you offer him a drink of water and you say to yourself, I wish it were poisoned. He suddenly drops dead. You later discover that poison had somehow gotten into the water supply. Did you intend his death? Does *desire* equal *intention*? or is *expectation* also required?

4. You decide to kill your enemy, who lives in the next town. You get your gun, jump into your car, and drive there. On the way, you accidentally run over and kill a man, who turns out to be your enemy. Can you intend the end or goal, but not the particular *means*?

5. You are mountain climbing with your friend, and your ineptitude causes his accidental death. Suppose you later discover, through psychoanalysis or introspection, that you really hated him. Can you have an intention and not be *aware* of it?

> In vain the sage, with retrospective eye,
> Would from the apparent what conclude the why,
> Infer the motive from the deed, and show
> That what we chanced was what we meant to do.
>
> —Alexander Pope

6. Are we always the best judges of our own intentions? Albert

Speer asserts in his memoirs, *Inside the Third Reich,* that he went back to Berlin at the end of the war to say good-bye to Hitler, but elsewhere that he went to warn Lüsschen to leave. Do you always believe the person who claims to be doing something, not for the money, but for the principle of the thing?

7. Can you intend an action if you are drunk? drugged? brainwashed? hypnotized? sleepwalking? Must an intentional action be *consciously* intended?

8. Oedipus intended to marry Jocasta; unknown to him, she was his mother. Did he intend to marry his mother? Is *belief* an element of intention? Remember the problem of the "referential opacity" of intentional or psychological verbs (Chapter 7): you cannot safely replace one description of a person by another, in propositions involving knowledge, belief, etc.

9. Can you intend to win at roulette? Can you intend (for the tenth time!) to give up smoking? Is *ability* an ingredient of intention or is hope enough? or must that hope be a rational hope?

10. You come upon your enemy lying down and you shoot him. (I'm sorry these examples are all so gory.) But it turns out that he was already dead. Can you intend the *impossible*? (Can you intend to find the greatest prime?)

11. Suppose your enemy was falling from the top of the Empire State Building; you shoot him as he passes the fifty-eighth floor. Can you intend the *inevitable*? (But we are all on our way to dusty death!)

12. The price of movie admissions goes up, and you decide not to go. Can you intend *not* to do something? Intentionally not acting may be called *forbearance*.

13. Kitty Genovese was murdered on the night of March 16, 1964, on a street in Forest Hills, New York, and no fewer than thirty-eight people living in apartment houses nearby heard her scream and saw her trying to escape; not one person intervened or even called the police. Did these onlookers intend her murder? If you, a good swimmer, ignore the cries of someone in the water calling for help, do you intend that

he drown? What if you are a poor swimmer? Can you intentionally *not act* when (unlike example 12) you may be said to have a moral obligation?

14. Old Karamazov was killed by his epileptic servant Smerdyakov; but Smerdyakov made Ivan realize, afterward, that it was he, Ivan, who wanted his old father dead: Smerdyakov was only carrying out Ivan's intention. Can you intend that *someone else* act? Can you intend someone else's *action*?

15. When may intentional behavior be equated with the following of *rules*? When you play chess, is every move intended to checkmate your opponent? Can you "play chess" and intend to lose?

16. Is behavior intentional when it is persistently directed toward a *goal*? Are bird migrations intentional? the motions of a sunflower?

17. So much crime and violence seem wanton, purposeless, unmotivated. Hannah Arendt has coined the phrase "the banality of evil." Is stealing or shooting "just for the hell of it" intentional?

18. As you are walking downstairs, you trip, and thrust your hand out to break the fall. Was your action intentional or *reflexive*? (Can the knee jerk reflex ever be intentional?)

19. As you are driving your car, a dog suddenly runs in front of you; you slam on the brakes. Was your action intentional or *reactive*? (Unlike the case of a knee jerk reflex, you have a motive.)

20. A commuter on a railroad, disgusted by the heat, dirt, delays, and crowds, decides on the spur of the moment to refuse to pay his fare. Is his action intentional or *impulsive*? (Note that there has been no deliberation.)

21. You are a kleptomaniac and cannot resist "swiping" something from a department store counter. Is your behavior intentional or *compulsive*?

22. At dinner, you are asked to pass the salt, and you do. Is your action intentional or *conventional*?

23. You are a chain smoker and reach for a cigarette. Is your action intentional or *habitual*?

24. The telephone rings while you are working and you reach to answer it. Is your action intentional or *automatic?*

25. Income tax time has come around again; you hate to pay taxes, but you do. Is your behavior intentional or *obligatory?* Or, your child is kidnaped, and a ransom is demanded. Is your payment intentional or *coerced?*

These examples illustrate the thesis that it is difficult, perhaps impossible, to pinpoint a mental act called intention. In Latin *intendo (arcum)* means "I aim (my bow)." It was thought that the mind could somehow be aimed or directed at a target; the usage survives in "this is what I aim to do." But, like trying to isolate the act of "volition" by subtracting "my arm goes up" from "I raise my arm," isolating the act or entity called "intention" seems hopeless. Like other "states of consciousness" (Chapter 18), intention seems intuitively clear at the outset, but becomes under scrutiny quite hazy. And the "mental act" often is a fiction: if I say, "I promise to meet you tomorrow," but do not do so, would you accept my excuse that, although I did indeed say "I promise," I was merely uttering the words and had no intention of meeting you? Can one justify saying the words and withholding a mental commitment? No—not because it is impossible to lie (nothing easier!), but because the spoken words *are* performatory: they *are* the commitment. Nothing is added to, or subtracted from, the words "I promise" by thinking "I intend (or do not intend) to keep this promise";[1] nor by saying, "I promise to keep my promise."

Actions and Reasons for Actions

Intentions are sometimes referred to as causes of human actions, but I think that is misleading. Intentions are better understood as motives, or reasons, which serve to characterize or describe an action and to explain why it was done. Human actions are not

[1] The "intentional fallacy" in art criticism is reference to what the artist or poet intended to do, as a criterion for evaluation of the finished product. We see how inappropriate this is in Chapter 21.

caused merely because they are intended. Your hunger may be the *reason* why you eat, but it does not *cause* you to eat: you might steadfastly refuse to eat no matter how hungry you are. Hamlet's actions were impelled by revenge, but they were not caused by revenge. Thus, such motivations as hunger or revenge are explanatory ex post facto, but have no predictive value since they may always be resisted.

The concept of action is logically primitive: it defies analysis into, or reduction to, or explanation by, any simpler concept. It is the person who acts (Chapter 17), that is, who is said to *do* the acts: he does not *cause* them. Thus, "I cause my hand to rise" is equivalent to "I raise my hand." If my knee jerks, or if I sneeze, I have not acted at all, or done anything; rather, something has happened *to* me, like falling down, or contracting a disease. An action must be within my power or ability to do or to refrain from doing. Borderline instances of an action might be shivering, or fainting, or falling in love(?). The reason for an action need not be an intention; other possible reasons for action are habits, dispositions, tastes, obligations, desires, and wants. All of these are legitimate answers to the question, why did you do such and such? To be rational (Chapter 16) is to *act* in accordance with *reasons*; it is always justifiable to ask *why* about any person's action.

The action of a person differs from the same movements made by an animal. If a monkey pushes a chess piece, that is not an action. We laugh when Mark Twain complains about the size of the mosquitoes in Arkansas: once, on Election Day, he says, they were caught trying to vote. The feeding or sexual activities of an animal consist of muscular contractions; but these activities by a person also involve a context: his motives, knowledge, environment, and values. A man standing near me on the subway turns to me and says, "The decimal system wasn't introduced into Finland until very late." What is he doing? transmitting information? quoting Norman Douglas? being friendly? mistaking me for someone else? being initiated into a fraternity? responding to a dare? I cannot say what he is doing without knowing the surrounding circumstances. Events often cannot be described adequately without contextual knowledge. Max Weber defines actions as "human behavior insofar as the acting individual attaches a subjective meaning to it." This is one of the reasons offered for the claim that the sciences which deal with human actions require the use of the special method called *Verstehen,* or empathy, which we considered in Chapter 11.

Difficulties with the Concept of Action

But there are serious difficulties with this traditional account of human action. An action can usually (and perhaps always) be described in more than one way. Like all of the events that science tries to explain (Chapters 9 and 10), human actions permit of diverse categorization; how, then, can they be simply identified or individuated, so as to be attributed without ambiguity to a purpose? The following five sentences, for example, describe the same action: I move my hand; I turn the water faucet; I fill the drinking glass; I assuage the invalid's thirst; I do a charitable deed. Consider another example: I flex my finger; I flip the electric switch; I illuminate the room; I scare off the burglar; I alarm the entire community. My action may be intentional under one description but not under another. The dean expelled the student for "setting fire to the library"; but the student claims what he was doing was "protesting the imperialist war." G. E. M. Anscombe has recently stressed the problems involved in this sort of referential opacity, which is one of the difficulties of meaning and naming discussed in Chapter 7.

Not only may an action be variously described, but it is not at all clear how to separate an action from its consequences: flexing your finger versus pulling the trigger; pulling the trigger versus releasing the bullet; releasing the bullet versus starting the revolution. Some philosophers have tried to define a class of actions as "basic," that is, not done by doing something else: thus, stopping your car is not a basic action, but stepping on the brake is. Others have selected certain actions as "atomic" if they cannot be subdivided into parts: thus, stepping on the brake incorporates the flexing of your leg muscles. Perhaps even that action is not atomic, since it may be said to include a separable act of exertion, or trying. Is raising my arm a different kind of action from raising a book? Sartre maintains there is no distinction between action and intention, since it is our action which informs us of our intention; but surely an action (unlike an intention) must be overt—it must "interfere with the world." Forbearance (as in examples 12 and 13 of intention) does not become action unless there is some reason to act. A private decision is not ordinarily an action.

We find, thus, that the concept of action resists analysis almost as strongly as the concept of intention. We must use these terms with great care; their imprecision seems ineradicable, like that of "mind" and "body" in Chapter 18. However, "action," like "person," seems to me indispensable; it must be taken as logically primitive, and metaphysically ultimate.

Freedom, Determinism, and Fatalism

Also ultimate, I would maintain, is a core of personal freedom. I would deny that you can ever be caused to do what you really do not want to do. Threats, blackmail, and the power of a totalitarian government may always be resisted: your enemies may throw you into jail, or even kill you, but they can never compel you to act. The commander of the *Pueblo* was free not to give up; prisoners of war could stand firm; the old Bolsheviks at the Moscow Trials did not have to sign phony confessions; many victims of the Spanish Inquisition, in fact, did not recant under torture. Post-hypnotic suggestion and brainwashing cannot make you do what you profoundly object to doing. Do unconscious motivations (e.g., your resentment of your friend resulting in his "accidental" death) cause you to act against your will? or is it not rather that you acquiesce in your hidden desires and fears? An "irresistible impulse" may in fact be merely an unresisted impulse: do we not succeed in resisting many impulses while a police officer is watching us?

This drops us into the dead center of one of the hoariest of philosophical problems: are persons free agents? Mark Twain once said, there's nothing hard about giving up smoking: I've done it myself a dozen times. The problem of freedom of the will has likewise been solved many times.

It is an important problem because *free will* lies at the intersection of two fundamental but perhaps incompatible convictions: the subjective or inward phenomenological certainty of *freedom*; and *determinism* (Chapter 1), the insistence that every event has a cause. Shall I move my finger to the left or to the right? The answer seems intuitively irresistible: I can move it in either direction; there is no compulsion on me either way; I can deliberate and decide; having moved my finger to the left, I realize in retrospect that I could have moved it to the right (that is why remorse and repentance seem so genuine). Freedom is a postulate on which we all act.

Determinism must be clearly distinguished from fatalism. *Fatalism* asserts not that every event has a cause, but that every event has been preordained; that the causes of events are outside ourselves; that whatever occurs does so regardless of what we do; that we cannot act, since events are beyond our control; that there are no alternatives; that deliberation is illusory. It is an ancient doctrine. No one can refute it, since it is vacuous of content—whatever happens or fails to happen is taken by the fatalist as substantiating his claim; nothing whatever could be evidence against it. The irrefutability of fatalism is built into it, like the self-proclaimed infallibility of a sacred writing. If you point this out, the fatalist says your argument, too, is preordained. Determinism likewise can be neither proved nor disproved; but determinism is not a metaphysical doctrine, it is a postulate for action. Its efficacy is pragmatic: it is the refusal to abandon the search for causes.

If, as determinism asserts, *all* events have causes, why should not "free" human actions have causes? Are our "free" choices, in fact, determined? The Stoics thought that people could not help acting as they do. Spinoza asserted that if a falling stone could think, it would say it is falling of its own free will. He argued that man is also determined, but it is by forces emanating from his own nature: a free human act is not arbitrary or spontaneous, but is performed in accordance with reason, that is, based on an understanding of the whole; it is done *sub specie aeternitatis,* not on the impulse of the moment. The irrational or angry man is not free. The fourth part of Spinoza's *Ethics* is titled "Of Human Bondage, or the Strength of the Emotions."

But is it true that the will is free only if it is guided by reason?

Duns Scotus and other "voluntarist" philosophers deny this. They assert the priority or superiority of the will over the intellect. In André Gide's *Lafcadio's Adventures,* a man tries to prove that he is free by suddenly and spontaneously killing an unknown fellow passenger on a train. (The police are baffled by the absence of a motive.) Can one's freedom be established in this way? or by suicide?

Free Choice

A free action, as Hume, Mill, and Russell have pointed out, is not one which is uncaused or undetermined, but rather one which is uncoerced, or uncompelled. Thus, anyone observing my behavior, and knowing my dispositions, character, habits, training, temperament, and so on, would be able to predict my "free choices." Human actions are as predictable as any other events; that is, they may be seen to be "constantly conjoined" with previous events, and explained by regularities or general laws. St. Augustine reconciled human freedom with divine foreknowledge. And Marx argued that revolution is inevitable—not in spite of our choices, but because of what we will choose.

Freedom from *external compulsion* ("when the moving principle is outside" in Aristotle's phrase) is then the only sort of freedom which counts. But when is this condition met? Compulsion of course need not be physical duress: your choices are also influenced by social customs (are you free to be a cannibal, or to commit incest?) ; by climate and geography (crimes of violence are seasonal—they tend to increase during the khamsin or mistral) ; by class and family background; by education; by conditioning; by habits; by health; by drink and drugs (if the angry man is not free, how could the drug addict be?); by wealth or poverty. One speaks of personal character as if it were an ultimate; but surely it is continually molded by training and learning and experience. "I am a part of all I have met," says Tennyson's Ulysses. Character alone is so tenuous a foundation for prediction and explanation that, no matter *what* you do, although most people would be surprised, someone is sure to say, isn't that just like him! If you add to the roster of external influences the Freudian theory that our true motivations are buried and concealed from us, we emerge as puppets whose "free" choices are entirely illusory; voluntary acts thus cannot be clearly distinguished from compulsive acts. There is nothing free or accidental in our choice of profession or spouse or politics. The structured personality is fixed in early childhood: whether you will become a criminal or a poet is then determined. (If your choices depend on your parents, and their choices are also determined by *their* parents, is everything then somehow contained in the first living cell?) Even that stubborn intuition of free choice in moving your finger: could it possibly be deceptive? Do you know for certain that you are not in a state of post-hypnotic suggestion as you move your finger to the left? John Locke cites this case: you get up in the morning and decide upon reflection not to leave your apartment that day; your staying at home seems a completely free choice. Unknown to you, however, someone has padlocked your door while you were asleep.

Is my free choice one in which I weigh all the factors and then decide in accordance with my *dominant motive?* I can go to Grand Central Station by subway or by taxi or by foot. The subway is fastest; a taxi is most comfortable; walking is cheapest. My free choice is based on whether time or comfort or money is uppermost at the moment. But then isn't "free choice" a tautology? If I have become a compulsive time-saver, for example, a miser, in what way is my choice a free one? If my psychoanalyst relieves me of these compulsions and tells me to "take it easy," then is my new choice free? In each instance, my dominant motive has been changed.

Responsibility

If freedom of choice, then, is to be dismissed as illusory, how can we ever hold people responsible for their actions? Is *tout comprendre, tout pardonner?* In Samuel Butler's *Erewhon,* a judge about to pass sentence on a criminal admonishes him:

It is all very well for you to say that you came of unhealthy parents, and had a severe accident in your childhood which permanently undermined your constitution; excuses such as these are the ordinary refuge of the criminal. . . . There is no question of how you came to be wicked, but only this—namely, are you wicked or not? . . . You are a bad and dangerous person.

The man's crime was that he caught consumption; he had been given a solemn warning the year previous, when he had been found guilty of bronchitis. How indeed shall we differentiate between succumbing to disease and succumbing to temptation? Should no one ever be held responsible for crimes, as Clarence Darrow urged? We cannot divorce morality—that is, what I *ought* to do—from ability—that is, what I *can* do. Thus, I do not feel that I ought to swim the English Channel, nor become the world's chess champion, nor learn Sanskrit perfectly overnight. Why then ought I give up smoking? or be brave? or resist temptation? Can the scope of my ability be clearly delineated at all?

Science of Human Behavior

The analysis of human actions indeed seems tangled. But some conclusions may be drawn. No aspect of human freedom makes a science of human behavior impossible. We can find out whether there are objectively verifiable regularities in what people do, without having to refer to mental acts of choice or intention. Explanatory general laws of behavior may be stated causally—for example, frustration tends to cause aggression, and disintegration of the home causes adolescent lawlessness—even though motives are not mental thrusts or causes. Causes are not in competition with motives or with reasons. To justify a man's action by ascribing motives to him—for example, Hamlet wanted revenge—serves not only to describe or characterize his action, but also to explain it. Revenge is a disposition. It needs a situation to trigger it; yet that situation might never come to pass (just as this soluble piece of chalk may never be put into water) ; but that is exactly the nature of explanation by disposition. When the law declares a person responsible, that usage is sui generis, in effect performatory or ceremonial: there may be good reasons for punishing someone for the possession of contraband, for example, or for the accidental adulteration of milk, or for vagrancy, even though these crimes may involve no action or intention.

Self-Determination by the Growing Person

As for the conflict between freedom and determinism, let us remember that these are methodological postulates, not metaphysical dogmas. Determinism means that people will never abandon their search for the causes of events; it is verified as a postulate by our continued discovery of regular connections between kinds of events. Freedom, likewise, is not a gift from heaven, but a postulate; it is verified (that is, made true) by our acting freely. Heredity and environment impose their constraints, as I have shown, but these restrictions are not irresistible. If you predict correctly what I will do, based on what you know I have already done, you have not thereby made my choice the less free. A man's freedom must be asserted, and demanded; as James puts it, the first act of a free man ought to be to declare his freedom. The model of human behavior that equates free choice with action in accordance with a dominant motive is simplistic and inadequate; first, because it abstracts from the fluidity of most situations, and the variety of ways in which situations of choice may be described; second, because it fails to recognize that the person is a process. Herein lies the crucial role of intelligence, as Dewey stresses: moral responsibility is genuine because human beings *grow*. My character is not a bare battlefield on which ignorant armies clash by night: it is progressively structured by my restrictive shaping of the possibilities open to me. I begin to make myself as soon as I am born, and I continue to make myself until I die. My freedom and my responsibility both are grounded in that fact. My every choice changes me and therefore affects my future choices. A motive which I should always have, is so to choose as to anticipate and direct my future choices and to expand the unknown scope of my ability; in brief, to grow. If we are compelled to be free, as Sartre puts it paradoxically, it is because we ought to grow. This is not indeterminism, but *self-determination*.

Just as the world presents itself to us as open and malleable; just as the species *Homo sapiens* has unknown evolutionary potentialities; so the individual person is an unfinished animal. He is never complete while alive. Of all of the thousands of lives which are open to him, he becomes only the one person he finally chooses to create. His future is free—not because it is uncompelled, or unpredictable, but because he has a core of freedom if he insists on it. What he has become is only instrumental to his future growth. Every man is a self-made man.

21

Form in Art

SOME OF THE DIVERSE senses in which we speak of art are suggested when we contrast art with life (*ars longa, vita brevis*); or art with science (intuition versus conceptual knowledge, according to Croce); or art with nature (Aristotle says that a flower differs from a sculpture in that its "principle of growth" is within itself, whereas the principle of growth of a sculpture is imposed on it from the outside); or art with what is without value; or the fine arts with the practical arts; or the arts with the crafts.

> *Queen*:   More matter, with less art.
> *Polonius*: Madam, I swear I use no art at all.

What, indeed, is "art"? "We have no art," say the people of Bali, "we do everything as well as possible." Until the Renaissance, such activities as painting, sculpture, and architecture were usually associated with carpentry and building; the term "aesthetics" was not coined until the eighteenth century. Ancient Greece had no art in our sense (the Greek *techne*, usually translated as "art," is closer to our "skill" or "craft"), nor did ancient Egypt, nor did medieval Europe.

Classification of the Arts

Attempts to classify the different kinds of art often begin with the medium employed; but most traditional distinctions have been eroded. Sir Joshua Reynolds once objected to Ghiberti's sculptured bronze gates for the Baptistery in Florence because "they overstepped the limits that separate sculpture from painting." Do these limits still exist? Are they defined by the materials used? or by a distinction between two-dimensional and three-dimensional works? or by the use of color? Where does collage fit? Is Chinese calligraphy (which uses pictographs) to be classified as painting? How does sculpture differ from architecture? Both employ mass, shape, line, light, and shadow; you can walk into the sculptures of Henry Moore and Barbara Hepworth, and apprehend them from the inside. Is a mobile a sculpture?

How do we categorize the performing arts? Where are the boundaries between classical ballet and modern dance? between dance and drama? Where does mime fit in? It combines the dancer's expressiveness with the actor's ability to represent. The Japanese Noh drama is music and choreography built around the barest plot; it is so nonliterary that the lines need scarcely be intelligible. Grotowski defines his Polish Laboratory Theatre as "a totality of human behavior" in which "the spoken word can act as a sort of awning which hides the play." How does the cinema fit in to the arts? Like early Elizabethan drama, films were at first considered to be entertainment rather than art. The cinema is an entirely new art, arising not from an obscure creative urge, but from a technical invention. The film is not just a play which has been photographed; motion is essential to it; *montage* is its unique method for creating meanings by the sequence and juxtaposition of images into visual metaphors. André Malraux distinguishes between cinema and theater: in the theater, conversation is ceaseless, but films "*break into* dialogue after long stretches of silence, just as a novel breaks into dialogue after long narrative passages."

Nelson Goodman has proposed classifying the arts into the *autographic,* in which the artist acts on the same physical materials that the viewer later perceives (painting and sculpture), and the *allographic,* in which he makes use of an independent code (for example, language and sounds). But all classification seems to be vexation!

Art functions within human experience in many ways: to express the imagination (Shelley); to purge the emotions through pity and terror (Aristotle); to promote the class struggle (Marx); to advance universal brotherhood (Tolstoy); to enhance morality ("the essential function of art is moral," bluntly says D. H. Lawrence); to criticize life (Matthew Arnold); to help live the good life (Pater, Dewey); to contemplate (Schopenhauer); to bring you "face-to-face with reality" (Bergson); to help you relax (Matisse); and, of course, to serve no function at all, but simply to exist for its own sake.

Art and the Imitation of Nature

The most ancient and honorable function of art is the "imitation of nature." Nowadays the term "imitation" is pejorative; the "mere imitator" is scorned. However, the thesis here means that it is the world outside of the artist which is the source of his inspiration, or the reservoir for his ideas. Hamlet urges, hold the mirror up to nature! Monet describes a painting as *"une fenêtre ouverte sur la Nature."* Leonardo da Vinci advises the painter to look at women's faces by twilight, when their secrets can best be perceived. Successive revolutions in the history of painting have all proclaimed themselves "truer to nature;" in their turn, impressionism, pointillism, cubism, futurism, and so on claimed to capture "what we really see." In the fourteenth century, however, Boccaccio wrote, "There is nothing which Giotto could not have portrayed in such a manner as to deceive the sense of sight." (There is a charming anecdote told that, when Juan Pareja stood next to the portrait of him painted by Velázquez, no one could be sure which indeed was the portrait.)

Nature is the source of inspiration even for artists who deliberately distort what they think is "out there": consider the mannerism of El Greco, the fantastic art of Bosch, and the surrealism of Magritte and Dali. The same contention applies to literature: Kafka and Joyce are no less indebted to the world about them than Balzac and Zola. Nature is an aesthetic norm for the artist even when he disagrees with Matthew Arnold that he should "see the object in itself as it really is."

The function of art in the imitation of nature is obviously a complex one. This notion has been ridiculed by Virginia Woolf: "Art is not a copy of the real world; one of the damn things is enough." And by Picasso, who, when he was told that his portrait of Gertrude Stein didn't look like her, said, "Never mind, it will." And by Matisse, who, when a visitor to his studio suggested, "Surely the arm of that woman is too long?" replied, "Madame, you are mistaken. That is not a woman; that is a picture." Philip Ernst painted a picture of his garden and omitted a tree that spoiled the composition; then, "overcome with remorse at this offense against realism," he cut down the tree. Is a color photograph more faithful to nature than a black-and-white one? Chinese Buddhist painters aim for "the spirit of nature" and try to "purify it of materiality" by not using any color at all. The Nuremberg Chronicles, a medieval historical document, "represented" 198 popes by 28 different woodcuts; 224 kings by 54; 69 cities by 22. "Art is not Nature," said George Moore, "Art is Nature digested. Art is a sublime excrement." And Kokoschka announced, "I am the last painter to use his eyes."

Aristotle and Plato differ significantly on art and the imitation of nature. Aristotle believes that what the artist "imitates" is the quintessence of the particular thing he sees; thus, what Cézanne paints is the universal Apple which is only imperfectly embodied in any particular apple. The artist "completes what nature cannot bring to a finish. The artist gives us knowledge of nature's unrealized ends" or universals (Chapter 1). Plato, on the other hand, regards art as inferior to nature, since the particular apple which the artist copies is itself only a copy of the universal Apple, which is truly real. Art is for Plato thus twice removed from reality; partly for this reason he eliminated art from his perfect state.

The claim that the artist derives inspiration from the world outside is implicitly denied, in an interesting way, by certain works of art that exemplify rather the involuted self-reflection of the artist's mind itself. Thus André Gide's *The Counterfeit-*

ers is the "journal of a novelist who is writing a novel about a novelist who is keeping a journal about the novel he is writing." Nabokov's *Pale Fire* purports to be written by the editor of a poet's autobiography; but the editor unwittingly reveals himself to be insane. *Hamlet* contains a play within a play; Claudius watches the play; Hamlet watches Claudius; Polonius watches Hamlet; we watch them all. In a similar way, Velázquez' painting *Las Meniñas* (in the Prado) shows a mirror so placed that the observer is drawn into a self-contained and isolated world. And the movie *8 1/2* is about the making of a movie, itself. In all of these works of art we never get outside the mind of the artist, so to speak.

Art as a Language

We often ask about a work of art (but never about a flower), what does it *mean*? We expect it to communicate something to us: but exactly how? If art is to be considered a language, it is so only loosely and metaphorically. Lusty, rowdy gaiety is clearly suggested to us by Bosch's rural scenes; cheerful serenity by Vermeer's interiors; nameless menace by the landscapes of Chirico; the evils of fascism by Picasso's *Guernica*; and poised energy by Myron's *Discus Thrower*. Meyer Schapiro has recently shown that Christian and Jewish artists, painting the same biblical account of Moses at the battle with the Amalekites (Exodus 17:9-13), represent Moses differently in order to communicate their theological views. The text reads, "when Moses held up his hand, . . . Israel prevailed." Christian painters depict Moses frontally, with both arms raised, so that his posture is like that of Christ on the cross. Jewish painters show Moses in profile, so as to eliminate the suggestion that Moses was a forerunner of Christ. Certain symbols are well-established iconographically: the bats and dogs in Dürer's *Melencolia;* the arrows that identify St. Sebastian. But I am less persuaded that the attenuated sculptures of Giacometti communicate (as has been claimed) the "one-dimensionality of man"; and I am rather reluctant to accept Ernst Fischer's assertion that the

Moses of Michelangelo was not merely the embodiment of the self-aware Renaissance personality, but was "also a commandment in stone to Michelangelo's contemporaries and patrons: 'This is what you ought to be like. The age in which we live demands it. The world at whose birth we are all present needs it.' "

In music, likewise, some compositions are avowedly program music (Wagner's *Liebestod,* Strauss' *Thus Spake Zarathustra*). But why did Berlioz remove the program notes he wrote for his *Fantastic Symphony?* Erik Satie remarked, on first hearing a piece by Debussy called "Morning-Noon-Afternoon," "I liked especially that little bit around 11:30." Perhaps the most appropriate dictum on music as a language is Felix Mendelssohn's "The meaning of music lies not in the fact that it is too vague for words, but that it is too precise for words."

If we are to think of the literary arts as a language, then we must regard the words as functioning both cognitively and expressively. But what information is being communicated by Wallace Stevens' "Death is the mother of beauty"? or by Shelley's

> Life, like a dome of many-colored glass,
> Stains the white radiance of Eternity

or by the delightful imagery of Stephen Spender's

> Eye, gazelle, delicate wanderer,
> Drinker of horizon's fluid line.

Can we be reasonably sure of what *Hamlet* tells us? or *Moby Dick?* or *The Waste Land?* Are there really ghosts in *The Turn of the Screw?* Sometimes the language of poetry is artfully ambiguous: in Milton's *Paradise Lost* is the line

> Nor did they not perceive the evil plight

—well, did they perceive it or didn't they? The answer is apparently that they did and they didn't.

An extreme position on this issue is taken by Carnap: for him the language of the poet expresses his feelings just as a gesture would, or a cry, or a grunt; it is emotive and noncognitive; it conveys no knowledge. In this view, a sonnet is closer to a stamp of the foot than to a proposition. But surely such a view is misguided; it is like worrying about how the names used in fiction can denote. Art conveys information without striving for or attaining the rigor of science.

"Thou shalt not commit a social science!" says W. H. Auden. Art enhances human experience by its hints at the ineffable, by the interplay of multiple meanings, by suggestive overtones, allusions, and atmosphere. The meanings "leak through," so to speak. It is not a defect that when Hamlet cries,

> O, that this too too solid flesh would melt

he may be saying not "solid," but "sullied." Nor would *Hamlet* be a better play if we were sure whether or not Gertrude connived at her husband's murder. William Empson cites the Chinese poem

> Swiftly the years, beyond recall.
> Solemn the stillness of this spring morning.

What makes these phrases a poem? The sentiment is elevated, and the lines are terse, spare, compact, and closely connected; but why are "the years" and "this morning" juxtaposed? Why are the years "swift" and the morning "solemn" and "still"? It is this provoking ambiguity which permits and requires the reader to supply his own answers; and the greater the latitude left the reader, often the richer the poem. We must perforce choose between two inconsistent statements in science or in philosophy, but never between two poems. "Critics quarrel with other critics," says Santayana, but "with an artist no sane man quarrels." That is also why poetry is so difficult to translate—often the "creative misunderstanding" (Valéry) is lost. You cannot replace the rain in Hemingway's *Farewell to Arms* by any other symbol; nor can you substitute anything for the falling camellia blossoms in Japanese drama (which suggest that a beheading is to come).

The Artist's Intention

If art is to be regarded as a language, the question then becomes, what does the artist intend to communicate? Idealist philosophers such as Croce and Cassirer hold that the objective value of art depends on the harmony between the artist's inner intuition and its external expression, that is, between the "poet's vision and his handiwork." But, as we have seen (Chapter 20), intention as an explanatory category is quite confused; how do you determine it, if it is not fully realized in the work of art? Do you ask the artist? Do you read his letters, notes, or autobiography? Do you look at the title of the work (e.g., Brancusi's *Bird in Space*)? or at the epigraph (e.g., the quotation from Heraclitus in Eliot's "Burnt Norton")? Do you consult the artist's psychoanalyst? What about the intention of insane poets such as Christopher Smart? What of unconscious intentions? or of irony? A. E. Housman's poem "1887," written for Queen Victoria's Golden Jubilee, praises the Englishmen who died for the Empire; it ends with the lines

> Get you the sons your fathers got,
> And God will save the Queen.

When the critic Frank Harris congratulated Housman on his priceless irony, Housman exploded: that was pure patriotism!

Uncertainties about the intention of the artist prompted a movement called the "New Criticism".[1] Its advocates maintain that the work of art is public and self-sufficient; it is "detached from the author at birth." To evaluate a poem or a painting on the basis of what its creator may have intended is to appraise a phantom—the work of art as it might have been or should have been: we must consider it only as it actually is. What the artist may have "had in mind" is not part of the perceived work; to refer to it is the *intentional fallacy*. We ought not see in Shakespeare's *Hamlet* an implausible familiarity with the Oedipus complex. We should cope cheerfully with such "put-ons" as Robert Rauschenberg's reply to a French art dealer who asked him to paint a portrait of Iris Clert, "This is her portrait if I say so."

By avoiding the intentional fallacy, we can take with a grain

---

[1] This approach may be traced to the following sources: Matthew Arnold's claim that literature, rather than religion, is central to a civilization and therefore requires a "high seriousness"; T. S. Eliot's incorporation into poetry of philosophy, psychology, and anthropology; I. A. Richards' practical criticism; T. E. Hulme; William Empson; and Monroe Beardsley.

of salt certain allegedly "explicative" critical antics: for example, in interpreting Dylan Thomas' line

And from the windy West came two-gunned Gabriel

the critic Elder Olsen explains that the poet had in mind the constellation Perseus, for the man Perseus (who decapitated Medusa) had two weapons (his sword and Medusa's head); the two guns recall the Wild West, and therefore the game of poker, and therefore other card games, and therefore trumps, and therefore the last trump, and therefore Gabriel. If this explanation helps us better to enjoy that line, fine! But all we ever have is the line, and not the professed contents of Dylan Thomas' brain. Joseph Conrad's short story "The Secret Sharer" is about a young sea captain on his first voyage in command. The captain protects a stowaway who is a murderer and a fugitive. The simple adventure has profound and ambiguous overtones—of delusion, homosexuality, the force of authority, the conflict between morality and justice, the story of Cain and Abel, the *doppelgänger,* Conrad's own life. There is little point in inquiring what the author's "real" intention was, or what the "true" interpretation is: any hypothesis which can be supported by evidence in the text ought to be thoughtfully examined and joyfully experienced. To insist on the "real meaning" [2] is to mistake literature and art for idealized science. A work of art is not a sense datum; it is not merely something perceived, but rather something interpreted. And in the richness, multiplicity, and range of its legitimate interpretations lie its fertility and vigor as a work of art.

What Is a Work of Art?

I have so far left a *work of art* undefined. To begin with, of course, it is a physical object. It consists of shapes or colors or

[2] An old anecdote is worth telling. Robert Browning was once asked what he had meant by a poem he wrote many years before. When I wrote that poem, he is supposed to have replied, God and Robert Browning knew what I meant. Now only God knows.

movements or sounds or other things that stimulate the senses. [3]
But whatever the materials, they must be composed or organized or shaped in a special way. Aestheticians and critics speak
of such requirements as harmony, balance, contrast, stress, proportion, centrality, theme, development, accent, rhyme, focus,
and so on; but none of these is necessary. The essential requisite is that the materials be so *formed* that they are finally experienced as a *unity,* whether they extend timelessly through
space (as do painting and architecture) or whether they cumulate nonspatially through time (as does music). The frame of
a painting, the pedestal of a statue, the proscenium in a theater,
the silence that precedes and follows a piece of music, and the
space around a cathedral all act to enclose the work of art in
what Rilke called a "circle of solitude." Thus it is experienced
as an isolated, unified, instantaneous presence.

Form, one of the fundamental concepts in philosophy, is perhaps impossible to define. Form, along with structure, system,
and order, are pretty much the same, says Josiah Royce,

> . . . whether they appear in a Platonic dialogue, or in a modern
> text book of botany, or in the commercial conduct of a business
> firm, or in the arrangement and discipline of an army, or in a
> legal code, or in a work of art, or even in a dance or the planning
> of a dinner. Order is order. System is system. Amidst all the variations of systems and of orders, certain general types and characteristic relations can be traced.

It is these most general features which logic studies. We may
speak of the common form of two sonnets, or of two major
scales, or of two "A" propositions; we say that a man's arm and
a bird's wing have homologous forms; that optical and electrodynamic waves have the same form; that ice and steam are
different forms of water. The story of Faust is given distinct
forms in Marlowe's play, Goethe's poetic drama, Berlioz' opera,
and Thomas Mann's novel. The way in which we put things
together, or take things together—what we decide to abstract as

---

[3] Why are tastes and smells rarely if ever the materials for a work of art?
Brillat-Savarin wrote an aesthetics of gastronomy; Huysmans, in *A Rebours,*
described an organ for combining odors. Is it because tastes and smells do not
lend themselves to structuring? or because they are received by us chemically?
or because they are too closely associated with biological needs?

similar in different contexts, how we use universals (Chapter 1) —is a primary aspect of how we organize experience and understand the world.

> *Hamlet.* Do you see yonder cloud that's almost
> in shape of a camel?
> *Polonius.* By the mass, and 'tis like a camel indeed.
> *Hamlet.* Methinks it is like a weasel.
> *Polonius.* It is backed like a weasel.
> *Hamlet.* Or like a whale?
> *Polonius.* Very like a whale.

Form of a certain kind, as we will shortly see, is of the essence in the concept of a work of art.

Five Quandaries

To define the work of art as sensuous materials formed into a unity, however, and to stop at that point, would be to commit the reductive fallacy. The status of "work of art" is not imputed to anything unless that thing is embedded in a certain social context which relates the observer and the artist. This may be illustrated by five quandaries:

1. *Forgeries.* The Metropolitan Museum of Art in New York announced on December 7, 1967, that it had removed from display a bronze horse supposed to have been sculptured about 475 B.C. This "quintessence of the ancient Greek spirit" was suddenly declared a modern fraud, made in 1920. The museum's *Handbook* at the time described the horse as summing up "in an eloquent way the achievements of the Greek sculptor in this period," and added that "the artist's conception has endowed it with an additional quality which is essentially Greek—a quiet beauty which removes it from the individual to the typical." Why was this exquisite sculpture, admired for decades by millions, placed in storage? How did it change?[4] Similarly, the fake "Vermeers" painted during the

---

[4] I am happy to report that a later investigation seems to have reestablished the sculpture's authenticity, although it is still somewhat problematical.

1930s by Van Meegeren are so good that some art experts continued to maintain that the paintings were authentic even after Van Meegeren announced his hoax. Why were the paintings removed from the galleries? They had delighted many observers. In 1762, James MacPherson published some "translations" from the third-century Gaelic bard Ossian; they were greatly admired by such notable literary figures as Blake, Herder, and Chateaubriand; Goethe wrote, "Homer has been superseded in my heart by the divine Ossian." But when it was revealed that MacPherson himself had written the poems, no one took any further interest in them. On August 2, 1961, some prankish B.B.C. announcers in London broadcast an "avant-garde composition by Piotr Zak" entitled "Mobile for Tape and Percussion." The "music" was a random collection of whatever sounds could be made by banging on whatever objects happened then to be in the studio. The problem presented by forgeries in the arts is not that intelligent and responsible critics may be deceived, but rather that whatever interest may be retained in paintings, sculptures, poems, and so on, that are exposed as forgeries, they are no longer accepted as works of art.

2. *Copies.* Modern techniques of reproduction are so fine that only the expert can distinguish an original painting from a replica. If the differences are virtually indiscernible, why then do we perceive and appreciate originals and replicas so differently? Why was there such excitement about whether or not the portion of a statue found in the basement of the British Museum was *the* Aphrodite of Praxiteles?

3. *Non-persons.* Paintings produced by monkeys, or by babies trailing their fingers in water colors, no matter how attractive, are regarded only as curiosities, never as works of art. This poem was recently published:

> While life reached evilly through empty faces
> While space flowed slowly o'er idle bodies
> And stars flowed evilly on vast men
> No passion smiled.

Not a masterpiece, surely, but one has read worse poetry. It was composed by a digital computer. When you now reread the poem, will you do so in the same way? (*pace,* Wittgenstein!) Computers have also composed music that could pass in the concert hall for second-rate Haydn—that is, until you discover its composer.

4. *Intention.* Stephen Dedalus, in Joyce's *Portrait of the Artist As a Young Man,* asks, "If a man hacking in fury at a block of wood make there an image of a cow, is that image a work of art?" What if it is produced idly, or inattentively—while doodling, even while sleepwalking?

5. *Nature.* Dewey supposes, in *Art As Experience,* that

> . . . a finely wrought object, one whose texture and proportions are highly pleasing in perception, has been believed to be a product of some primitive people. Then there is discovered evidence that proves it to be an accidental natural product. As an external thing, it is now precisely what it was before. Yet at once it ceases to be a work of art and . . . now belongs in a museum of natural history.

Definition of a Work of Art

Analysis of these five quandaries indicates that nothing is a work of art unless it is deemed to be intentionally *formed*; that is, that materials (colors or shapes or sounds or whatever) are arranged (or composed or manipulated) into a unity, by a *person,* for the *sake of doing so* (regardless of any other motives) and in order to evoke a *response* to the artist from some other person. Monkeys, babies, and computers are not persons. Neither is nature. Men who hack furiously or inattentively or somnambulistically do not intend to evoke any response. A painting or a poem falsely attributed by its creator to someone else violates the requirement that the work of art be intended by the artist as he himself forms it to evoke *your* response to *him,* even if he knows nothing about you, nor you about him. The forger wants you to respond to someone else. (No child ever shows you another's mudpies.) Every poet wants a publisher, every composer a performance, every actor an audience, every painter a showing. Every artist feels unfulfilled without a perceiver; in the limiting case (alone on a desert island?) the intended ultimate perceiver may well be the artist himself at a later time. Why do we all scorn the copy or the replica, however beautiful? Because it lacks the personal forming. And it is through the art of alien or remote cultures that we expect to attain intimate and fertile insight into them.

This analysis also clarifies the basis for three traditional distinctions: between the work of art and the artifact; between the arts and the crafts; and between the fine arts and the practical (or applied) arts. In the first member of each of these pairs, the forming is primarily for the sake of doing so; in the second, it is primarily utilitarian. Likewise, "hack art" is seldom formed for its own sake: greeting card verses, advertising art, television and radio commercials, passport photographs, waxworks, and so on. We sort out borderline cases (decorative maps, quilts, chess pieces, etc.) by this same criterion: were they formed for intrinsic or utilitarian purposes?

Role of the Person

The personal requirement also explains why a beautiful object made by a factory or corporation is not deemed a work of art. And how rare is a successful collaboration by two artists. Perhaps the dramatists Beaumont and Fletcher, or Erckmann-Chatrian, or Hart and Kaufman are exceptions; but few music lovers are happy with the arrangements of Bach by Busoni, or with the completion of Mozart's *Requiem* by Süssmayer, or with the orchestration by Ravel of Mussorgsky's *Pictures at an Exhibition*. No one can "finish" Schubert's *Unfinished Symphony*. Opera may be regarded as a combination of arts, so that the composer and the librettist (e.g., Gilbert and Sullivan, or Mozart and DaPonte) are not so much collaborating on a single work of art as each rather "doing his own thing." Some Renaissance painters employed assistants to fill in the backgrounds, but the assistants were clearly not collaborators. Only when Renoir became too arthritic to hold a brush firmly did he engage someone to make sculptures for him from some of his paintings.

The term "folk art" is generally applied to the anonymous creations of many hands—folk song, folk dance, the old sagas and epics, and so on. Perhaps the medieval cathedrals and tapestries should also be so regarded.

I am not in this analysis committing the intentional fallacy—I hope!—since I am not suggesting that a work of art be evaluated on the basis of what the artist may have intended. Nor am I disputing my earlier claim (in Chapter 20) that it is difficult, perhaps impossible, to pinpoint a mental act called "intention." Rather, I am pointing out that the status of "work of art" is never ascribed to anything unless we *impute* to a person (rightly or wrongly) the intention to form materials as stated. We have no more assurance that we do this correctly than we have about any other empirical proposition. When a museum piece is reclassified as a forgery and stowed away, it is because we have changed our imputation. (The term "work of art" is of course being used here in a value-neutral sense.)

Weakening of Formal Requirements

The restless outpouring and diversification of artistic activity in recent years has tended to diminish formal requirements in the arts. It would be quaint to recall that Vitruvius said that a temple to Mars ought to be in the Doric order, and to Venus in the Corinthian; or that Plato described music in the Mixolydian mode as mournful, in the Ionian as enervating, and in the Phrygian as healthful. The dictum that "form follows function" now seems inadequate: few people are offended today if a bank looks like a colonial cottage or like a Greek temple, or if a church looks like a fish or like a boat. And, although Robert Frost once said, "I'd as soon write free verse as play tennis with the net down," other artists disagree. We are offered paintings that are solid black; music consisting of four minutes and thirty-three seconds of silence; ballets in which the "dancers" lie motionless on the floor; poetry made up entirely of advertising slogans and railroad timetables strung together; movies of an "actor" sleeping soundly for hours; dramas consisting of the stenographic court record of legal trials; "happenings"; holes dug in the desert; and piles of automobile tires. A Brillo box and a urinal have become works of art when suitably isolated. Mere selection, or change of place, or assemblage, or highlighting, or enlargement of scale seems to count as forming. Increasing reliance on unplanned, chance, or "aleatory," elements approaches the point at which the artist abdicates. It is this consideration which makes for much of the perplexity in experiencing some modern art.

Some contemporary experimentation, however, runs in the opposite direction, namely, toward maximum formal control: Joyce's *Ulysses*, for example, or serialism in music, in which a series of pitch intervals serves as the unifying technique for the control of the rhythm, dynamics, tone-color, and duration of an entire composition.

It is worthy of note that, just as there seem to be no human communities anywhere without language, so also might art serve as the criterion of the human. The primitive peoples who lived in Altamira and Lascaux some twenty thousand years ago painted pictures on the walls of their caves; but the most highly developed animal species, those which can use tools, follow instructions, and solve problems, produce nothing which can be called art. If there is a constant in human nature, perhaps it is this passionate interest in *form*, this craving to discover or impose order on experience.

22

Creativity

THE EXPLANATION of creativity has been a problem ever since Thomas Aquinas reminded us that God created the world out of nothing—*ex nihilo*—and Leibniz added that the world is the work of God just as the poem is the work of the poet. How can something be made out of nothing? To be creative is not quite the same as to be inventive, or talented, or innovative, or expressive, or artistic, or productive, or intelligent, or spontaneous, or divergent, or unpredictable, or energetic, or anything else. The quandary was noted by Freud: "Before the problem of the creative artist, analysis must alas lay down its arms"; and by Jung: "The creative act will forever elude the human understanding." (Of course I am using the word "creative" in its strict and value–neutral sense, and not in the laudatory or loose Madison Avenue sense.)

What is it that the artist *adds* to his materials to create a work of art? Does he, as Michelangelo said, reveal the statue by chipping away the excess marble? Does he rearrange or reshuffle what is already there and somehow transform it? According to B. F. Skinner, a man writing a poem, like a hen laying an egg, or like a woman having a baby, merely mediates and transmits only what was there before. In an eloquent passage in *Tristram Shandy*, Laurence Sterne asks:

> Tell me, ye learned, shall we for ever be adding so much to the bulk—so little to the stock? Shall we forever make new books, as apothecaries make new mixtures, by pouring only out of one vessel into another? Are we for ever to be twisting and untwisting the same rope? for ever in the same track—for ever at the same pace? Shall we be destined to the days of eternity, on holy days as well as working days, to be shewing the relics of learning, as monks do the relics of their saints—without working one—one single miracle with them?

Does the creative person look at the world in a new way—free of the need to do anything about it, and by this fresh approach show us what the world is really like (Bergson)? Is creativity equivalent to violence (Sorel)? to masturbation (Anthony Burgess)? to play and the discharge of surplus energy in the "sheer plenitude of vitality" (J. C. F. Schiller, Herbert Spencer)? But many people who are violent or masturbate or play are not creative.

Is the creative always associated with the different, or the new? Is it "the ultimate metaphysical principle by which *novel* beings are created" (Whitehead)? But every single thing in the world is different from every other (as the "identity of indiscernibles" maintains; see Chapter 12) and is therefore new. And, although every event indeed has roots in the past (which is the claim of determinism), no event is identical with a previous event. The computing device about which the inhabitants of Lagado boasted to Gulliver is no longer a fantasy: such a machine can now be programed to follow syntactical rules for combining words or sounds or other elements; each such combination will be new.[1] Another difficulty with the view of the creative as the novel is what Bernard Berenson once called the "originality of incompetence." The inferior dabbler often experiences the same turmoil and "creative enthusiasm" as the genius.

Does the creative artist *know in advance* what his work will be? If he did, he would already have it completely in hand! The

---

[1] Note that it is possible to produce a denumerably *infinite* number of combinations from a *finite* number of component parts or elements (e.g., poems out of words, melodies out of notes, chemical compounds out of elements, chess games out of chess pieces), provided only that the components may be used more than once, and that there is no limit imposed on the length of any combination.

artist is never sure: his material may resist him in unanticipated ways; he can predict neither how this work will turn out nor the development of his future career. Jerome Bruner has called creativity "effective surprise." When Haydn heard the first performance of his *Creation* he burst into tears. "Did I write that?" he asked. Wallace Stevens perhaps put it best when he said that a poem of his was "what I wanted it to be without knowing before it was written what I wanted it to be, even though I knew before it was written what I wanted to *do*." Joyce worked on different portions of *Ulysses* all at once, as if it were a mosaic, and continued to do so (by means of telegrams to his publisher) while it was in press.

How does the artist know when his work is finished? Hemingway rewrote the last chapter of *A Farewell to Arms* forty times; and every museum director can tell you about the painter who steals into the gallery, the night before the exhibition is to open, to add a few final brush strokes. Mozart wrote, in a letter, that

> when I am feeling well and in good humor . . . thoughts come in swarms and with marvelous ease. . . . Once I catch my air, another comes soon to join the first, according to the requirements of the whole composition. . . . Then my mind kindles—the work grows— I keep hearing it and bring it out more and more clearly, and the composition ends by being completely executed in my mind, however long it may be.

But Mozart left over a hundred unfinished works! Paul Valéry said, "a poem is never finished, it is only abandoned." Giacometti lamented, "There is no hope of achieving what I want. . . . I go on painting and sculpting because I am curious to know why I fail."

A long tradition makes the artist not active, but rather the passive recipient of inspiration. Plato describes how the artist's soul is temporarily replaced by the gods, who dictate his words; the poet is "enthusiastic" (literally, possessed or filled by gods) and "ecstatic" (literally, standing beside himself) . More recently, Max Scheler says, "The artist is only the mother of the work of art: God is the father." But perhaps divine inspiration has today been superseded by the Freudian unconscious.

Another ancient line of thought makes the creative artist irrational. Shakespeare tells us

> The lunatic, the lover, and the poet
> Are of imagination all compact.

Think of the many creative persons who have been on the verge of insanity (or beyond!) —Poe, Dostoyevsky, Van Gogh, Nietzsche, Schumann, Nijinsky, Kafka, Verlaine, Virginia Woolf. Think of the artist's reliance on the stream of consciousness; on free association; on dreams (Coleridge's "Kubla Khan"). Aristotle, however, disagreeing with Plato, views the artist as a sober, hardworking citizen, with no nonsense about irrationality or divine possession.

Can we learn something about the creative process from the artists themselves? Unfortunately, no approach could be less illuminating. Note these samples:

Picasso:

> I take a walk in the forest. . . . I get an indigestion of greenness. I must empty this sensation into a picture. Green dominates it. The painter paints as if in urgent need to discharge himself of his sensations and his visions.

Jacques Barzun describes a conversation in which Richard Wagner once

> tried to explain . . . to Berlioz how the perfect work of art grew from an inner capacity which received objective impressions from without, and transformed these according to the laws of general metaphysics and individual psychology into a product which, etc., etc. "I understand," replied Berlioz, "we call it digesting."

Matisse:

> I try to find a color that will fit my sensation. There is an impelling proportion of tones that can induce me to change the shape of a figure or to transform my composition . . . a moment comes when every part has found its definite relationship and from then on it would be impossible for me to add a stroke to my picture without having to paint it all over again.

Rice Pereira:

> The traveler is just a pilgrim . . . values change with each voyage. Sometimes one gets a glimpse of the bridge to eternity before it disappears like a rainbow. . . . In one sense my work gives structure and dimension to *thought* in time.

Would it help to observe artists going about their work? Proust could write only in a cork-lined room; Schiller needed the smell of rotten apples; Dickens needed London street noises; Wagner needed female scarves or fetishes; De Quincey, Poe, and Baudelaire needed drugs. Jackson Pollock brooded over a twenty-foot canvas for weeks, and then painted the whole thing in a three-hour burst. Leonardo da Vinci spent days staring at the wall of Sta. Maria della Grazie, while the prior who had commissioned him to paint a mural approached apoplexy. Apparently, the creative process can be pinned down neither by outside observation nor by introspection.

Freud and Jung

The Freudian analysis of artistic creativity assimilates it to dreams and daydreams, which reveal unfulfilled wishes and latent instinctual forces. The libido, or reservoir of psychic energy, is utilized to full satisfaction in childhood. But cultural barriers frustrate the libido as we grow up, and the impulses which society tries to exclude from consciousness break loose as neuroses or myths or slips of the tongue or, when suitably altered for acceptable public expression, as art. Art, says Freud, is a compensatory activity: "happy people never make fantasies." Art releases what the censor represses. I offer, without comment, some examples of Freudian analysis of creativity: Leonardo painted the Virgin and St. Anne leaning over the child Jesus, who is located between them—because Leonardo was successively raised by both his mother and the wife of his father. Picasso painted the dove as a symbol of peace because his father was an academic painter who copied stuffed pigeons, and the pigeon is a phallic symbol. Beethoven as a boy was the victim of "a maniacal and castrating passion." Goethe suffered from premature ejaculation. Lewis Carroll's Wonderland is a womb. (Kenneth Burke maintains that the poetry of John Keats really deals with capitalism and socialism and that Hume's criticism of causality is a bachelor's unconscious skepticism of potency and progeny.)

Jung posited the "collective unconscious" as the reservoir of archetypes, or primordial images, into which the artist unconsciously dips for his ideas. Certain stories, images, and forms reappear at all times and in all places, because they are part of the human being's congenital equipment (Frazer's *Golden Bough* is a great collection of recurrent primitive myths). "It is not Goethe who creates *Faust*," declares Jung, "but *Faust* who creates Goethe." The sculptor Henry Moore, a disciple of Jung, affirms:

> There are universal shapes to which everybody is subconsciously conditioned and to which they can respond if their conscious control does not shut them off . . . for example, rounded forms convey an idea of fruitfulness, maturity, probably because the earth, women's breasts, and most fruits are rounded.

But Jung's hypothesis of a collective unconscious is unfalsifiable; it is consistent with any art, any dream, any experience, any event.

Perhaps the clearest insight into creativity is to be gained from this paradigm by Vincent Tomas of the *noncreative* act:

> The rifleman knows what he ought to do to hit the bull's-eye . . . what position he ought to assume, how he ought to adjust the sling, where exactly he ought to place his left hand, where he ought to place the butt so that it fits his shoulder and cheek, what the sight picture ought to be, how he ought to exhale a little and then hold his breath when the sight picture is correct, and how he ought to squeeze off the shot without knowing exactly when the explosion will come, so that he won't flinch until after it is too late to spoil his aim.

By contrast, the creative act never requires following rules blindly; it never calls for finding the single correct answer. It always demands choosing—even when there is no reason for one choice rather than another. The medium is recalcitrant; it makes its own demands. "All things resist being written down," says Kafka. Eliot puts it, in "Burnt Norton":

> Words strain,
> Crack and sometimes break, under the burden,
> Under the tension, slip, slide, perish,
> Decay with imprecision, will not stay in place,
> Will not stay still.

The artist corrects, erases, changes; he does not give expression to whatever first comes into his head. The artist criticizes his work as he creates it. The medium interacts with the artist's ideas, and he reshapes his ideas as he goes on. It is not as if he were solving a puzzle which has only one solution. The creative may be opposed to the academic, to the imitative, to the derivative, to the repetitive, to doing things by rules, or by accident, or according to a plan, or as a means to an end. What, then, is it? I fear it continues to defy precise analysis. Like Einstein's *Einfühlung* or Peirce's "flash" as the source of a scientific hypothesis (Chapter 10), or like the sudden illumination in solving a problem in mathematics, perhaps creativity is another aspect of the quintessentially human.

23

Man Is the Measure

THE SUN RISES and sets, and rises again; the seasons recur; the tides predictably surge and ebb. Nature is replete with its own rhythms. Why then do I claim that it is man who is the measure of all things?

It is because these natural periodicities are neither necessary nor unique nor eternal; and because man can take account only of what man can know. And, as we have come to realize in so many different contexts, what man can know hinges on what man is. Our perception is active inquiry, not passive reception. We human beings select what we determine to be fact, by means of hypotheses that we design to answer our questions, allay our doubts, appease our curiosity, and augment our understanding. Thus fact and hypothesis are complementary; observation and theory are mutually reinforcing. We use the tools of logic to structure our concepts, to regulate our inquiry, to articulate our discourse, and to validate our inference. We resolve that certain propositions are analytic; that is, that we will maintain the fixity of certain meanings in the face of Hell and high water. We contrive vocal sounds into symbolic statements, which bite on to the world meaningfully. We do all this as we guide our hands and brains, in order to describe and explain the world and make it finally more amenable to our ideals. Thus there is an irreducibly anthropocentric surd in knowledge.

If whatever we come to know—about ourselves, or our society, or our past, or the world—is shaped by our characteristic sensory equipment, and circumscribed by our finite biological capacities; if we must cook our raw sensations before we can digest them; if neither the self nor the world has a determinate structure apart from our conceptual apparatus; if our categories seldom become watertight containers for the things they are intended to sort out; if nothing "out there" corresponds to the symbols of logic; if there are (as there now seem to be) limits to the completeness of formal systems; if some portions of the universe are (as physics now seems to assert) forever beyond our ken; if no synthetic proposition can be known to be true a priori; if our explanations inevitably presuppose an implicit context; if the "truth" is best understood in terms of what we do to achieve our purposes; if we impute causes, and select universals, in order to facilitate our direction of the flux of events; if language and behavior are guided by complex and subtle rules which (as now seems probable) cannot be stated fully in propositions; if we are ensnarled in an (apparently intractable) linguistic entanglement; if there are no purposes in nature other than the ones we introduce; if *Homo sapiens* is merely the end product pro tem. of random mutations in certain chemicals; if the person can be neither entirely identified with his body nor clearly differentiated from it; if (as now seems painfully evident) our concepts of "mind" and "body" are deficient; if the difficulties in self-knowledge seem insuperable; if we cannot easily resolve the dialectical tension between such strong ethical convictions as the right to privacy and the right to knowledge; if our experience is likely always to exceed our knowledge; if the mind fits the world only loosely— why, these are some of the dimensions of the human condition.

But it would be adolescent folly to think that what all this entails is romantic despair, or nihilism, or radical skepticism, or solipsism. Just because we have no absolute certainty in empirical propositions, it does not follow that anything goes! Our scientific knowledge is cumulative, self-corrective, and as reliable as we can make it. Just because no cosmic plan guarantees the attainment of all our goals, it does not follow that we are helpless drifters. Only the infant thinks the world was made for him! Just because rationality is not precisely definable, or because different domains of inquiry encounter various obstacles, it does not follow that there are no objective standards. A philosophic or scientific claim which is not justified by appropriate reasons is not to be taken seriously.

The exigencies of living in the world are always with us; but "the world" is not a fixed datum; it is increasingly subject to some control. At various stages in our growth, we may discover built-in limitations to our knowledge; but not (so far as we can tell) to our curiosity, nor to our craving to impose form and order on the flux, of which we are ourselves a part. It is this need which produces metaphysics and science and geometry and history and poetry and art; these are some of the bridges from mind to the world. Just as the world is partly malleable, so are the human species; and the society; and the person. Each is what it has come to be, but the constraints imposed by the past are not irresistible. The person while alive remains unfinished, in a constant process of self-creation, as recalcitrant to his own creative efforts as words are to a poet. The person is as much an effect of his actions as a cause. Every man is a self-made man. Thus, having begun this journey with Protagoras, perhaps I may conclude with Shakespeare:

We know what we are, but we know not what we may be.

Guide to Further Reading

This section is a selective listing of books that are highly recommended. These books are intended to supplement rather than to document the text. Many of them are available in editions other than the ones specified. Those which have an unusually good bibliography are marked with an asterisk.

For information on any of the philosophers or movements or issues discussed in this volume see the *Encyclopedia of Philosophy*,* ed. Paul Edwards (New York: Free Press, 1967).

For the recent historical background of contemporary philosophy see John Passmore, *A Hundred Years of Philosophy** (London: Duckworth, 1957).

For a representative group of readings from classical and contemporary sources illustrating the variety of points of view on many problems see Paul Edwards and Arthur Pap, eds., *A Modern Introduction to Philosophy** (New York: Free Press, 1965).

I. The following group of works is concerned with general issues in epistemology and metaphysics:

Austin, J. L. *Sense and Sensibilia*. New York: Oxford University Press, 1964.

Ayer, A. J. *Language, Truth, and Logic*. London: Gollancz, 1958.

275

————, ed. *Logical Positivism.** New York: Free Press, 1959.

Blanshard, Brand, *Reason and Analysis.* La Salle, Ill.: Open Court, 1962.

Carnap, Rudolf. *The Philosophy of Rudolf Carnap.** Edited by P. A. Schilpp. La Salle, Ill.: Open Court, 1963.

Feigl, Herbert, and Sellars, Wilfrid, eds. *Readings in Philosophical Analysis.* New York: Appleton-Century-Crofts, 1949.

Flew, Antony, ed. *Logic and Language.* 1st and 2d series. Oxford: Blackwell, 1960 and 1961.

Hospers, John. *An Introduction to Philosophical Analysis.* 2d ed. Englewood Cliffs, N. J.: Prentice-Hall, 1967.

Krikorian, Yervant H., ed. *Naturalism and the Human Spirit.* New York: Columbia University Press, 1944.

Nagel, Ernest. *Logic without Metaphysics.* Glencoe, Ill.: Free Press, 1956.

————, and Brandt, Richard R. *Meaning and Knowledge: Systematic Readings in Epistemology.** New York: Harcourt, Brace, 1965.

Polanyi, Michael. *Personal Knowledge.* New York: Harper & Row, 1964.

Reichenbach, Hans. *The Rise of Scientific Philosophy.* Berkeley and Los Angeles: University of California Press, 1956.

Russell, Bertrand. *The Philosophy of Bertrand Russell.** Edited by P. A. Schilpp. Evanston, Ill.: Library of Living Philosophers, 1946.

Urmson, J. O. *Philosophical Analysis: Its Development between the Two World Wars.* New York: Oxford University Press, 1960.

Waismann, F. *Principles of Linguistic Philosophy.* Edited by R. Harre. New York: St. Martin's, 1965.

II. This section lists books that are somewhat more specialized in logic and in the philosophy of science:

Čapek, Milič. *The Philosophical Impact of Contemporary Physics.* New York: Van Nostrand Reinhold, 1961.

Carnap, Rudolf. *Philosophical Foundations of Physics.* Edited by M. Gardner. New York: Basic Books, 1966.

Feigl, Herbert, and Brodbeck, May. *Readings in the Philosophy of Science.** New York: Appleton-Century-Crofts, 1953.

Hempel, Carl G. *Aspects of Scientific Explanation.** New York: Free Press, 1965.

KUHN, THOMAS S. *The Structure of Scientific Revolutions.* Chicago: University of Chicago Press, 1963.

NAGEL, ERNEST. *The Structure of Science: Problems in the Logic of Scientific Explanation.* New York: Harcourt, Brace, 1961.

NEURATH, OTTO, CARNAP, RUDOLF, and MORRIS, CHARLES, eds. *International Encyclopedia of Unified Science,* 2 vols. Chicago: University of Chicago Press, 1955.

POPPER, KARL. *The Logic of Scientific Discovery.* New York: Basic Books, 1959.

QUINE, W. V. *From a Logical Point of View.* New York: Harper & Row, 1961.

————. *The Ways of Paradox.* New York: Random House, 1966.

————. *Word and Object.* Cambridge, Mass.: M.I.T. Press, 1960.

SCHEFFLER, ISRAEL. *The Anatomy of Inquiry.** New York: Knopf, 1963.

STEBBING, L. SUSAN. *Philosophy and the Physicists.* New York: Dover, 1958.

STRAWSON, P. F. *Introduction to Logical Theory.* London: Methuen, 1952.

SUPPE, FREDERICK, ed. *The Structure of Scientific Theories.* Urbana: University of Illinois Press, 1974.

WARTOFSKY, MARX. *Conceptual Foundations of Scientific Thought: An Introduction to the Philosophy of Science.** New York: Macmillan, 1968.

III. On the specialized problems of the social sciences:

BRODBECK, MAY, ed. *Readings in the Philosophy of the Social Sciences.** New York: Macmillan, 1968.

KAUFMANN, FELIX. *Methodology of the Social Sciences.* New York: Oxford University Press, 1944.

NATANSON, MAURICE, ed. *Philosophy of the Social Sciences, a Reader.** New York: Random House, 1963.

IV. On history:

DRAY, WILLIAM H., ed. *Philosophical Analysis and History.* New York: Harper & Row, 1966.

MEYERHOFF, HANS, ed. *The Philosophy of History in our Time.* Garden City, N.Y.: Doubleday Anchor Books, 1959.

WHITE, MORTON. *Foundations of Historical Knowledge*. New York: Harper & Row, 1965.

V. On physics, written for the nonphysicist:

BARNETT, LINCOLN. *The Universe and Dr. Einstein*. New York: Mentor Books, 1950.

BRIDGMAN, P. W. *A Sophisticate's Primer of Relativity*. New York: Harper & Row, 1965.

EINSTEIN, ALBERT, and INFELD, LEOPOLD. *The Evolution of Physics*. New York: Simon and Schuster, 1938.

EINSTEIN, ALBERT. *Philosopher-Scientist*.* Edited by P. A. Schilpp. Evanston, Ill.: Library of Living Philosophers, 1949.

MARGENAU, HENRY. *The Nature of Physical Reality*. New York: McGraw-Hill, 1950.

VI. On mathematics:

NEWMAN, JAMES R., ed. *The World of Mathematics*. 4 vols. New York: Simon and Schuster, 1956.

WEYL, HERMANN. *Philosophy of Mathematics and Natural Science*. Princeton: Princeton University Press, 1949.

VII. On biology and evolution:

HANDLER, PHILIP, ed. *Biology and the Future of Man*. New York: Oxford University Press, 1950.

MUNSON, RONALD, ed. *Man and Nature: Philosophical Issues in Biology*.* New York: Delta Books, 1971.

SIMPSON, GEORGE GAYLORD. *The Meaning of Evolution: A Study of the History of Life and of its Significance for Man*. New Haven, Conn.: Yale University Press, 1949.

WENDT, HERBERT. *The Sex Life of the Animals*.* New York: Simon and Schuster, 1965.

VIII. On philosophical psychology, or "philosophy of mind":

BORGER, ROBERT, and CIOFFI, FRANK, eds. *Explanation in the Behavioural Sciences*. Cambridge: Cambridge University Press, 1970.

JAMES, WILLIAM. *Psychology: The Briefer Course.* Edited by Gordon Allport. New York: Harper Torchbooks, 1961.

RUSSELL, BERTRAND. *The Analysis of Mind.* New York: Macmillan, 1921.

RYLE, GILBERT. *The Concept of Mind.* New York: Barnes & Noble, 1949.

VERNON, M. D. *The Psychology of Perception.* Baltimore: Penguin, 1962.

VON WRIGHT, GEORG HENRIK. *Explanation and Understanding.** Ithaca, N.Y.: Cornell University Press, 1971.

WITTGENSTEIN, LUDWIG. *Philosophical Investigations.* New York: Macmillan, 1953.

Since most of the interesting material in this relatively new area of philosophy is in periodical form, the following paperback anthologies are useful:

ANDERSON, ALAN ROSS, ed. *Minds and Machines.* Englewood Cliffs, N.J.: Prentice-Hall, 1964.

CHAPPELL, V. C., ed. *The Philosophy of Mind.* Englewood Cliffs, N.J.: Prentice-Hall, 1962.

GUSTAFSON, DONALD F., ed. *Essays in Philosophical Psychology.* Garden City, N.Y.: Doubleday Anchor Books, 1964.

HAMPSHIRE, STUART, ed. *Philosophy of Mind.* New York: Harper & Row, 1966.

HOOK, SIDNEY, ed. *Dimensions of Mind.* New York: Collier, 1961.

PITCHER, GEORGE, ed. *Wittgenstein: The Philosophical Investigations.* Garden City, N.Y.: Doubleday Anchor Books, 1966.

IX. On linguistics and the philosophy of language:

BLACK, MAX. *The Labyrinth of Language.** New York: Mentor Books, 1968.

HOOK, SIDNEY, ed. *Language and Philosophy.* New York: New York University Press, 1969.

LEHMANN, WINFRED P. *Descriptive Linguistics: An Introduction.* New York: Random House, 1972.

SEARLE, JOHN R. *Speech Acts.* Cambridge: Cambridge University Press, 1969.

X. On the intersections of philosophy, ethics, and law:

MORRIS, HERBERT, ed. *Freedom and Responsibility.** Stanford: Stanford University Press, 1961.

XI. On philosophical problems in art:

Gombrich, E. H. *Art and Illusion: A Study in the Psychology of Pictorial Representation.* Bollingen Series. Princeton: Princeton University Press, 1961.

Kennick, W. E., ed. *Art and Philosophy: Readings in Aesthetics.* New York: St. Martin's, 1964.

Weitz, Morris, ed. *Problems in Aesthetics.* 2d ed. New York: Macmillan, 1970.

Index

Index

283